CLARITY

A SIMPLE METHOD
TO FIND YOUR DIRECTION
IN A WORLD FULL OF NOISE

CAM MERCHANT

WILEY

First published 2026 by John Wiley & Sons Australia, Ltd

ISBN: 978-1-394-43294-3

NATIONAL LIBRARY OF AUSTRALIA

A catalogue record for this book is available from the National Library of Australia

Registered Office
John Wiley & Sons Australia, Ltd. Level 4, 600 Bourke Street, Melbourne, VIC 3000, Australia

For details of our global editorial offices, customer services, and more information about Wiley products visit us at www.wiley.com.

Wiley also publishes its books in a variety of electronic formats and by print-on-demand. Some content that appears in standard print versions of this book may not be available in other formats.

Cover design by Wiley
Cover Image: © Beyhes Evren/Getty Images

Set in 11/16 pts and Palatino LT Std by Straive, Chennai, India.
Printed and bound by CPI Group (UK) Ltd, Croydon, CR0 4YY

C9781394432943_260826

The manufacturer's authorized representative according to the EU General Product Safety Regulation is Wiley-VCH GmbH, Boschstr. 12, 69469 Weinheim, Germany, e-mail: Product_Safety@wiley.com.

To my younger self: I wish you had known these pillars when you were going through your darkest times. But I don't regret those days. What you went through and survived has allowed you to step into your purpose—and create something that I hope will serve and help others going through similar times. If even one person is helped by this book, it was all worth it.

I'm incredibly proud of you for holding on. Thank you for turning your pain into purpose.

And to Jules, Ollie and Carter: you are my clarity.

Contents

Before we begin...

Before we dive in, I want to start with honesty.

Writing this book has been one of the hardest things I've ever done, and I got married to a complete stranger on national television, so that's saying something. The writing was hard not because I don't believe in the process I've outlined in the following pages—I absolutely do; I'm living proof it works—but because I know I can't possibly get it right for everyone. Your life, your story and your experiences are completely different from mine, and I want to acknowledge that from the very beginning.

I'm not here as an expert with all the answers. I'm not a psychologist or medical doctor. I'm someone with lived experiences who has been at the bottom of the barrel in life and found their way back. I'm not saying I have it all figured out and life's perfect, far from it, I'm just genuinely proud of how I managed to find my way back to where I am today, and proud to share it with the intent to help you on your way. I'm now a practitioner of positive psychology and wellbeing and an advocate for mental health and fitness.

Above all that, I'm someone who genuinely cares about other human beings and wants to help them find a little more within themselves.

So, I'm here as a human; someone who's walked through confusion, loss, purpose, trauma and joy, and found a way to make sense of it all through what I now call the Clarity Method.

This isn't a 'fix-you' book. It's a 'walk-with-you' book. I'm not here to change you but to walk alongside you and help you hear yourself again. You're not behind; you are exactly where you need to be right now. I believe by picking this book up you're ready to do the inner work. You are trusting that when you invest your time into you right now, you're giving yourself the opportunity to become more aware of yourself, your emotional state and your surroundings. This will help you develop a clarity that will benefit all aspects of your life, helping you create an elevated version of yourself you can be proud of. That's the starting point.

You believe in the process and trust it because you want something more. You are not doing it because somebody has told you you're supposed to do it. You do it because you genuinely believe this is the way. I'm here to remind you that even through all the noise, through everything you've been through, clarity is possible.

My hope is that by the end of this book you simply understand, learn and know yourself a little more than you did before.

You should be proud of the courage you've shown to start this journey. Thank you for being here and joining me on it.

Introduction

The hospital ceiling had 72 tiles. I know because I counted them, multiple times. When you're lying in a bed you never imagined would be yours, in a place you never thought you'd find yourself, you start counting things: ceiling tiles, cracks in the paint; anything to avoid counting the choices that led you here.

The walls were white with a splash of light blue. It was the kind of colour scheme designed to make you feel like everything wasn't so bad and you were simply at a day spa—as if the right colour could make you believe you'd chosen a wellness retreat instead of checking yourself in to a mental rehabilitation facility because you couldn't trust yourself to stay alive in the outside world.

It was two weeks into my stay. I would stay six weeks total, but I didn't know that yet. All I knew was that I'd spent the first two weeks resisting. I'd been fighting against the process, telling myself I didn't belong here, that I wasn't that bad, that I could handle this on my own the way I'd always handled everything: by pushing through, by performing, by pretending. Denial is a comfortable room, until it becomes a coffin.

I remember the day my parents drove me to the facility. I remember stepping out of the car, legs shaking, and walking toward the glass doors that led to the reception area. As those doors slid open, I thought, *So, this is what rock bottom looks like*. It wasn't a dramatic crash or like a scene from a movie. It was just automatic doors, fluorescent lights and a waiting room that smelled like disinfectant and despair. *This is it,* I remember thinking. *This is where people go when they've run out of places to hide.*

I signed myself in. My parents stood beside me, and I could see in their eyes the same thing I felt in my chest—grief for the person I used to be and terror about who I might become if this didn't work.

I was 29 years old. From the outside, my life had looked successful. I was the former professional cricketer travelling the world, the guy people saw smiling and laughing in person or on the screens of post-match interviews like nothing was ever an issue, like he had it all figured out and life was fun. No-one who saw me like this knew about the sleepless nights and the racing thoughts that wouldn't stop. They didn't know about darkness that had been creeping in for years, ever since a wave changed everything.

Uncovering my trauma

I was 20 years old when the Indian Ocean earthquake hit on 26 December 2004, causing what became known as the Boxing Day tsunami. I was on holiday in Thailand with both my parents and, in a matter of minutes, the world as I knew it was rearranged. I saw the ocean become a wall of destruction. I lost my parents for over 12 hours and saw things that no person should see. I survived, but something inside me didn't make it back home.

I didn't know it then, and wouldn't know it for years, but trauma often doesn't announce itself. It moves in quietly, unpacking its bags in the corners of your mind, rearranging the furniture of your soul while you're busy trying to appear normal. It whispers lies that sound like truth. It convinces you that the darkness is just who you are now, that the anxiety and discomfort in any social gathering is simply part of your personality, and that the emptiness is something everyone feels but nobody talks about.

For years, I ran from this trauma and these thoughts. I threw myself into cricket, work, relationships—anything that would keep me too busy to feel. Until finally I realised I couldn't outrun what lived inside me. Eventually, the running stopped working.

And so I ended up in a room counting ceiling tiles and resisting the very help I'd asked for.

Deciding to make a change

Two weeks in, something shifted. Maybe this shift was due to exhaustion; maybe it was grace. Or maybe I had finally run out of excuses. Whatever the cause, somewhere between breakfast and lunch on an ordinary Tuesday, after retelling my story over and over again to anyone who would listen in the hope it would somehow change everything, I stopped fighting. I stopped pretending I was fine and stopped telling myself I didn't need this. I finally realised if I wasn't willing to change, nothing would change.

For the first time in years, I became willing to see my life as it actually was, not as I wished it to be or as I performed it for others, but as it truly was. I started to see the habits that weren't serving me, the thoughts I'd been avoiding, and the patterns that kept leading me back to the same dark places.

It was terrifying. But it was also the first moment of genuine clarity I'd had in years. *Oh,* I thought. *This is what I've been hiding from. This is what's real.*

The therapists had been saying things to me for two weeks, but I hadn't been listening, not really. Now, with the walls down,

I started to hear. I started to understand that the mess I was in wasn't something that had happened to me. Yes, the tsunami was real. Yes, the trauma was valid. Yes, my cricket career and the identity I'd tied to that had ended. But the life I'd built since then—including the coping mechanisms, the avoidance and the pretending—was based on choices I had made.

I was able to acknowledge this without blame or shame. It was just the truth. And with that truth came something unexpected: power. If I had been choosing patterns that led me here, I could choose different patterns that led somewhere else. I might not make changes overnight or easily, but the possibility was there. For the first time in years, I felt something other than despair. I felt responsible.

But here's what the movies don't show and most people don't tell you about those moments of clarity in hospital beds: the breakthrough doesn't mean the work is done. It means the work can finally begin. Because three weeks later, still inside those walls, the darkness came back harder than before.

Choosing between darkness and the light

It was late in the evening and I was alone in my room. The television was on, but I couldn't hear it. It was just a blur of movement and light while something much louder screamed inside my head.

You're never going to get better.

You're a burden.

This pain will never end.

There's a way to make it stop.

I sat on the edge of the bed, sweat dripping from clenched fists as I resisted the voices in my head. At the same time, part of me was drawn to the relief offered in the form of surrender and in the choice that felt like freedom.

The tears came before I made any decision. They hit the sheets like drops from a leaking tap. Tap. Tap. Tap. A rhythm of grief for the life I thought I'd have and terror of the life I was living.

'This could be the end', something whispered. 'You could be free from all of this. No more pain. No more suffering. No more pretending. No more fighting a war you've already lost.'

I looked down. I looked at what was in my hand: enough saved-up pills to send me into the abyss.

And then came a different voice, quieter and kinder. It was a voice I hadn't heard in so long I'd forgotten even existed.

'You haven't done everything yet, mate.'

The words cut through the noise like light through a crack in a door. And then the voice kept going.

'You've achieved so much but you've got so much more to do. You haven't found your soulmate yet. The one. You haven't had a family. You haven't become a father—something you've always wanted. There's still so much you said you wanted to do. Don't give up now. Don't throw it all away when there's still so much road ahead.'

I paused. I breathed. Something in my chest shifted. The change was not a feeling but a knowing, coming from deep in that place where truth lives before the mind can argue with it. I knew the voice was right. I had spent so long fighting to survive that I'd forgotten I was fighting for a life I hadn't even built yet. This life was still possible. There was a woman I hadn't met, children I hadn't held and a purpose I hadn't discovered. A different version of myself was still possible. I just hadn't become it yet.

The darkness had been telling me I had nothing worth staying for. But the light was reminding me I hadn't yet created what was worth staying for.

'That's the point', the voice seemed to say. 'You have to stay to build it. It's possible.'

I wiped my eyes and I made a decision that would change everything. *Okay,* I thought. *If I'm going to do this, if I'm going to stay and fight for this life, then I'm going to do it properly. No more half measures. No more grey areas or excuses. Line in the sand. All in.*

I wasn't going to continue on the same path, sinking into victimhood, waiting for someone else to save me and running from the feelings that terrified me. Instead, I was going to learn to actually feel these feelings and sit with them. I was going to learn the signals my body was giving me, to understand that the anxiety in my chest wasn't a death sentence but data. My body wasn't my enemy; it was trying to tell me something I hadn't been willing to hear.

I was going to figure out who I actually was beneath all the performance, all the achievement, all the ways I'd defined myself by what I did instead of who I was and all the ways I'd let society tell me who I should be.

I was going to build new habits, new routines and new ways of being that would serve the man I wanted to become instead of the man I'd been pretending to be.

And eventually—not yet, but eventually—I was going to stop isolating. I was going to let people in. I was going to discover that the healing I'd been searching for alone had been waiting for me all along, found in the connections I made with others and presenting my gift as service to help those also feeling the same.

But first, I just had to be willing to begin.

I didn't know it then, but that moment and that decision was the first step of an eight-step journey. It was the start of a journey I am incredibly proud of, which would take me from that hospital room to a life I couldn't have imagined. I can now sit back and see that the worst day of my life turned out to be the best day of my life. That day led me to this exact moment right now.

> *You are exactly where you are meant to be right now.*

The first steps of my recovery

Recovery wasn't linear. Let me be clear about that. I didn't walk out of that facility six weeks later as a changed man with all the answers. I simply walked out as a man who had finally stopped pretending he didn't need to change. I remember giving myself grace in that moment, though. I knew change wasn't going to be easy and it wasn't going to happen overnight, or even the next day, next week, month or year. But I believed it would happen if I gave myself a chance and I gave myself permission. And I believed it would be worth it.

The years that followed were filled with setbacks and many moments of doubt. I had days when the old voices returned and I had to fight to remember why I'd chosen to stay. I went back to cricket coaching because it was the only work I knew with an essence of joy. Still, I'd have days when I was coaching and think, *Is this it? Is this all my life will ever be?* I knew nothing was wrong with what I was doing, because helping kids and adults was a privilege. I just envisioned more.

But something had shifted in me that night in the hospital. I was no longer waiting for life to happen to me. I was showing up for it, even when showing up felt impossible.

I started paying attention to my thoughts instead of being controlled by them. I started taking ownership of my choices instead of blaming my circumstances. I started building small rituals that kept me grounded when the world felt chaotic. I started reaching out instead of retreating in.

And slowly, so slowly I almost didn't notice it happening, the life I'd dreamed about in that dark hospital room began to take shape.

The cricket coaching wasn't the end but a stepping stone. It was a safe place to heal during the real work of personal growth and figuring out what was next. And when I was ready, truly ready, in a way I couldn't have forced or faked, the universe opened a door I never expected.

'Hey', it seemed to say. 'Do you want to get married on a television show?'

It sounds absurd, doesn't it? From psychiatric facility to reality TV. But that's the strange alchemy of a life lived with clarity: things start connecting in ways that make no logical sense but feel exactly right.

I said yes. And on that show, I met Jules. She wasn't just a partner. She was proof that the voice had been right. Everything had been waiting for me—the soulmate I hadn't found yet, the family I hadn't created yet and the life I hadn't built yet. I'd just had to keep going long enough to receive it. It took me 13 years but it started with a single decision.

Why I wrote this book

I wrote this book because I remember saying to myself at my worst: *If I can find a way out and make my way back to the joyous, authentic and loving human being I knew I was then I would dedicate my life to empowering others to find a way too.*

Maybe you're in your own version of that hospital room. Maybe you're feeling the same quiet desperation, and you've also hidden it so well that no-one around you suspects. Maybe you have a nagging sense that life has more to offer and you're meant for something bigger, brighter and bolder. Because it is available to you, but you may not be able to see the path forward through all the noise.

Maybe you've picked this book up because the word 'clarity' called to something inside you—a hunger and a hope; a small voice that whispers, 'There has to be another way'.

Maybe things are going along swimmingly but you're just looking for a little more clarity and direction in your life and your identity, or to know yourself a little better than you did last year, which is certainly my hope for you. Maybe you're just curious for a little growth so that you have something to give, which is where I believe meaning in life comes from. Or maybe you're looking to develop a little more peace through the accelerated learnings provided in the following pages.

No matter why you've found yourself here, I want you to know something: I see you. I see you because I've been you. And I want you to know that you holding this book and even simply being curious about finding clarity tells me something important about you. It tells me that somewhere beneath the confusion and the doubt, a part of you hasn't given up. And that part of you is right. That part of you wants more for you because it truly believes you deserve it, and so do I.

This book is not just about my journey. It's about yours. And it's not just about feeling better. It's about redesigning how you experience and live your entire life, the way you want to and on your terms.

Over the following pages, I'm going to share the eight steps, or what I now call the Clarity Method, that took me from rock bottom to a life I'm genuinely proud of. This isn't a perfect life, or one without struggle or doubt or dark days. But it is a life of clarity, where I know who I am, what I want and how to find my way back to centre when the world gets loud.

I didn't invent my eight pillars in a vacuum. They're based on principles I discovered through years of therapy, research, trial and error, and, most importantly, lived experience. I've tested them in the fire of my own recovery and refined them working with countless others who were searching for the same thing I was.

My eight pillars are Willingness, Awareness, Accountability, Regulation, Identity, Habits and discipline, Connection and contribution, and Integration. I outline how the pillars work together in chapter 3, and then delve into each one in much more detail in chapters 4 to 11. For now, let me tell you this: they work, and not because they're magic, but because they're true. They'll work for you if you're willing to do more than just read this book. You also need to do the work.

To help you with this work, I've included exercises through the following chapters. Please do them. Grab a journal, write in the margins or use the companion Clarity Workbook available via my website (cameronmerchant.com). Do whatever works for you. Have the uncomfortable conversations with yourself that this journey requires.

> *Knowledge without action is just entertainment.*

And you didn't pick up this book to be entertained. You picked it up because you want something to change.

I'm not here to give you the answers; I'm here to ask you the questions. I can give you the map and walk beside you, but you have to also walk the path.

So, here's my promise to you. I'm going to be open, raw and honest and show up with all my heart for you, even while my doubts and insecurities still find ways to present themselves. Right through writing this book, I've dealt with thoughts like, 'Who am I to be writing this book?', 'Leave it to the experts, mate', 'No-one will read this' and 'You really think you can help people?' But I've worked through these thoughts because of my main mission and purpose: you.

You too will feel fear, discomfort and self-doubt along the way. You will try to convince yourself that you are okay, that you can stay where you are. That is completely normal. However, if you commit and step out of the familiar and give yourself permission and lean into this process and show up for this journey—really show up, with honesty and courage and a willingness to be uncomfortable—you will not be the same person on the other side. You'll have tools to calm the storm when life gets chaotic. You'll have deeper connections and a sense of purpose that makes getting out of bed feel meaningful. Most importantly, you'll have a way back to yourself whenever you get lost.

Because you will get lost. Life will knock you off course. Things will go sideways. The confusion will return, the noise will get loud again, and at times you will forget everything you've learned. That's not failure. That's being human. The gift of this work isn't that you'll never struggle again. The gift is that you'll know how to find your way home to you.

Just because the past didn't turn out exactly like you wanted doesn't mean your future can't be better than you ever imagined. I know this because I've lived it. I sat in that hospital room with the weight of the world crushing my chest and no clear picture of what tomorrow could look like. Now I wake up next to the woman I love, grateful for kids I adore, doing work that matters and living a life that my former self couldn't have dreamed possible but would be so proud of.

The distance between those two realities isn't due to luck or magic or some special advantage I had that you don't. It's due to clarity.

Clarity is power. Clarity breeds mastery. And it's available to you too. The journey you're about to begin will take you through my eight essential pillars—from Willingness to Integration—that build on each other. We'll walk through each one together.

One more thing before we begin. You may be reading this in a dark place. You may be closer to my hospital room than to my current life. You may be wondering if clarity is even possible for someone who's lost as much or hurt as deeply as you have.

If that's you, hear me when I say you are not too broken for this. You are not too far gone. You are not the exception to every rule of recovery.

The voice that tells you it's too late, that you've messed up too badly, that other people can change but you can't, is lying. It's the same voice that lied to me in that hospital room. And I'm living proof that it can be wrong.

Some part of you, however small, however buried, picked up this book because it believes change is possible. Feed that part. Trust that part. Let that be the voice you listen to as we walk this path together. You matter. Your life matters. The clarity you're seeking isn't just for other people; it's for you too.

Over 13 years ago, I sat on the edge of a hospital bed with a choice in my hands. I chose life. I chose clarity. I chose a significantly better direction than the one I was currently on. And that choice, made in the darkest moment of my existence, led me to everything beautiful I have today. And I am so grateful for it.

Now it's your turn and I'm extremely excited for you and to start this with you.

Noticing the pressures and noise around you

Before jumping into the rest of the book, let's pause for a quick reflection exercise. Think about where in your life you feel the most 'noise' right now, and where you feel even a tiny bit of calm. Connect also to how you personally define 'calm', because this will give so much more meaning and power to how you answer and respond.

Let's be real — life can feel like a pot that's always on the boil. The heat doesn't disappear; it just changes levels. And when life is boiling, clarity becomes harder to access.

Right now, my pressures are completely different to yours. I'm in the thick of raising two little humans, Ollie (five) and Carter (almost two), while writing this book and cheering on my wife, Jules. My dad just had double open-heart surgery. Life is wonderful but a lot. I'm managing it with a smile because of the processes I've learnt over the years, and which I'm sharing with you in the coming pages.

This book does not offer a 'one size fits all' approach. In the following chapters, I share the processes and methods that, after years of fumbling and stumbling in my own life, I now realise worked for me. I'm sharing them with you so that you might be able to do the same and find a way that works for you.

So, to start this process, what pressures and noise are you currently sitting with?

(continued)

Perhaps your pressures come from some of the following:

- family
- finances
- relationships
- work or career
- university or education
- politics and the state of the world
- identity, diversity and belonging
- social media
- health
- expectations versus reality.

This list is just to prompt you. No doubt you'll have your own pressures too. Take a moment now to name them.

And maybe you're facing noise such as:

- mental noise (overthinking)
- social noise (opinions, comparison)
- digital noise (phones, content, distraction, social media)
- emotional noise (fear, doubt, pressure)

Think about how this noise is affecting you.

In this book, I'm going to call these pressures and this noise 'disturbances'. Disturbances are the things that shake you and pull you away from yourself. You don't find clarity by ignoring these disturbances and pretending you're fine. You find it by getting honest about what's boiling.

Write down your disturbances. What's turning the heat up on your pot right now? It's okay to be open and honest. Once you define what's disturbing you, you can start creating solutions that actually fit you. This is what this book is all about. You can't always turn the pressure off, but you can learn how to manage the heat.

This isn't about becoming someone new. It's about remembering who you already are. That's what the Clarity Method is here to help you to do — find your clarity and enjoy this life the way you want to, through whatever challenges come your way.

Your personal glossary

Throughout this book, I use words like 'purpose', 'calm', 'clarity', 'instinct' and 'trust'. But I don't want to assume my meaning is the same as yours.

Clarity begins with language. The words you use carry personal energy, memory, emotion and history. They shape the meaning you live. You need to define them consciously—because undefined words quietly run your life.

I've shared here my definitions for terms I've used through this book. My goal is to make these words feel less intimidating and more personal, so you can connect to them as we continue throughout this book together. If my definitions resonate with you, use them as your own. If they don't, take some time now to write down your personal definitions. Let the words become yours.

My personal glossary

Calm The space within you where nothing needs to be rushed, fixed or forced; the presence of being at ease and in control

Clarity Seeing things as they are—without judgement, pressure or perfection

Confidence The quiet belief that you'll figure it out no matter what happens, not because you have all the answers, but because you trust yourself to handle whatever comes

Courage When you're not sure if you can, but decide that you will regardless even when fear is present

Direction The path you choose to move toward, guided by your values, not your circumstances

Discipline Choosing what matters most over what feels easiest

Identity The story you believe about who you are—and who you're becoming

Instinct Your body's first truth before doubt, logic or overthinking

Ownership Taking responsibility for your choices, reactions and direction without blame or excuses

Presence Being fully where you are, instead of mentally living somewhere else

Purpose The reason you get out of bed when no-one's watching; your why

Soul The quiet part of you that feels, the place where joy, grief, pride, shame and hope live

Trust Believing in yourself, your path and the process, even when you can't yet see the outcome

Part I

Understanding the power of clarity — and how to get there

Chapter One

The clarity crisis

From the outside at least, Sarah had everything. She had the corner office with floor-to-ceiling windows overlooking Sydney Harbour and the six-figure salary that had doubled in five years. Her Instagram feed was full of weekend brunches and sunset yoga sessions and blessed captions that made her former university friends green with envy. She had a relationship, and a body, that looked perfect in the photos. She had a life that looked perfect in her feed.

And yet, at 3.17 am on an everyday Tuesday, Sarah lay awake in her $4000 bed, staring at the ceiling, heart racing, mind spinning, asking herself a question she couldn't answer: 'What do I actually want?'

She didn't mean what she was supposed to want—what her parents expected, what LinkedIn and Instagram said success looked like or what the algorithm had convinced her she needed. What did she actually want? The question terrified her, because after 34 years of achieving, optimising and climbing, she realised she had no idea.

She had followed the script perfectly: study hard, get the degree, land the job, climb the ladder, hit the metrics, post the wins, repeat until... what? Until she was lying awake at 3 am with everything she'd been told to chase, feeling more lost than she'd ever felt in her life?

Sarah isn't a real person, but she is every person.

How the modern world stole your ability to see

I've met hundreds of versions of 'Sarah' in my work, thousands, maybe. These people may have different faces, different postcodes and different specifics, but they have the same hollow look in their eyes. And they whisper the same confession like it's a shameful secret: *I have everything I was supposed to want, and I've never felt more confused about my life.*

They come to me not because they're failing. They come because even though they're succeeding by every external measure, it feels like nothing.

It might be the high achiever who's burnt out but can't stop, or the entrepreneur who built the business and lost themselves in the process. Or it could be the parent who's so busy providing for their family they've forgotten who they are outside of that role. Maybe it's the young professional drowning in options, paralysed by the fear of choosing wrong. It might even be the retiree who worked their whole life for freedom, only to discover they have no idea what to do with it.

They're all staring at the same question, just with different ceiling tiles: 'What do I actually want?'

So let me ask you the same question: 'What do you actually want?' When was the last time you honestly asked yourself that? I'm not asking what you've been told to want or looks good on paper or impresses other people. What do you want? When was the last time you sat with that question—without distraction, without noise, without rushing past it—and answered it honestly?

Most people don't. They move through life chasing outcomes they never consciously chose, ticking boxes they never designed and living scripts they never wrote. And then one day, they arrive—and feel nothing.

Here's the truth. It doesn't matter what you want because it's yours to want. There is zero judgement here. It's your personal choice and desire and can be anything. It could be:

- inner peace
- financial freedom
- status
- fame
- self-worth
- love
- family
- contentment
- happiness
- fulfilment.

There is no hierarchy here and no right or wrong answers, because your desires are yours. They don't need to be justified and they don't need approval. This is about honesty.

But here's where most people get stuck. They think wanting something is enough. It's not. At the core of every desire, no matter how big or small, is one thing: clarity. This clarity allows you to see what you truly want and understand why you want it. And this clarity helps you to map the path to get there. Without clarity, desire turns into confusion. With clarity, desire turns into direction.

After a decade of asking people what they truly want, the pattern I've noticed is clear. The problem isn't that they don't want enough, or that they lack motivation, discipline or opportunity. The problem is that they can't see clearly. And in the modern world, that's not a personal failing. It's a society-wide epidemic. We are living through the greatest clarity crisis in human history. That might sound dramatic, but it isn't.

To use a real-life example, can I ask you a question? How many streaming services do you currently have? How many TV channels do you have available? And have you ever sat on the couch with your partner and spent hours arguing trying to pick a movie? Chances are, you watched nothing but trailers and eventually gave up, exhausted with all you actually achieved was frustration with each other and an argument. What a time! I miss the days of DVDs and VHS at the video store. Once that decision was made and you brought it home, that was it. Strap in. If you don't know what these are, please go ask your parents. You had to get down to the local store and physically hand-pick the movie you wanted to watch but once you were back on the couch, the decisions had all been made. The biggest frustration was if the actual VHS or DVD wasn't behind the one you had chosen because it was already rented out. That was a sad moment.) Remember that? Good times.

The explosion of streaming and viewing options is a simple yet easy way to illustrate the concept of the clarity crisis. But simply having too many options is not the real crisis.

You now have access to more information than every human who lived before 1900 combined. You can learn almost anything, connect with almost anyone, buy almost anything, and become almost anything. The barriers that limited every previous generation—such as geography, class, access and information—have largely dissolved. A study from Cornell University reveals that a person makes an average of 35 000 decisions every single day.

And yet this access to more information and more options hasn't made us happier overall. According to the World Health Organization

(WHO), anxiety disorders have increased by 25 per cent globally since 2020. Depression rates have doubled in the past two decades. In Australia alone, according to the Australian Bureau of Statistics (ABS) National Study of Mental Health and Wellbeing, 2020–2022, 42.9 per cent of adults (16 to 85 years) had experienced a mental disorder at some point in their lives. That's nearly half the population struggling to cope over their lifetime. The rates among young people are even higher. The same ABS study found nearly 40 per cent of 16 to 24 year olds had experienced a mental health disorder in the previous 12 months.

We have more options, access and freedom than ever. And yet we are also more confused, overwhelmed and lost than ever. (Maybe try mentioning this when you are next on the couch with your partner trying to pick a movie. It might ease the tension a little. Good luck.)

This is the clarity crisis. It's not a motivation problem. You don't need another productivity hack or morning routine or goal-setting framework. You don't need more information about how to succeed. You need to be able to see.

You need to see:

- your life as it actually is, not as Instagram filters it to be
- what you genuinely want, not what you've been programmed to chase
- your path forward, not the thousands of possible paths that fragment your attention.

And to see all this, you need to see yourself clearly, not the performance you've mistaken for your identity.

> *We don't have a motivation problem. We have a clarity problem.*

Every time you haven't acted, every self-help book you've abandoned, every New Year's resolution that dissolved by February, every time you've known what to do but couldn't make yourself do it, wasn't because of weakness or lack of willpower. It was caused by confusion masquerading as motivation failure.

You can't act decisively on a life you can't see clearly. You can't pursue a vision that's buried under noise. You can't move forward when you're standing in fog so thick you can't see your own feet.

The first step isn't another strategy. The first step is clarity.

The paradox of more

Put simply, more options plus more noise equals less clarity. I know—it seems counterintuitive. Shouldn't more options mean more freedom? Shouldn't more information mean better decisions? Shouldn't more access mean more opportunity?

In theory, yes; in reality, however, no.

Have you ever been to a restaurant with a truly extensive menu? I mean every choice of every cuisine you can imagine and a choice of every dish within that cuisine. Chances are, you simply felt bamboozled (and still hungry). You're exhausted before the drinks have even been served.

Similar to the streaming options example, the decision in front of you becomes overwhelming. As the sweats start to build, perhaps you look around, hoping to be inspired by what everyone else is eating, but all you see are your friends and the wait staff waiting on you and your decision. Your choice suddenly has the potential to ruin the evening, all because you didn't know what you wanted and had too many options to choose from. That's a bit like life when you have less clarity.

Now imagine your good friends, let's call them Steve and Marlene, are sitting across the table from you. They're vegans and, lucky for them, the menu only offers four vegan options. They have been able to make a clear and decisive choice in a matter of moments and move on. Why? Because they know who they are, what they want, and what they can and can't have. They weren't going to spend their time and precious energy looking at the meat dishes. The choice is simple, and that's clarity (in a food kind of way).

I'm not saying we all have to be vegans, but when you know who you are, what you want, how you're going to get it and how it's going to work for you in a world full of options, your life just gets a little easier. Confusion is expensive. It costs you your time, energy, relationships and peace and, in this instance, your evening with Steve and Marlene.

Psychologist Barry Schwartz spent decades researching in this area and what he calls the 'paradox of choice'. His findings revolutionised how we understand modern decision-making and modern misery.

In one famous study, researchers set up a jam-tasting booth at a grocery store. Over one weekend, they offered 24 varieties: on another weekend, just six. The results were staggering. When 24 options were available, only 3 per cent of people who tried the jam went on to buy any. When six options were available, 30 per cent of tasters bought jam. The stores saw ten times more purchases, simply by reducing options.

But here's the part that matters most: the people who faced 24 options didn't just make fewer purchases. Those who did buy jam also reported feeling worse about their decisions. They second-guessed their choice. They wondered about the options they didn't pick and felt less satisfied with what they had. Ever felt that way before?

Schwartz summarised this paradox perfectly: 'The fact that some choice is good doesn't necessarily mean that more choice is better'.

Now multiply that jam booth by every domain of your life:

- *What career should you pursue?* You have thousands of options, and the internet will show you success stories for all of them.
- *Who should you date?* Swiping left or right offers infinite potential partners, each one potentially better than the last, so why commit?
- *Where should you live?* The world is your oyster. You can work from anywhere. Every city has its advocates.
- *What should you believe?* Every worldview has its defenders. Every lifestyle has its influencers. Every choice has its cheerleaders and its critics.
- *What should you eat?* You have more diet options and philosophies than ever in human history, each with its own research, gurus and armies of true believers ready to argue in the comments.

This is your brain on modern life: paralysed not by lack of options, but by abundance of them. You're exhausted not by too few possibilities, but by too many. And you're not lost because the path is blocked, but because you can see thousands of paths but have no map.

Confusion is expensive. It costs you time, energy, relationships and peace. Ask yourself:

- How many hours have you spent scrolling, researching and comparing options, and still not deciding?
- How much energy have you wasted worrying about whether you made the right choice? (Have you decided on that movie yet?)

- How many nights have you laid awake, mind racing through possibilities, unable to find peace?
- How many relationships have suffered because you were too distracted, too overwhelmed and too mentally elsewhere to be present?

> *Confusion isn't neutral; confusion is catastrophically expensive. And the modern world is a confusion factory running at maximum capacity.*

The noise machine

If too many options create confusion, too much noise makes this confusion permanent.

Johann Hari, author of *Stolen Focus,* spent years investigating why our attention spans have collapsed. His research revealed something disturbing: our focus is being split by too many tasks and interruptions. According to the 2025 Microsoft Work Trend Index, the average Australian worker is interrupted every two minutes by 'meetings, emails, or pings'. And according to research led by Gloria Mark (and published in the research paper 'No task left behind?'), it takes approximately 23 minutes to return to the same level of focus after each interruption. (I'm certainly included in this disrupted focus, by the way.)

If you're interrupted every two minutes but need 23 minutes to recover, you never actually achieve deep focus at all. You spend your entire day in a shallow, fragmented state, present enough to respond, but never present enough to think.

And that's just work. You're likely also distracted by:

- notifications
- news alerts
- social media pings

- personal emails that demand an immediate response
- texts from friends
- updates from apps you forgot you had
- articles that tell you everything you believed is wrong
- videos that make you feel inadequate
- comment sections that make you lose faith in humanity.

Cal Newport, author of *Deep Work*, calls dealing with all this 'context switching' and his research shows it's not just inefficient; it's also cognitively devastating. Every time you shift your attention, your brain pays a 'switching cost'. Over a day, those costs accumulate into what he calls 'attention residue': a fog that makes deep thinking nearly impossible.

You cannot hustle your way through confusion. You cannot productivity-hack your way to clarity. You cannot optimise a life you can't see.

I often think about this in relation to our need to take photos or videos of precious moments that were just meant to be enjoyed and appreciated. Instead of just being present, we're often already thinking how the moment will look on social media. We can walk away with a gallery full of images yet zero recollection of what that moment actually meant and how it made us feel. The distraction of capturing a moment on camera can prevent our minds and souls from capturing it.

The noise isn't accidental. Some of the smartest engineers in the world have spent billions of dollars figuring out how to capture and hold your attention. The apps on your phone were designed by people who understand your psychology better than you do and their incentive is to keep you scrolling, not to help you see clearly.

This isn't a conspiracy theory. It's their business model.

> *Attention is the currency of the digital economy — and you are paying with your clarity.*

The 'monkey mind'

Around 2500 years ago, the Buddha described the state of 'kapicitta'—having a monkey mind.

Picture a monkey in a jungle, swinging from branch to branch, never still, never settled, grabbing at every new thing that catches its eye. Chances are, that's your mind on a normal day—jumping from thought to thought, worry to worry, and plan to fantasy to regret to comparison to fear. (Once again, this is also very me.)

The Buddha wasn't speaking metaphorically. Modern neuroscience has confirmed what contemplatives knew millennia ago: the default state of the untrained mind is chaos.

Research from psychologists Matthew Killingsworth and Daniel Gilbert at Harvard University found that on average people spend 46.9 per cent of their waking hours thinking about something other than what they're doing. In other words, for almost half your life, your mind could be somewhere else. You could spend half your life not actually present for your own experience.

And here's what makes it worse: the study found that mind-wandering is directly correlated with unhappiness. The more your mind wanders, the more miserable you feel, regardless of what you're actually doing.

This wasn't a problem our ancestors faced to the same degree. For most of human history, the external environment demanded attention. You had to watch for predators. You had to track your food. You had to pay attention to your surroundings because your (and your tribe's) survival depended on it. Now the external environment demands distraction. It's engineered to pull your attention in every direction simultaneously. And your monkey mind, which was already restless, has been given a jungle of infinite branches to swing from.

In the modern world, most of us have become servants to our minds. We don't choose our thoughts; they choose us. We don't direct our attention; it gets hijacked. We don't see clearly; we see whatever the noise and the algorithms and the anxious monkey decide to show us. More often than not, we try to do one task but then start another task without finishing or even remembering what we originally started. (Or is that just me?)

Finding clarity is about taking back control. It's training the monkey and deciding what you pay attention to instead of letting attention happen to you.

The cost of confusion

I worked with a man recently—let's call him David, because that was his name—who was a successful property developer and family man in his mid-40s. On paper, David was living the dream. In reality, he was slowly drowning.

David came to me not because of a crisis but because of a creeping sense that something was wrong. 'I wake up tired', he told me. 'I go through the motions. I'm successful by every measure but I feel like I'm failing at everything that matters.'

When we dug into his life, the picture became clear: or rather, the picture of unclarity became clear. David received over 200 emails per day. He was on 17 different group chats. He had three streaming subscriptions, two news apps and a social media habit he was embarrassed to quantify. He was 'connected' to thousands of people online and genuinely close to almost none of them.

His morning started with his phone. His day was then a series of reactions to other people's priorities. His evening was a numbing scroll until sleep. This routine had been set to repeat for years.

'I have no idea what I actually think anymore', David said. 'I have no idea what I actually want. I just respond to whatever's in front of me.'

David wasn't lazy or unmotivated. David was buried so deep in noise that he'd lost sight of his own life.

His confusion was costing him:

- *His presence with his kids:* He was always distracted, always checking something else and never fully there.
- *His health:* He felt he had no time to exercise and no energy to cook, and paid no attention to his body's signals.
- *His marriage:* He and his partner were two people sharing a house but not sharing a life.
- *His creativity:* The ideas that used to excite him had dried up under the weight of constant input.
- *His peace:* He couldn't remember the last time his mind had been quiet.

David is not unusual. Instead, he is normal. David is what happens when you try to live a human life inside an inhuman amount of noise. Many researchers, including Dr Andrew Huberman, neuroscientist at Stanford School of Medicine, have documented what happens to your brain and body when you're in a state of chronic confusion and overwhelm. Impacts include elevated cortisol, disrupted sleep, impaired immune function, accelerated ageing and reduced cognitive capacity. Confusion isn't just uncomfortable; it's physically damaging.

> *The world continues to get louder. You need to get clearer.*

This is the choice we all face. The world isn't going to get quieter, the options aren't going to decrease and technology isn't going to stop competing for your attention. The noise and distraction are not going away.

You have a choice: learn to see through the noise or spend your life reacting to it.

The clarity crisis questionnaire

Take a moment now to assess your own clarity crisis. Grab a pen and your journal (or my companion workbook).

Rate each of the following statements from one (never) to five (constantly).

Mental noise:

1. I feel overwhelmed by the number of decisions I have to make.
2. I find it hard to focus on one task without my mind wandering.
3. I scroll through my phone without really knowing why.

Life direction:

4. I'm not sure what I actually want from my life.
5. I often wonder if I'm on the right path.
6. I find myself comparing my life to other people's and feeling inadequate.
7. I feel stuck but can't identify exactly why.

Present moment:

8. I struggle to be fully present, even with people I love.
9. I feel like life is happening to me rather than being lived by me.
10. I'm tired even when I've had enough sleep.

Add your score for each question to give you a total out of 50.

Scoring:

- *10–20 — mild clarity crisis:* You're experiencing some fog, but you can still see your path.
- *21–30 — moderate clarity crisis:* The noise is winning more often than not.
- *31–40 — severe clarity crisis:* You're lost in the storm and need a way out.
- *41–50 — critical clarity crisis:* Emergency clarity intervention is required.

Whatever your score, know this: recognising the problem is the first step to solving it. Most people never even get this far. They assume confusion is normal, busyness is virtue and overwhelm is just the price of modern life. It isn't. Clarity is possible. And the fact that you're reading this book means you're ready to find it.

The clarity crisis isn't your fault (but it is your responsibility)

You didn't choose to be born into an era of infinite distraction. You didn't choose to have a brain that evolved for a world that no longer exists. You didn't choose to have algorithms designed by geniuses whose sole purpose is capturing your attention. You didn't choose the comparison, hustle and fear culture that permeates every screen. This was the water you were born into, and fish don't choose the water.

But, and this is crucial, you do choose what happens next. You get to write the next chapter of your life through the way you respond. You can choose to write your story in pen, pencil or texta. (I personally love those BIC four-in-one coloured pens. I used to use them at school for all my homework and tests. Each paragraph would be in a different colour and in CAPITAL LETTERS because I wanted to make it pop and be exciting for the teachers to read. This didn't help me finish exams on time, but I figured they had to read so many exams, surely they needed a little more joy in their life, and maybe they would give me a few extra marks for creativity? That never happened, but it does show I've always been one for others.)

Back to you. You can choose to:

- stay lost or learn to see
- keep reacting or start responding
- blame the noise or build your signal
- remain a victim of the clarity crisis or become its victor.

You always control your response to the events around you.

> *You can't outrun unclear thinking, but you can outgrow it.*

The path forward

The eight pillars I'm about to share with you are the path out of the clarity crisis. They're not abstract philosophy or feel-good platitudes. They're the concrete practices that took me from a psychiatric hospital to a life of genuine peace, purpose and presence.

The pillars are Willingness, Awareness, Accountability, Regulation, Identity, Habits and discipline, Connection and contribution, and Integration. Each pillar builds on the last and, together, they form a complete system for moving from confusion to clarity, not once, but again and again, whenever life gets loud.

But what is clarity, exactly? I don't mean the dictionary definition but the lived experience. I mean the feeling in your body when the fog lifts and the power that comes from finally being able to see.

Once you understand what clarity actually is—what it feels like, what it makes possible and what it gives you access to—you'll be willing to do whatever it takes to find it. So that's what the next chapter is all about.

Chapter Two

Clarity is power

The morning it happened, I wasn't expecting anything. I was three weeks into my stay at the facility. Breakfast was finished and a group session was being held in an hour. I was sitting in the common room, one of those sterile spaces designed to feel comfortable but never quite succeeding, staring out the window at nothing in particular.

My mind was doing what it always did: racing, replaying conversations, rehearsing fears, and jumping from past regret to future catastrophe with barely a breath in between. In other words, the usual chaos; the same monkey swinging from branch to branch. And then, without warning, it stopped—not gradually or through any effort. It just... stopped.

For a moment, I thought something was wrong. The silence was so unfamiliar it felt like a malfunction. Like when that refrigerator you've tuned out suddenly switches off and you realise how loud it's been all along. But nothing was wrong. Something was finally right.

I looked at the garden outside the window; really looked at it. I saw the way the morning light caught the leaves, the slight movement of branches in the breeze, and the green that was really 100 different greens. I'd seen that garden every day for three weeks, but I'd never actually seen it. And in that moment of seeing, that moment of the noise falling away and the world coming into focus, I felt something I hadn't felt in years.

Peace.

This wasn't the absence of problems. My problems were still there. The trauma was still there. The work ahead was still there. But for the first time in longer than I could remember, I wasn't being crushed by them. I could see them clearly, almost from a distance, like looking at a map of difficult terrain instead of being lost inside it. *Oh,* I thought. *This is what I've been missing. This is what clarity feels like.*

It lasted maybe five or ten minutes. Then the noise crept back in, the thoughts returned, and I was back to being the confused, struggling version of myself I'd been for years. But those five minutes changed everything. Now I knew clarity was possible. I'd felt what it was like to see, think and be clearly, even for just a moment. And I became determined to find my way back.

What changes when you can finally see

Before considering what clarity is, let's first have a quick look at what it is not:

- *Clarity is not the absence of problems:* You can have massive challenges and still see clearly. In fact, clarity often reveals problems you've been avoiding, which is uncomfortable but ultimately liberating.
- *Clarity is not certainty:* You don't need to know how everything will work out. You don't need a five-year plan or

a guaranteed outcome. Clarity is about seeing the next step, not the entire staircase.

- *Clarity is not related to intelligence:* I've met brilliant people who can't see their own lives clearly and simple people who possess profound wisdom about what matters. IQ has nothing to do with it.
- *Clarity is not perfection:* It's not some elevated state that only monks achieve after decades of meditation. Clarity is available to anyone, including you, including now.

So, what is clarity? Here's my definition, forged in the fire of my own recovery and refined through years of helping others find theirs. Clarity is the ability to see your life as it truly is, without the distortion of fear, the fog of confusion or the filters of other people's expectations—and to know, with quiet certainty, what your next step should be.

That's it. It's not a mystical experience or a permanent state of enlightenment. It is just the ability to see and the knowledge of what to do next. When you find your personal clarity you take on only what you can control and stop worrying about the noise you can't.

Clarity is knowing what matters. Letting go of noise. Choosing your direction and taking action because when you can see clearly, anything is possible.

> “*Clarity is power. Clarity breeds mastery.*”

I've said those words thousands of times. They've become something of a mantra for myself and the community I'm so lucky to talk to. But I want you to understand why they're true, not just inspirationally, but also practically and scientifically.

When you can see clearly:

- you stop wasting energy on paths that don't serve you
- the opinions of others lose their power to destabilise you
- you access a kind of confidence that doesn't depend on external validation.

That's real power, not power over others, but power over your own mind, your own choices and your own life.

And mastery? Mastery is what happens when clarity becomes consistent, when you're not just occasionally seeing clearly but building a life around that clarity.

The neuroscience of seeing clearly

Science has now uncovered that our brains are physically different when we're operating from clarity versus confusion.

Your brain has two key regions relevant here: the prefrontal cortex and the amygdala. The prefrontal cortex sits right behind your forehead. It's the newest part of the brain evolutionarily, and the part that makes humans human. It handles executive functioning such as planning, decision-making, impulse control and complex thinking. The amygdala came much earlier in our evolution. It's your brain's alarm system, constantly scanning for threats and triggering the fight-flight-freeze response when it detects danger. It kept your ancestors alive when sabre-toothed cats roamed the earth. It's fast and powerful and doesn't consult your rational mind before acting.

These two regions are in constant competition for control of your behaviour. They're so important they are even being discussed at my son Ollie's new school, and he's only five. (It's actually pretty cool—he comes home and tells me about his brain and how it operates. I guess his teachers are hoping to help them regulate big emotions when feeling overwhelmed and help parents with those meltdowns we all try to deal with. It's an absolute gift and I only wish we'd all learned something similar at school.)

When you're stressed, anxious, overwhelmed or confused, your amygdala takes over. It floods your system with cortisol and adrenaline, preparing you for physical danger. Your heart rate increases. Your breathing becomes shallow. Blood flow shifts away from your prefrontal cortex toward your muscles.

This is brilliant if you need to run from a tiger. It's catastrophic if you're trying to make a thoughtful decision about your career, your relationship, your life direction or even just the kind of milk you want to buy at your local supermarket. Meltdown, aisle 3!

When your amygdala is running the show, you literally cannot think clearly. This isn't a character flaw; it's biology. Your prefrontal cortex goes offline when your threat-detection system is activated. Likely you can remember saying something in an argument that you immediately regretted, or making an impulsive decision when stressed that made no sense in hindsight. You can know what the right choice is and still not be able to access that knowledge when you're overwhelmed. Your prefrontal cortex knows, but your amygdala has the wheel.

The good news is this process works also in reverse. When you're calm, regulated and present, when you've done the work to quiet the alarm system, your prefrontal cortex comes back online. You can access your full cognitive capacity and see options you couldn't see before. You can make decisions aligned with your values rather than your fears. Daniel Kahneman's Nobel Prize–winning research confirmed this. Most of our decisions are made on fast, emotional autopilot, but we can train ourselves to slow down and engage our full thinking capacity.

The clarity compound effect

In *Atomic Habits,* James Clear introduced the concept of the aggregation of marginal gains. This is the idea that small improvements, compounded over time, produce remarkable results. If you can get 1 per cent better every day, for example, you'll be 37 times better after a year. This uses the formula for compound interest, and the same principle applies to clarity. I call it the 'clarity compound effect', and it works like this:

Small moments of clarity × consistency = transformation

You don't need to achieve enlightenment, retreat to a monastery or overhaul your entire life in one dramatic gesture. You just need small, consistent moments of clear seeing.

If you can have five minutes of genuine presence with your morning coffee, guess what? That's clarity. One decision made from a calm state instead of reactive panic is clarity. A single conversation where you're fully listening instead of planning your response is clarity. Pausing before sending that angry email back to Karen and instead asking, 'What do I actually want here?' is clarity. Each of these moments is tiny and almost insignificant in isolation, but they compound.

Every time you access clarity, you're strengthening the neural pathways that make clarity easier for you to access next time. Every time you pause instead of reacting, you're training your brain that pausing is an option. Every time you see through the noise, you're building the mental muscles that help you see through the noise faster tomorrow.

In making these kinds of choices, you're working with the neuroplasticity of your brain, which is its ability to rewire itself based on experience. Practising clarity literally changes your brain.

Think about a pathway through the jungle that has been walked on thousands of times. That path is clear and easy to walk on. If you decide to cut a new path, that track will be small and thin. If you don't walk that path again it would just grow back. The easier option would be to walk the original path. But what would happen if you decided to walk that new path numerous times instead of the old path? Eventually, you would create a clear path that was easy to access and the old path would grow over. In essence, that is how your brain works.

Back in 2021, I started forging a new path without really being aware of the science behind it. Every day, first thing in the morning, I chose to focus on three positive emotions of love, energy and self-belief. Over time, these helped to create a neural highway of positive emotions. I just started with the following very simple mantras:

- I am loved.
- I am strong.
- I am amazing.

Now they weren't perfect by any means and neither was I. Parts of me didn't even believe them, but I stuck with them. Walking a new path is hard, and I fell off at times and was tempted to go back to the old, easier path. The mantras have certainly changed over the years but, at the time, they were what I needed. They made me feel safe. Once I started to change the narrative, I started to change my state and eventually my story—and then I did start to believe, wholeheartedly.

Through committing to this habit, my neural pathway is now well established. When I wake up, it automatically gives me this incredibly positive, kind and energetic start to the day. This, in turn, has allowed me to change in other areas. We all have to start somewhere, and I encourage you to give yourself permission to take what feels best for you and just start.

> *You don't need to see the whole staircase. You just need to see the next step clearly.*

You don't have to solve your entire life today or go from total confusion to perfect clarity in one leap. You just need to see a little more clearly today than you did yesterday, then a little more clearly tomorrow and then the day after. The compound effect will do the rest.

Clarity versus certainty

The distinction between clarity and certainty almost got me during my recovery. As humans, most of us want certainty. I wanted to be certain that the work would be worth it, that I would get better and I wouldn't relapse. I wanted to be certain my life would turn out okay.

But certainty isn't available to humans. The future is genuinely unknown. You cannot have certainty about things that haven't happened yet, and pretending you can is just another form of delusion.

What I learned, slowly and painfully, is that clarity doesn't require certainty. In fact, the desperate need for certainty is often what blocks clarity. Think about it: when you demand certainty before acting, what happens? You wait. You gather more information and research endlessly. You seek opinions, run scenarios and try to eliminate all risk. And while you're doing all that, you're not moving. You're not learning or getting feedback from reality. You're stuck in your head, trying to think your way to a guarantee that doesn't exist.

Clarity takes a different approach. Clarity says, 'I can see enough to take the next step. I'll take it, see what I learn, and then look for the next step from there'. Clarity is about direction, not the destination. Clarity provides a compass, not a GPS with turn-by-turn navigation. Clarity is knowing enough to move, not knowing everything before you start.

Around 2000 years ago, Stoic philosopher Seneca advised,

> It is not that we have a short time to live, but that we waste a lot of it. Life is long enough, and a sufficiently generous amount has been given to us for the highest achievements if it were all well invested.

Waiting for certainty is not a good investment. It's a form of hiding. And the years you spend waiting for the certainty of the perfect moment are years you could have spent learning, growing and finding your way.

> *If you knew what was coming, you would stop stressing and start celebrating.*

I say this to people all the time, and it usually takes them a moment to understand what I mean. If you could see your life five years from now—see that you made it through this difficult season, that you figured it out and you're okay—you wouldn't spend today in anxious paralysis. You'd trust the process and act. You'd do the work without needing a guarantee. You'd stop stressing and start celebrating.

Okay, if someone had said this to me while I was on my bed in hospital, when I felt I had absolutely nothing going for me and was on the edge of the end, I would likely have thrown my leftover sandwich at them and told them to get out. But looking back on it now, it all makes sense. I know now I just have to trust the process and focus on just the next moment.

You can't see five years from now, but you can choose to act as if the outcome will be worth it. You can choose faith over fear. You can choose movement over paralysis.

That's clarity combined with courage, so start celebrating!

What clarity makes possible

When clarity becomes consistent, everything shifts. I've seen this in my own life, and in the lives of thousands of others. Clarity makes decisions easier, not because you have all the information, but because you can see what actually matters. The noise falls away. The opinions of others become interesting rather than controlling. The 'right' choice becomes obvious not because it's guaranteed to work, but because it aligns with who you are.

Let me give you an example here to illustrate this further. I recently worked with Michelle, who had been paralysed for two years about whether to leave her corporate job and start her own business. She had two years of pros and cons lists, two years of asking everyone's opinion and two years of second-guessing herself.

When Michelle and I worked on her clarity, when she finally got quiet enough to see herself clearly, the decision quickly became obvious. Her circumstances hadn't changed, but she could finally see what she actually wanted underneath all the fear and external expectations. She started her business and it's thriving. She's certainly faced some hurdles, but she created the clarity she needed to back herself and jump.

Clarity also makes relationships healthier. When you can see yourself clearly, you stop needing others to validate your worth. When you can see others clearly, you stop projecting your wounds onto them. When you can see the dynamics in your closest relationships clearly, you can address what's really happening instead of fighting about surface symptoms.

I've watched couples on the brink of divorce pull back from the edge, not because their problems disappeared but because they finally got clear on what they each needed and whether they could provide it for each other. Sometimes that clarity saved the marriage. Sometimes it allowed them to end it with love instead of bitterness. Both are victories and both require clarity.

Clarity even makes the impossible feel possible, and this one still amazes me. Perhaps you've heard of the phenomenon in psychology known as 'learned helplessness'—the state where someone has failed so many times that they stop trying, even when success becomes available. They've learned to believe that their situation is hopeless.

Clarity dissolves learned helplessness, not through positive thinking or motivational slogans, but through accurate seeing. When you see your situation clearly, including your own role in it, the options you've been blind to and the resources you've discounted, 'impossible' often turns out to be 'not yet attempted'.

People don't gain new abilities with this breakthrough, but finally see the abilities they already had. I often tell people, 'Everything you need is within you'. Clarity allows you to see that.

The clarity experience

When clarity arrived for me, the whole weight of the world seemed to lift from my shoulders, and I felt like I could breathe again and trust what was ahead.

Here's what clarity might feel like for you:

- *Physical sensations:* Your body relaxes, not into collapse but readiness. Your shoulders drop, your jaw unclenches and your breathing deepens. The brain fog dissipates, and you have a sense of being settled in your own skin and present in your body rather than trapped in your head.
- *Mental experience:* Your racing thoughts slow down, not by force but by loss of interest. The thoughts that seemed so urgent reveal themselves as noise, and they lose their grip. What remains is spaciousness—room to think, see and choose.
- *Emotional quality:* You feel peace, but not passivity. You feel a quiet confidence that doesn't depend on external circumstances. You might still have problems to solve, but you no longer feel like those problems are crushing you. You're standing beside them rather than under them.
- *Decision-making:* You become better at making decisions. Options that seemed equivalent suddenly have different weights. One path feels right, not because you've logically eliminated all others, but because something in you recognises it as aligned. The choice becomes 'obvious'.
- *Relational shift:* Other people seem more themselves. You're not projecting your fears or needs onto them but actually seeing them, maybe for the first time. And they often notice something is different about you, even though they may not be able to name it.

This is what I tasted that morning in my room, and it's available to you. Perhaps not permanently at first, but increasingly as a skill you develop, a state you can access when you need it and a home base you learn to return to.

> *Clarity isn't a destination; it's a home you learn to find your way back to.*

Taking a clarity pause

I talk about calming the nervous system to find clarity in much more detail in the Regulation Pillar (chapter 7), but the following is a single practice that can help you create a moment of clarity even before you've learned the full system.

I call this practice the 'clarity pause':

1. *Stop:* Whatever you're doing, pause. Physically stop moving if you can. This interrupts the momentum of reaction.
2. *Breathe:* Take three conscious breaths. Inhale through your nose for four counts. Hold for four counts. Exhale through your mouth for six counts. This activates your parasympathetic nervous system and starts to bring your prefrontal cortex back online.
3. *Ask:* Consider one question: 'What do I actually want here?' Don't think about what you think you should want or what others might want you to want. What do you actually want in this moment?
4. *Listen:* Wait for an answer. It might come as a word, a feeling, an image or a knowing. Don't force it. Just wait.

That's it. Stop. Breathe. Ask. Listen.

Do this the next time you feel overwhelmed, confused or reactive — perhaps before you send an important email, in the middle of an argument or when you wake up at 3 am with a racing mind.

This practice won't solve everything. But it will give you a taste of what clarity feels like. And that taste, like my five minutes back in my room at the mental facility, will show you what's possible.

The cost of staying unclear

Over this and the previous chapter, I've described the benefits of clarity and the costs of confusion.

You also need to consider the deeper costs to your life caused by confusion and lack of clarity. These include the opportunities you miss, the relationships you damage, the time you waste and the person you never become.

Every year spent confused is a year not building what matters to you. Every decision made from confusion creates consequences you'll have to clean up later. Every relationship filtered through confusion is a relationship with fog between you.

I wasted the years between the 2004 tsunami and my hospital room. I may have been incredibly busy, but busy and clear are not the same thing. I was running in circles, working hard to go nowhere and putting enormous energy into a life that wasn't actually mine.

That's what confusion does. It lets you feel productive while making no progress. It lets you be busy while staying stuck. It lets you exhaust yourself in motion that generates no movement.

> “*Confusion is expensive, but clarity is compound interest on your life.*”

Chapter Three

Introducing the Eight Pillars of the Clarity Method

When I met Marcus at one of my wellbeing workshops, he looked like a man who had already given up. He was 43 years old, recently divorced and just made redundant from a finance job he'd held for 16 years. His adult daughter had stopped speaking to him after the separation. He wasn't sleeping, was drinking too much and had gained 20 kilograms in six months. And underneath all of it, I recognised something in his eyes immediately, because I'd seen it in my own reflection years before.

He was lost; completely and utterly lost. My heart sank. I knew and felt his pain. I've been there.

'I don't know who I am anymore', Marcus told me. 'Everything I thought I was—the job, the marriage, the father—it's all gone. I feel like I'm drowning in the middle of my own life.'

I said, 'Marcus, what if I told you that everything falling apart is actually the beginning of everything coming together?' At the time, he looked at me like I'd lost my mind, but that conversation was now 18 months ago.

Today, Marcus runs his own consulting business. He's lost the weight and repaired his relationship with his daughter. He's in a new relationship with a woman who, as he puts it, 'sees me for who I actually am, not who I was pretending to be'. He meditates every morning. He sleeps through the night. He knows exactly who he is and what he wants.

He is the same man, with the same history and same circumstances that brought him to my door. Yet, he's living a completely different life. What changed is that he walked the eight pillars with me. His journey may not have been perfect, linear or without setbacks. But step by step, pillar by pillar, Marcus rebuilt himself from the inside out.

This chapter is your introduction to that same journey.

The architecture of transformation

The Clarity Method is the architecture of transformation I discovered through my own recovery and have since refined through years of working with people seeking the same thing: a way out of the fog.

These aren't abstract concepts I invented in a vacuum. They're the distilled wisdom of what works, drawn from ancient philosophy, modern neuroscience, psychological research and the lived experience of real people making real changes in their real lives.

Each of the eight pillars, outlined in the following table, matters, as does the order and the integration. Skip one, and the structure wobbles. Rush through one, and you'll find yourself circling back later. This isn't a checklist to work through. It's a journey back to yourself.

The eight pillars in the Clarity Method: An overview

Pillar	Core question	What it unlocks
1. Willingness	'Am I ready to begin?'	The decision to engage with life again
2. Awareness	'What's really happening?'	Seeing clearly for the first time
3. Accountability	'What am I responsible for?'	Owning your life without shame
4. Regulation	'Can I feel safe in my body?'	Learning to calm the storm within
5. Identity	'Who am I beneath everything?'	Remembering the real you
6. Habits and discipline	'Who am I becoming daily?'	Becoming who you say you want to be
7. Connection and contribution	'How do I heal through others?'	Expanding beyond yourself
8. Integration	'How do I sustain this?'	Living with clarity, not chasing it

Each pillar builds on the one before it. The questions progress from basic readiness ('Am I willing?') through self-understanding ('Who am I?') to sustained practice ('How do I sustain this?').

This isn't random. This is architecture. And like any architecture, it follows principles that can't be violated without consequences.

The map you've been missing

Most people who feel lost aren't actually lost; they just don't have a map. Think about it: if you woke up in an unfamiliar forest with no idea where you were, you'd likely feel panic, confusion and overwhelm. You might run around in circles, exhausting yourself while making no progress. You might sit down and give up, convinced there's no way out.

But if you were handed a map of the forest, with your location marked and a clear path to safety signposted, everything would change. The forest or your circumstances haven't changed, but your relationship to those circumstances has transformed completely. You can see, and when you can see, you can move.

The Eight Pillars of Clarity are that map, helping you move from willingness, to awareness, to ownership, to stability, to self-trust, to consistency, to connection, and to a life that feels like yours again and that you can certainly be proud of.

That's the journey. That's what's waiting for you on the other side of this book, and I'm excited for you and proud of you for being here with me.

As you prepare to start your journey, let's look at each pillar in a little more detail.

Pillar 1: Willingness — the decision to begin

Everything starts here. You're not waiting for motivation or the perfect plan; you just need willingness. Willingness is the moment you stop waiting for life to change and decide to change your relationship with life. You can always find a reason not to do something, so you need to figure out why you must nail this right now.

Willingness comes before motivation, not after. You don't get motivated and then act—you act and then motivation follows. In my hospital room, I wasn't ready or motivated, but I was willing. And that willingness was the crack that let the light in. This led me to my why and purpose that I lean into everyday.

Pillar 2: Awareness — seeing clearly for the first time

Once you're willing and you have your why, the next step is learning to see. Awareness is the practice of observing your life, your thoughts and your patterns as they actually are, not as you wish they were or fear they might be. It's uncovering what's serving you and what is not.

Awareness starts the moment you step back and realise, *I am not my thoughts. I am the one observing my thoughts.* The moment you can observe a pattern, you're no longer controlled by it. You cannot change what you refuse to see.

Pillar 3: Accountability — owning your life without shame

This is where most people get stuck, and it's also where everything pivots. Accountability is taking ownership of your life, not with blame or shame, but with the recognition that you are the common denominator.

In the Accountability Equation, Event + Response = Outcome. You can't control the events, but you always control your response. Nobody is coming to save you. That's the bad news. You don't need saving. You need ownership. That's the good news.

Pillar 4: Regulation — learning to feel safe in your own body

You can have all the awareness and accountability in the world, but it won't matter if your nervous system is constantly in survival mode. When your amygdala is activated, your prefrontal cortex goes offline. You cannot think clearly because your body believes it's in danger.

Regulation is the practice of calming your nervous system so clarity becomes possible. Most people try to think their way out of anxiety, but this doesn't work. You have to breathe your way through it and feel your way back to safety.

Pillar 5: Identity — remembering who you are beneath everything

With a regulated nervous system and a willingness to take ownership, you're finally ready for the deeper work: discovering who you actually are, not who you've been told to be or the labels you've accumulated, but the real you.

Growing up, I built my entire identity around being a cricketer. When this was stripped away, I didn't know who I was, what my values were or what my strengths and life skills were because I'd never asked the deeper questions. Most of us haven't, so digging deeply is what this pillar is all about.

Pillar 6: Habits and discipline — becoming who you say you want to be

Identity without action is just philosophy. This pillar is where clarity becomes behaviour and insights become habits. The person you want to become meets the person you actually are — one day at a time, one choice at a time.

Discipline isn't punishment. Discipline is care for your future self. Show me your habits, I'll show you your future. If you change the habits, you change the beliefs. Change the beliefs, you change the identity. And change the identity, you change your life.

Pillar 7: Connection and contribution — healing through relationship and service

The first six pillars are largely about you. This pillar is where your journey expands beyond yourself. You can do all the inner work and still feel empty if your life isn't connected to something larger than you. Humans didn't evolve for isolation. We're wired for belonging.

At one point in my recovery I faced a choice: I could go home, close the curtains and sink back into darkness, or I could drag myself to the nearby oval and help a young cricket player with his technique. This turned into a sliding door moment that changed the trajectory of my life. We heal in connection. We suffer in isolation.

Pillar 8: Integration — living with clarity, not chasing it

The final pillar isn't a destination but a way of life. Integration is the practice of maintaining clarity when life gets loud again—because it will. The noise never permanently disappears and the old patterns don't vanish forever.

What changes is your relationship to all of it. Integration is the difference between someone who got better once and someone who knows how to stay well. It's the difference between a peak experience and a transformed life.

Why this order matters

You might be wondering whether you could start with the Habits Pillar instead of the Willingness Pillar, or whether you could skip the Regulation Pillar and go straight to the Identity Pillar. Well, you could try and many people do, but they almost always end up circling back.

Here's why the order matters:

- *You can't sustain change without stability:* This is why Regulation (Pillar 4) must come before Habits (Pillar 6). If your nervous system is constantly dysregulated, any habits you build will collapse under the first wave of stress. You need a regulated foundation before you can build consistent action on top of it.
- *You can't know yourself without owning yourself:* This is why Accountability (Pillar 3) comes before Identity (Pillar 5). If you're still in victim mode and still blaming others for your situation, you'll never get honest enough to see who you really are. Ownership clears the path for self-discovery.
- *You can't contribute from an empty cup:* This is why Connection (Pillar 7) comes late in the sequence. Trying to show up for others when you're depleted, confused and unregulated doesn't help anyone. It just creates co-dependency and burnout. You must fill your own cup before you can pour into others.
- *You can't integrate what you haven't built:* This is why Integration (Pillar 8) comes last. You don't have anything to sustain until you've walked the journey. Integration is the practice of maintaining the clarity you've developed through Pillars 1 to 7.

Think of this process as being like constructing a building. The foundation must come before the walls and the walls must come before the roof. You can't hang pictures until the walls are up. You can't move in until the roof is on.

The same is true for personal transformation. Architecture supports becoming who you're meant to be, and these eight pillars are that architecture.

The clarity check-in

Before we dive into the pillars, I want you to take a snapshot of where you are right now, not where you want to be or where you think you should be, but where you actually are, today, across all eight dimensions of clarity.

Rate yourself from one to ten on each pillar. Be honest, nobody will see this but you. A rating of one means this area is completely absent from your life right now. A rating of ten means you're living it consistently.

1. *Willingness:* 'Am I showing up for life, even when it's hard?'
2. *Awareness:* 'Can I see my thoughts and patterns clearly?'
3. *Accountability:* 'Am I owning my responses instead of blaming my circumstances?'
4. *Regulation:* 'Can I calm myself when my body is activated?'
5. *Identity:* 'Do I know who I am beneath the labels?'
6. *Habits and discipline:* 'Am I doing the daily work that builds the life I want?'
7. *Connection and contribution:* 'Am I genuinely connected and giving from overflow?'
8. *Integration:* 'When life gets hard, does the work hold?'

Write your scores down. This is your baseline — your starting coordinates. When you finish this book and return to this page, you'll score yourself again. The distance between

(continued)

those two numbers is the transformation the Clarity Method made possible.

Your lowest score tells you where you need this book most. Your highest score tells you what's already strong. Both matter, because clarity isn't about fixing what's broken. It's about seeing all of it clearly.

Starting your journey

We're about to dive into each pillar in depth. In the next two parts, I've included one chapter per pillar, with content to help you understand the concept and content to help you practice it. By the end of the book, you won't just know about the eight pillars. You'll have lived them.

Here's how I recommend you approach what follows:

- *Read actively, not passively:* This isn't a book to skim but a book to engage with. Underline passages and write in the margins (or use the highlight and notes features if reading the ebook). Argue with me where you disagree. Make this book yours.
- *Do the exercises:* Every pillar has practices. Don't skip them. Reading about push-ups doesn't build muscle, and reading about clarity doesn't build clarity. You have to do the work. That work can be done in your own journal or my Clarity Workbook, but I do not recommend trying to do it on your phone or a computer, because these devices are where distractions live. Writing creates transformation.

- *Go in order:* At least the first time through. I know it's tempting to skip to the pillar that seems most relevant to your current struggle, but resist that temptation. The order matters and you need to trust the architecture. However, once you have gone through the pillars and feel more comfortable and at ease with yourself, it's perfectly okay to tap into a pillar that you feel you need to focus on in a certain season or circumstance in your life. If it serves you, then go with it and allow it to help you when needed.
- *Be patient:* This isn't a weekend project. Real transformation takes time. I spent 13 years getting from that hospital room to the life I have now. You might move faster or slower but, either way, rushing won't help. The compound effect rewards consistency, not speed. Remember, life is not a race.
- *Return when you drift:* You will drift and you will lose your way. That's not failure; that's being human. The gift of this framework is that you always know the way back. When life gets loud, return to Pillar 1. Ask yourself, 'Am I willing?' Then move through the sequence again.

As mentioned, you can access my Clarity Workbook (available via cameronmerchant.com) to practice the learnings in this book. This works alongside the pillars, providing a space where you can respond to the exercises, questions and actions in the following chapters. The Clarity Workbook becomes your personal playbook for life. It is a place where your thoughts, lessons, goals and breakthroughs live, ready for you to go with you wherever and return to whenever you need direction.

When you use the Clarity Workbook, or your own journal, in this way this book transforms into a living guide for your life. It becomes your own blueprint, with your next steps of clarity and growth, leading to the life you're intentionally building. You can then return to this blueprint whenever life gets noisy.

Remember, this isn't a book just to finish; it's your personal guide to live by.

The eight pillars in action

Let me return to Marcus, the man I introduced at the start of this chapter and who, when I first met him, looked like he'd already given up.

Here's how the eight pillars worked in his life over the next 18 months:

- *Willingness:* Marcus showed up. That was his first act of willingness. He didn't feel ready and he didn't believe the process would work, but he showed up anyway. He kept showing up, session after session, even when part of him wanted to give up. We connected him to his why to keep going.
- *Awareness:* We mapped his life honestly. For the first time, he looked clearly at his patterns, including the overwork, the emotional unavailability and the way he'd used achievement to avoid intimacy. The discoveries were painful, but they were also true.
- *Accountability:* This was the hardest pillar for Marcus. He'd spent months blaming his ex-wife, his employer and his daughter. When he finally asked, 'What was my part in

this?'—really asked it, without defensiveness—everything shifted. He couldn't change what they'd done, but he could own how he'd shown up.

- *Regulation:* Marcus had been self-medicating with alcohol and work. We replaced those with actual regulation practices, including breathwork, movement and sleep hygiene. For the first time in years, he could feel his emotions without being overwhelmed by them.
- *Identity:* 'Who am I without the job title?' This question broke Marcus open. We discovered that he'd built his entire sense of worth on external achievement. We rebuilt this sense of self on something sturdier: his values, his character and who he was choosing to become.
- *Habits:* Marcus adopted a new morning routine and daily meditation. He implemented weekly calls with his daughter and a monthly review of his goals. These small actions and habits, repeated consistently, closed the gap between who he wanted to be and who he actually was.
- *Connection:* Marcus reached out to old friends he'd neglected and to his daughter, with humility and apology. Eventually, he reached out to a new partner, but only after he'd learned to be whole on his own.
- *Integration:* Now Marcus lives the practice, not perfectly but consistently. He has tools for when the fog returns and he trusts himself to find his way back. He's not chasing clarity anymore; he's living from it.

Marcus is the same man, with the same history and the same circumstances. He's now living a completely different life. That's the power of the eight pillars. This isn't theory but transformation.

Your journey begins

You now have the map, so your next question is simple: are you willing? I'm not asking if you're ready, certain or feeling like a smooth path is guaranteed. I'm just asking if you're willing.

If you are, if something in you is saying yes even while another part is scared, just know that's okay. It's normal. We all feel it I'm with you every step as you turn the page.

Part II is where the real work begins. We'll take each pillar one at a time, going deep, giving you everything I have, holding nothing back.

> *"You can move from willingness, to awareness, to ownership, to stability, to self-trust, to consistency, to connection and to a life that feels like yours again. Hard times may last a long time, but an epic story can last a lifetime."*

Be so proud of yourself for coming this far. I'm so excited for you. Let's begin.

Part II

Building your internal foundations with pillars one to four

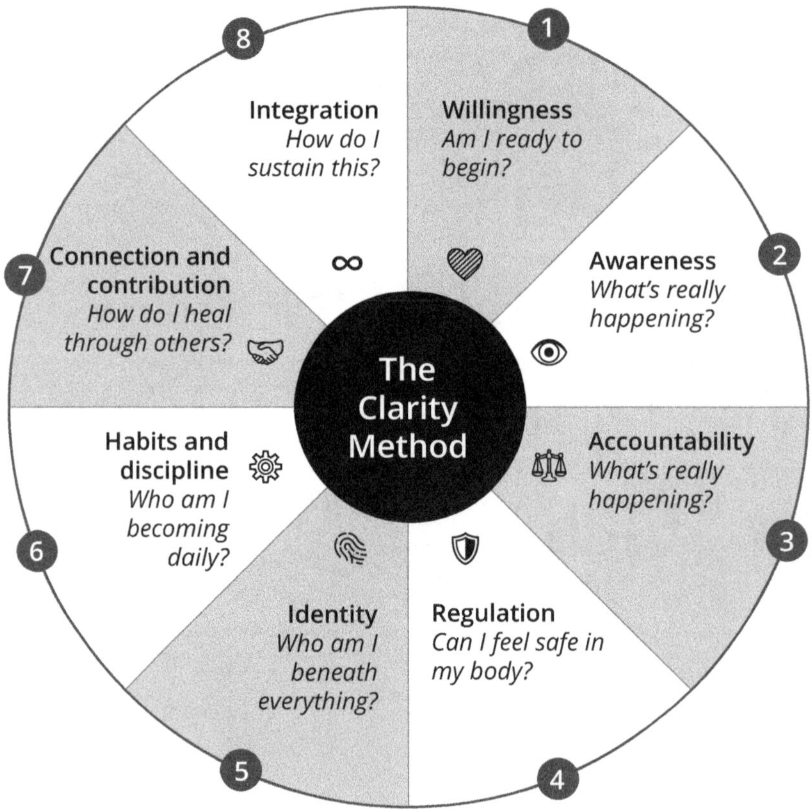
The Clarity Method
1
Willingness
Am I ready to begin?
2
Awareness
What's really happening?
3
Accountability
What's really happening?
4
Regulation
Can I feel safe in my body?
5
Identity
Who am I beneath everything?
6
Habits and discipline
Who am I becoming daily?
7
Connection and contribution
How do I heal through others?
8
Integration
How do I sustain this?

Chapter Four

Pillar 1: Willingness

> You don't have to see the whole staircase. You just have to be willing to lift your foot.

At certain moments in life, everything can feel stuck. It might not feel dramatically or catastrophically stuck, but just... the same. Have you ever felt that way? You're having the same thoughts, living the same patterns and having the same conversations. You have the same quiet feeling deep down that life could be different, but somehow you keep ending up right back where you started. I know that place well.

In the introduction, I talk about my early experience in a mental rehabilitation facility. Now let me tell you about what came immediately before this.

The decision to begin

I had found myself sleeping on a mate's couch in Sydney, not because I was on holiday or it was convenient, but because my life had quietly fallen apart and I was trying to piece it back together. Four weeks had passed since I'd returned from Canada (more on this in chapter 7). For four weeks, I'd been telling myself I was getting back on track and things were going to be okay. And, yet, nothing was really changing.

I'd experienced some superficial moments of light. You know the ones—those brief windows where you think, *Maybe things are turning around.* But underneath it all, the same thoughts kept circling. The same heaviness sat in my chest. The patterns hadn't changed and, deep down, I knew the truth. If nothing changed, nothing would change.

One night, after another long day of going over the same thoughts again and again, I ended up lying on the floor of my mate's bedroom just exhausted. I felt mentally worn down; the kind of tired that sleep doesn't fix. I stared into the abyss and thought, *There must be something I can do differently.* Because doing the same things and hoping for a different result wasn't working.

I now know you will remain the same until the pain of remaining the same is greater than the pain of change. And that's where I was on this particular night, so I finally picked up my phone and called a mate.

This person had walked a difficult path before me. He had been through rehab and done the hard work of rebuilding his life. I called him because I had no answers or idea what I was to do next. I needed some kind of direction and some kind of hope.

When he answered the phone, I tried to sound like I had things somewhat together. But he knew me too well and within a few minutes he simply said, 'Cam, you need to go to rehab. It will change your life. It might even save your life'.

I remember my immediate reaction. 'No chance.' Not because I didn't know he might be right, but because my mind instantly went somewhere else. What would people think? What would people say? I can't be seen doing that. I'm 'Cam, the professional cricketer who travelled the world and has a great life'. Surely, I had to keep that facade up. I tried to brush the suggestion off. 'I'm fine, mate. Everything's okay.'

But he didn't let it slide. After a short pause, he said something that completely stopped me in my tracks; something I will never forget that changed my life. 'Cam, do you realise that if you don't do anything right now, we'll be having this exact same conversation in a month's time?'

Everything went quiet. In that moment, I knew he was right. Nothing he said was dramatic or complicated. It was just painfully true. If I didn't change something, my life would simply repeat itself, and that wasn't good. I would still have moments, little glimpses of hope and temporary motivation, when things felt okay, but the overall pattern would remain the same. And a month later, I would be back on that same bedroom floor, having the same conversation.

That was the moment something shifted inside me. I didn't suddenly find motivation, excitement or confidence, but I did find willingness. And willingness is very different. Willingness isn't loud. It doesn't arrive with fireworks or big emotional breakthroughs. It's quiet. It's the moment you finally say to yourself, 'Maybe I don't have all the answers... but I'm willing to try something different'.

In that moment, something inside me softened and the weight I'd been carrying for weeks suddenly felt lighter. My problems didn't disappear, but for the first time in a long time, I stopped resisting the truth. I needed help and I was finally willing to do something about it. I made the decision to check myself into rehabilitation.

That decision simply meant I had taken the first step. But here's something incredibly important I've learned about change:

- Your life doesn't change the moment you feel ready.
- Your life changes the moment you become willing.

Most people wait for motivation. They wait until they feel confident, the fear disappears or the timing feels perfect, but those moments rarely come. And if you wait, it might be too late. Real change begins much earlier, when you reach the point when staying the same becomes more painful than trying something new.

When the discomfort of growth finally becomes less frightening than the discomfort of repeating your life, when willingness shows up, something powerful happens. You open the door to possibility, because willingness creates movement.

> *Movement creates opportunity, and opportunity is where transformation begins.*

Think about it like going to the gym. Say you've decided to start training in the morning. Your alarm goes off, but you just don't feel like it. Your body feels tired. Your mind tells you to stay in bed. You tell yourself you'll go tomorrow but if you show up anyway, even when you don't feel like it, something interesting happens. Perhaps you've been in this situation and know what it is. You never regret it afterwards. The hardest part wasn't the workout. The hardest part was being willing to start.

Life works the same way. You don't need to feel confident or have the perfect plan. You don't even need to know exactly where you're going. You just need to be willing to take the first step, because willingness gives your life a chance, and when you give your life a chance, anything becomes possible.

The myth of readiness

Here's the lie that keeps many people stuck: 'I'll start when I'm ready'. For example:

- I'll start the diet when I'm ready.
- I'll have the difficult conversation when I'm ready.
- I'll leave the job when I'm ready.
- I'll get help when I'm ready.
- I'll change my life when I'm ready.

Readiness feels like a prerequisite. It also feels responsible, like you're being smart and waiting for the right conditions before you commit. But readiness is a seductive, reasonable-sounding myth that will keep you waiting forever. You don't get ready and then start. You start and then get ready.

Think about it. Were you ready the first time you rode a bike or drove a car? Were you ready the first day of a new job or the first time you held your newborn child? Of course not. You were terrified and uncertain. You had no idea what you were doing but you did it anyway. And, in the doing, you became ready. In the action, you developed the capacity. The readiness came after the beginning, not before.

You don't have to feel ready; you just have to feel willing. This distinction is everything. Ready is a feeling that happens to you. You can wait your whole life for it and it might never arrive. Willing is a choice. It's something you do. It's available right now, regardless of how you feel. Ready waits for motivation. Willing creates it.

The Willingness Equation

Most people believe motivation works like this:

Motivation → Action → Results

First you feel motivated, then you take action, and then you get results. Makes sense, right? That's certainly what it feels like when we're stuck. We're waiting to feel motivated enough to move.

But research has proven this model is backwards. Here's how motivation actually works:

Action → Results → Motivation

You take action first—even small, imperfect action—and that action produces some kind of result. Even if these results are tiny, they generate motivation for more action. The motivation you're waiting for doesn't precede the action. It follows the action.

This is what I call the Willingness Equation:

Willingness + Small action = Motivation

You don't need motivation to start. You need willingness. The willingness to take one small action despite not feeling ready or knowing if it will work, and despite every voice in your head telling you to wait. That small action, just one, creates momentum. And momentum creates motivation.

> *Motivation is a visitor. Willingness is a decision.*

You can't control when motivation visits, but you can decide to be willing any time you choose—and that can be right now, if you want.

The science of starting

The research behind the power of starting is overwhelming.

In the field of psychology, for example, studies have looked at a treatment approach called 'behavioural activation'. This approach was originally developed for depression, based on a counterintuitive insight: depressed people don't lack motivation because they're depressed; they become more depressed because they lack action.

The traditional view was that depression caused withdrawal. Treat the depression, and the person would naturally become more active. Behavioural activation flipped this idea. What if withdrawal causes (or at least deepens) depression? What if the path out isn't waiting to feel better, but acting your way to feeling better?

The research validated this approach dramatically. Studies showed that behavioural activation, simply getting people to take action before they felt like it, was as effective as antidepressant medication for many patients. In some studies, it outperformed cognitive therapy.

Dr Christopher Martell, one of the pioneers of this approach, summarised it perfectly: 'Action precedes motivation'. And he didn't mean sometimes or in some cases. He meant this as a reliable, replicable principle of human psychology.

This same principle shows up across many different domains:

- Exercise research shows that people who commit to 'just showing up' at the gym, even without a plan to work out hard, exercise more consistently than those who wait until they feel motivated.
- Writing research shows that professional authors who write daily, regardless of inspiration, produce more quality work than those who wait for the muse.
- Habit research shows that the most powerful predictor of long-term behaviour change isn't initial motivation but the willingness to start before conditions are perfect.

The neuroscience explains why. When you take action, your brain releases dopamine—the motivation molecule. But dopamine isn't just released when you achieve something. It's also released in anticipation of achievement. Taking even a small step toward a goal signals to your brain that reward is possible, which triggers dopamine, which makes you want to take the next step.

This is why willingness creates motivation. The action itself, not the results, starts a neurochemical cascade that makes continued action easier.

The first step doesn't require motivation. It requires only the willingness to be momentarily uncomfortable. You just need the willingness to feel this momentary discomfort, to feel uncertain, scared and like you don't know what you're doing, for just long enough to take one small action. After that, the brain takes over, momentum builds and motivation appears, as if by magic.

But it's not magic. It's just the Willingness Equation in action.

The Zen of beginning

Perhaps you've heard the following famous Zen teaching: 'Before enlightenment, chop wood, carry water. After enlightenment, chop wood, carry water'.

When I first heard this, I thought it was about the mundane nature of spiritual life. Even enlightened people have to do the dishes, right? But I've since come to understand it differently. The teaching is about the nature of beginning and continuing.

Before enlightenment, you chop wood and carry water while waiting for transformation. You do the daily tasks and go through the motions while hoping something will change, looking for the moment when the motions become meaningful. After enlightenment, you realise that the chopping and the carrying were the transformation. The daily showing up was the path. You weren't waiting for enlightenment to arrive but building it, one piece of wood, one bucket of water at a time.

The willingness to do the ordinary thing, repeatedly, without needing it to feel extraordinary is the whole practice.

In the *Tao Te Ching*, Chinese philosopher Lao Tzu wrote, 'A journey of a thousand miles begins with a single step'. Many people quote this, but few people understand it. The point isn't that long journeys start with one step. The point is that the thousand-mile journey is nothing but single steps. At no point do you stop taking steps and start covering miles. The miles are made of steps—every single one of them.

The willingness to take this step, right now, is the willingness to take all the steps. You can only ever take one step at a time, and the future steps don't require your willingness yet. Only this one does.

> *The moment you stop waiting for permission is the moment your life begins.*

No-one is going to give you permission to change or tell you you're ready. No-one is going to tap you on the shoulder and say, 'Okay, now it's time'.

You give yourself permission. You decide you're willing. You begin and life changes. Give yourself permission.

What willingness actually looks like

Willingness in practice is showing up when you don't feel like it. It's not about performing at your best; it's just about showing up and starting before you're ready. Willingness is:

- getting to the gym even if you only walk on the treadmill for ten minutes
- opening the document even if you only write one paragraph

- making the call even if your voice shakes
- launching the business before you have the perfect plan
- having the conversation before you've rehearsed every word
- submitting the application before you're sure you're qualified.

Willingness looks like being bad at something on purpose. It's accepting that the first draft will be terrible, the first attempt will be awkward and the first months will be confusing. It's choosing to begin anyway, and letting the improvement come through iteration. Basically, it's me through this whole writing process. As I write this right now, it's 9.31 at night and the rest of the family are asleep. I've heated up some leftover pasta to try to stay as quiet as I can and not wake anyone. It would be so easy for me to just head to bed and pick up sometime tomorrow, but I'm still here right now with the willingness to figure this out, write perhaps imperfectly at first but at least taking another step regardless to see where it takes me.

Willingness looks like feeling scared and moving forward. You're not waiting for the fear to disappear, because it probably won't. You're moving while afraid and letting courage be the choice to act despite fear, not the absence of fear. Basically, you are giving yourself permission to suck at whatever you're attempting, so stop putting so much pressure on yourself and just dare to 'suck'.

Willingness looks like trusting the process without proof. You're acting as if the effort will be worth it, even though you can't know for certain. You're choosing faith in the journey when the destination is still invisible.

David Goggins, former Navy SEAL and ultramarathon runner, puts it this way: 'You have to be willing to go to war with yourself'. That might sound aggressive, but I understand what he means. The war isn't against all of yourself; it's against the part that wants comfort over growth, certainty over possibility and to stay the same over the pain of transformation.

Willingness is enlisting in that war, not once or dramatically, but every morning when the alarm goes off and the old voice tells you to stay in bed. Instead, you reframe that as you get up and reply, 'This is what I do now!'

Confronting the hidden benefits of unwillingness

If willingness is so powerful, why do we resist it? We resist because unwillingness has hidden benefits we don't like to acknowledge. For example:

- *Unwillingness protects us from failure:* If you never try, you never fail. Your potential remains theoretical—safely untested and permanently possible. The moment you attempt something, you risk discovering your limits. Staying unwilling keeps the dream alive, even if it keeps you asleep.
- *Unwillingness protects us from judgement:* If you don't put yourself out there, no-one can criticise what you create, reject what you offer or see you struggle. Unwillingness is a kind of hiding, and guess what? Hiding feels comfortable and safe.
- *Unwillingness gives us someone to blame:* If circumstances aren't right, if the timing isn't perfect or you're not ready yet, it's not your fault that your life hasn't changed. Unwillingness lets you stay a victim of external conditions rather than taking ownership of internal decisions.

- *Unwillingness preserves the familiar:* Change is uncomfortable. Even positive change disrupts the equilibrium of your life. Unwillingness keeps you in the known, even when the known is painful. 'Better the devil you know', the unconscious logic says.

I'm not judging these benefits. I've claimed all of them myself at different times. They're human and they're understandable, but they're also expensive. The comfort of unwillingness comes at the cost of your clarity.

Every day you wait for readiness is a day you don't spend building the life you actually want. Every moment you stay in theoretical potential is a moment you don't spend in actual growth. Every protection against failure is also protection against success.

Unwillingness has its payoffs, but the cost is your life.

Taking the movie test

Imagine your life is a movie, and you get to watch it in the cinema, on the big screen, with popcorn. You get to watch the whole thing. You're in the audience, watching someone who looks exactly like you live your exact life. You have the same job, same relationship, same habits, same excuses, and the same 2 am conversations with yourself. What would you be screaming at the screen?

You know that moment in a film when the whole cinema is thinking the same thing? *Just tell her. Quit the job. Get on the plane. Stop going back to the thing that's destroying you.* It's so obvious from the outside. The only person who can't see it is the character on screen—and, in this case, that's you. That's all of us. Whatever the audience would be screaming during a movie of your life is usually a very reliable indicator of where you should be putting your attention.

So why don't we do it? We're not procrastinating out of laziness. We're procrastinating out of fear—fear of what we'll find out about ourselves if we actually try. The upside of never trying is never having to feel the pain of failure. If you never step into the arena, you never have to face the scoreboard.

And, yeah, if you do the thing, you're going to lose sleep. You'll doubt whether it'll work. Your brain will serve up every worst-case scenario like a Netflix autoplay you didn't ask for. But the sleep you lose chasing something that matters is a different kind of tired to the sleep you lose avoiding it. One keeps you up with fear. The other keeps you up with fire. You know the difference.

The audience already knows what you need to do, and so do you. The only question is whether you're willing to stop watching from the cheap seats and step back into the screen.

> *You are the star of your movie. Stop watching your life from the audience. Get back on the screen.*

The willingness inventory

Let's get practical. I want you to answer the following questions honestly:

1. *Where are you unwilling?* Write down three to five areas of your life where you've been waiting to feel ready, waiting for better circumstances, waiting for motivation to strike.
2. *What's the hidden benefit?* For each area, ask yourself, 'What am I getting from staying unwilling? What am I protecting myself from?' Be honest, you'll always uncover something.

(continued)

3. *What's the cost?* For each area, ask yourself, 'What is this unwillingness actually costing me? What am I losing by waiting?'

The willingness reframe

Use your responses to reframe what you tell yourself. For each area you've identified, complete this sentence: 'I am willing to *[xxx]*, even though I don't feel ready, because *[xxx]*'.

The last part is the practice. You need to name your willingness and connect it to your deeper reason. For now, ask yourself what it is you actually want, and make it conscious and specific.

The ambivalence map

Now, you can get even clearer using the ambivalence map. Most people think resistance to change is a character flaw, but it's not. It's your nervous system weighing what you might gain against what you might lose. The part of you that says, 'Let's go' and the part that says, 'Not yet' are both trying to protect you. The trick isn't silencing one but hearing both clearly.

Draw a line down the centre of a page. On the left side, write, 'What I gain by changing'. On the right, write, 'What I lose by changing'. Fill both sides honestly. The gains are usually about your future self while the losses are usually about your current comfort. Both are real.

Now circle the one gain that creates the strongest feeling in your chest. That's your anchor. Then circle the one loss that feels most frightening. That's the dragon you'll need to face. You don't have to slay it today. You just need to see it clearly, because what you can name loses the power it held in the shadows.

The 24-hour willingness challenge

Here's something you can do right now, before you even finish this chapter. Choose one area of your life where you've been waiting for motivation. (You can use your responses from the preceding exercise.) Now identify the smallest possible action you could take in that area within the next 24 hours. And I mean small, so small it seems almost pointless.

When I was at my worst, crippled with anxiety and depression and almost unable to function, my room was a mess and the apartment dismal. Cleaning the whole apartment felt like a huge mountain to climb. But instead of going to bed having accomplished nothing, I knew that being willing to just do one small task would go a long way to potentially being able to do another small task tomorrow. At that time, my bedroom floor was covered in clothes (like I was trying to be environmentally friendly and create my own floor insulation). A load of washing was a huge task, but I was willing to just do one small thing for the day. Getting that load of washing in seemed like an enormous win at the time. And more small steps followed. Okay, the washing may have sat in the machine for the next three days but at least I'd made a start. Your small act doesn't have to be perfect at all; it just has to be something. Give yourself some grace in the meantime.

Consider the following small steps you could take in your life:

- *If you've been wanting to exercise:* Put on your workout clothes. That's it. You don't have to work out. Just put on the clothes.
- *If you've been avoiding a difficult conversation:* Write one sentence about what you want to say. You don't have to send it or say it. Just write one sentence.

- *If you've been wanting to start a creative project:* Open a blank document and write a working title. You don't have to write more. Just write the title.
- *If you've been putting off getting help:* Search for one therapist or counsellor in your area. You don't have to call. Just search.

The action should take less than five minutes, and it should be so easy that not doing it would be embarrassing. Work out what your action could be, and then do it; not tomorrow or when you feel ready, but today.

This is the Willingness Equation in action:

Willingness + Small action = Motivation

You're not waiting for inspiration. You're creating it. Willingness is the door and everything else is on the other side.

My willingness moment

When I was in rehab, I attended many group counselling sessions. In the first few, I held back. I sat in the circle and listened to other people share their struggles—people who were fighting battles I understood, speaking truths I needed to hear—but didn't speak myself.

Eventually, I was asked to share, and something happened that I didn't expect. Instead of giving the polished version, the 'doing great, thanks for asking' version, I finally let go and told the truth. I told the group about the 4 am weight on my chest. I told them my life was a shambles, that I was afraid of starting from scratch again and had virtually nothing going for me. I told them about the shame and embarrassment I felt about where I was and the potential judgement I would receive for being here. I told them I was afraid of the voice telling me to stay in bed, and that I'd come not because

I felt ready but because I was finally willing to try even when trying felt impossible.

After the meeting, a man maybe 20 years older than me approached. He looked at me with eyes that had seen things and said, 'What you shared in there, that took courage. And I want you to know something. The fact that you're here, that you keep showing up, that's the whole thing. That's the practice. You don't have to feel better to get better. You just have to keep showing up'.

I think about that man often. I don't even know his name, but his words landed in me like seeds.

You will remain the same until the pain of remaining the same is greater than the pain of change. That's where my willingness moments showed up for me. I knew I wanted change and couldn't accept the pain of remaining the same anymore, so I was willing to step forward, do something about it and show up. I was willing to lay it all out on the line and give all of myself for even a glimmer of peace and clarity, and I'm so glad I did.

Right now, you're here with me, willing to make a change. You keep showing up. That's everything in this moment and I'm so proud of you. I hope you are also proud of yourself, regardless of where you are right now. If you were able to put a load of washing on today, or even just pants, that's more than I could manage on my darkest days, so you're doing better than I was at one stage in my life. There's something to be very proud of.

You don't have to feel ready. You just have to be willing to show up.

> *The life you want is on the other side of the step you keep avoiding.*

Are you willing?

Finding your deeper why

In September 1942, a young psychiatrist named Viktor Frankl was arrested by the Nazis and transported to a concentration camp. Over the next three years, he would be moved through four different camps, including Auschwitz. He would lose his pregnant wife, his parents, and his brother to the concentration camps (either due to starvation and sickness or the gas chambers). He would be stripped of everything—his possessions, his profession, his dignity and his name (replaced by a number). He would be starved, beaten and worked to the edge of death.

He would also discover something that would change psychology forever. Frankl noticed a pattern among the prisoners. Some gave up quickly. They stopped eating, stopped moving and stopped trying. Within weeks, sometimes days, they were dead, not from the direct violence of the guards, but from what Frankl later called 'give-up-itis' (borrowing the term from American soldiers). They had lost the will to live.

But others survived circumstances that seemed unsurvivable. Prisoners who were older, weaker and sicker than those who died, somehow kept going. They endured starvation that should have killed them. They withstood brutality that should have broken them. They refused to die when death seemed like the only reasonable option.

The difference wasn't physical strength or luck. It wasn't even optimism in any simple sense. It was meaning. Those who survived had something to live for. They had a reason beyond their own comfort, and a why that was stronger than their suffering.

One man was sustained by the thought of his child waiting for him in another country, and another by a scientific manuscript he hadn't finished. Another was sustained by the simple belief that his suffering had a purpose he couldn't yet see. Frankl himself was carried by two things: his love for his wife (not knowing she had already died) and his determination to reconstruct the manuscript the Nazis had destroyed, a book about finding meaning in suffering. A book he was now living.

After liberation, Frankl wrote *Man's Search for Meaning*, which would go on to sell over 16 million copies. In it, he articulated the insight from Friedrich Nietzsche that had kept him alive: 'He who has a why to live for can bear almost any how'. That single sentence is the foundation on which you need to build your willingness.

Why willingness isn't enough

So far in this chapter, I've told you that willingness is the door and everything else is on the other side. The decision to show up—before you feel ready, before you feel motivated—is where transformation begins. All of that is true.

But here's what I now need to add: willingness alone will not sustain you. I learnt this in hospital at the very same moment I knew was ready and willing to get up and try life again because then I realised I didn't know what I was doing it for.

Willingness gets you started. It gets you out of bed on the hard mornings and taking the first step when every part of you wants to stay still. But willingness is a finite resource. You can white-knuckle your way through a day, maybe a week and maybe even a month. But eventually, the willingness muscle exhausts. The old voices get louder and the comfort of old patterns calls you back.

And in that moment, when willingness alone isn't enough, you need something deeper. You need a why. I don't mean a surface-level 'I want to lose weight', 'I want to be successful' or 'I want to feel better'. Those whys aren't strong enough to hold you when the storm hits. You need a why that sings to your soul and connects to something fundamental about who you are and what your life is for. You need a why you would crawl through fire to honour.

Think about an anchor. When the seas are calm, you don't really need it. The boat is fine on its own, bobbing around close to where you left it. But when the storm comes, when the waves crash and the wind howls and everything in you wants to drift, the anchor is the only thing that keeps you from being swept away.

> *Your why is your anchor. Without it, you will drift. With it, you can endure almost anything.*

The night my why saved my life

Back in the introduction to this book, I told you about the night in my rehab room when I sat on the edge of my bed with a choice in my hands, questioning everything. I told you about the dark voice that said, 'This could be the end. You could be free from all of this'. I also briefly told you about the other voice, the one that pulled me back from that edge.

I wasn't saved by logic. In that moment, I couldn't access logic. My prefrontal cortex was offline, flooded by despair, unreachable by reason.

And I wasn't saved by willpower. I had no willpower left. I was exhausted in a way that went beyond tired, down into the marrow of my bones.

It was the other voice. So let me tell you a little more about it. This voice didn't argue with my pain. It didn't tell me things would get better. It didn't offer platitudes. It asked me questions.

What is it you really want? More accolades with sport? No. *More travel?* Done that. *What about a companion? A loved one? A family? Someone to build a life with. What about her?* Her. The woman I hadn't met yet. The soulmate I still believed was out there, even though I couldn't have told you why I believed it. *You haven't found her yet.*

And then: *What about them?* Them. The children I hadn't had yet. The family I'd imagined since I was young. The father I wanted to become but hadn't yet become. The fleeting images of me playing in the backyard with my kids, laughing, running and playing. *You haven't held your child yet. You haven't seen their face. You haven't watched them grow.*

And finally: *What about you?* The real me. The me I sensed was possible but had never fully become. The me that was buried under years of trauma and coping and performance. *You haven't become who you're meant to be. You haven't lived the life that's waiting for you. Don't you want to find out what that life looks like?*

In that moment, I wasn't thinking about recovery plans or therapy appointments or the mechanics of getting better. I was thinking about Jules, even though I didn't know her name yet or have any idea what she looked like. I was thinking about the children I would hold, even though I couldn't have imagined their faces.

I was connected to a why that was bigger than my pain.

And that why—not willpower, not logic and not even hope in any traditional sense—gave me enough to choose a different path from the one I was contemplating.

I always say that my kids saved my life, and they would never even know. I'm forever grateful for them. Every morning, from when I first open my eyes, I'm grateful for my two beautiful boys.

The why that saves your life might be something you don't even have yet. But believing it's possible is enough. That little bit of hope you create can change everything.

Superficial whys versus deep whys

Most people have whys but, often, these whys are too shallow to hold weight. For example:

- 'I want to get healthy.' Okay, why?
- 'Because I want to have more energy.' Why?
- 'Because I'm tired all the time.' Why does that matter?
- 'Because. I don't know. I guess I should have more energy?'

See the problem? This surface why is based on a vague sense of what you should want. It has no emotional anchor. When the alarm goes off at 6 am and the bed is warm and the workout feels impossible, 'I should have more energy' is not going to get you up.

Now let's go deeper:

- 'I want to get healthy.' *Why?*
- 'Because I don't want to feel like this anymore.' *Why does that matter?*
- 'Because last weekend my kids asked me to kick the ball around in the backyard and I said yes but after five minutes I was bent over, hands on my knees, completely done. I watched them walk back inside and grab a device instead.' *Why is that so important?*
- 'Because in that moment I saw the future. Not some dramatic health scare, just a slow, quiet disappearing act. Saying no to more and more. Watching from the couch instead of being in it. Becoming someone my kids learn to stop asking. I don't want to be the parent on the sideline of my own family's life. I want to be in the middle of it, running, laughing, present and alive, for as long as I possibly can.'

And you don't need to have kids to feel this. Everyone has their version. Maybe yours was the hike you had to turn back from. The invite you said no to because you didn't have the energy. The moment you realised you'd stopped saying yes to the things that used to make you feel alive. The details are different. The feeling is the same.

That's a deep, weighty why. That's a why that will drag you out of bed at 6 am even when every cell in your body wants to stay asleep. Do you feel the difference? The surface why is intellectual. The deep why is visceral. The surface why lives in your head. The deep why lives in your chest. You feel it deeply within.

> *A shallow why collapses under pressure. A deep why becomes unshakeable.*

The 'five whys dig'

The 'five whys dig' is one of the most powerful exercises I know to uncover your deep why. The concept is simple: for any goal or desire, ask yourself 'why?' repeatedly, usually at least five times, until you hit bedrock and uncover something that feels fundamental, emotional and non-negotiable.

Here's how it works:

1. Write down something you want.
2. Ask yourself, 'Why do I want this?' Write down the answer.
3. Take that answer and ask 'Why?' again. Write down the new answer.
4. Repeat until you've asked 'Why?' at least five times.
5. Notice where you land. The final answer, or the answer where you feel the most emotional charge, is your deep why.

Here's an example:

- *What I want:* 'I want to build a successful business.'
- *Why?* 'Because I want financial freedom.'
- *Why?* 'Because I don't want to worry about money.'
- *Why?* 'Because I grew up watching my parents fight about money constantly, and I never want to put my family through that.'
- *Why?* 'Because those fights made me feel unsafe as a child, like the ground could collapse at any moment. I want my kids to feel secure in a way I never did.'
- *Why?* 'Because the greatest gift I can give them is a stable foundation—the freedom to dream without fear and take risks knowing they're held. That's the childhood I wished I'd had. That's the parent I'm determined to be.'

Notice the journey. We started with 'successful business' and ended with 'the father I'm determined to be'. We started in the head and ended in the heart. The deep why here wasn't about business at all. It was about healing a wound from childhood and creating something different for the next generation. A why such as this will get you through the hard days of entrepreneurship. 'Financial freedom' wouldn't.

The science of purpose

The research on the benefits of purpose and meaning is overwhelming and some of the findings might surprise you.

In the famous Blue Zones research, scientists studied the regions of the world where people live the longest—including Okinawa, Japan; Sardinia, Italy; Loma Linda, California; Nicoya, Costa Rica; and Ikaria, Greece. These regions have the greatest number of people aged 100 and above, and researchers looked at what similarities could be uncovered.

They uncovered expected factors such as diet and movement, but one factor stood out above almost everything else: purpose.

In Okinawa, they call it *ikigai*, 'a reason for being'. In Nicoya, it's *plan de vida*, 'life plan'. Every Blue Zone had a cultural framework for articulating and honouring one's sense of meaning.

Research has also quantified the benefits of this: people with a strong sense of purpose live an average of seven years longer than those without one. Seven years is not a marginal effect; it's transformative.

Purpose can also result in:

- lower rates of Alzheimer's disease and cognitive decline
- reduced risk of heart attack and stroke
- faster recovery from illness and surgery
- lower levels of inflammation (a key driver of chronic disease)
- better sleep quality
- reduced anxiety and depression.

Your why doesn't just help you endure hardship but can also change your biology.

People don't burn out from working too hard. They burn out from working on things that don't matter to them. Read that again and let it sit. How do you feel about that in your life? This insight reframes burnout entirely. You can work incredibly hard on something you find deeply meaningful and still feel energised. Or you can work moderately on something meaningless and feel depleted. The issue isn't the quantity of effort but the quality of connection to purpose.

When your why is clear and strong, sustainable effort becomes possible. When your why is absent or shallow, even modest effort feels draining.

Common mistakes in finding your why

Here are the mistakes I see people make when trying to find their deeper purpose:

- *Choosing someone else's why:* Your parents wanted you to be a doctor, for example, or society says success looks like wealth and status. A borrowed why will never sustain you because it's not connected to your soul. The question isn't, 'What should my purpose be?' The question is, 'What is my purpose, whether or not anyone else approves?'
- *Keeping the why too abstract:* 'I want to make a difference', 'I want to help people' or 'I want to live my best life' all sound nice but they mean nothing. A useful why is specific enough to guide choices, telling you what to say yes to and what to say no to.
- *Expecting the why to feel exciting all the time:* Your deep why isn't meant to give you constant motivation. It's meant to hold you when motivation disappears. Your why doesn't have to be fun. It has to be true.
- *Thinking you need to find one why:* You're a complex person with multiple values and multiple sources of meaning. You might have one why for your health, another for your work and another for your relationships. What matters is that each why goes deep enough to sustain you.
- *Waiting to 'discover' your why before acting:* This is a sneaky form of procrastination. Purpose isn't discovered through contemplation alone. It's discovered through action. Don't wait to find your why before you start. Start, and let your why reveal itself through the living.

Remember that certain stages of your life can also have a different why. I thought that cricket was my why and my purpose, but it turns out that it was just the stepping stone to finding my real why and purpose in life—which is what I'm doing now. You are allowed to do the same and evolve your why.

The 'why now?' reckoning

Hopefully, as you've made your way through this chapter you've started to dig into your deeper purpose. The 'five whys dig' has taken you from your head into your chest. You've found something real beneath what you thought you wanted. How does that sit with you?

But here's what I've learned: knowing your why isn't the same as owning it. You can feel the truth of something in your bones and still hit snooze and go back to scrolling. You can still wait for some imaginary version of yourself who's finally 'ready'.

The gap between insight and action isn't a knowledge problem but an urgency problem. And urgency doesn't come from pressure or deadlines. It comes from reckoning, from looking honestly at what you're losing while you wait.

The 'five whys dig' helps you uncover what's underneath what you want. Now it's time for some harder questions, including why must you act on this now and what's the real cost if you don't?

If you've uncovered your deep why via the 'five whys dig', hold it in your mind as you read through the following sections. Don't rush them. Sit with each one before coming up with some possible responses.

Why me?

First, ask yourself, 'Why is this my work to do and not something I can hand to someone else or hope fixes itself?' No-one else carries your specific wound, your specific hope and your specific vision for what life could be. When I was in that hospital bed, the people who loved me could hold my hand but the decision to get up was mine alone. Your deep why comes from you. That's not a burden. That's your assignment.

Why now?

Next, ask yourself, 'What is it about this exact moment in my life that's telling me something has to shift?' You're reading this book right now, not last year and not five years ago. That's not random. Something brought you here. Perhaps a conversation, a feeling or a quiet accumulation of days that weren't quite right. Maybe something your child said stopped you in your tracks. Maybe what brought you here is the hollow feeling you get on Sunday nights when you think about the week ahead. Your life has been knocking. This is you finally answering the door.

What's the cost of another year?

Now ask, 'If I'm sitting here in 12 months, exactly where I am now, what will that have cost me?' This one is meant to sting. We tell ourselves that staying still is the safe option, waiting is neutral and not changing doesn't cost anything. But it does. Every day you wait has a price tag paid in moments you'll never get back. This could be:

- time with your kids when they're small and still think you're a superhero
- years of health you could have had
- relationships that might have been saved if you'd started earlier.

I lost years to waiting. I don't say that for sympathy. I say it because I don't want you to pay the same price.

> *“Inaction isn't free. You're paying for it every day in a currency you can't earn back.”*

Who else is affected?

Next, ask yourself, 'Whose experience of me changes if I actually do this work?' Here's what most people miss about their why: it's almost never just about you. When you're disconnected, running on empty and operating from old patterns, the people around you feel it. You might think you're hiding it well, but people don't experience your intentions. They experience your presence. And when you're not fully there, they know.

Right now, the people around you don't need you to be perfect. They need you to be there. Think about the people who matter most. What do they get from you when you're living your why versus when you're not?

What becomes possible?

Now ask, 'If I commit to this fully, what does my life actually look like in two years?' While the first four questions are about reckoning, this one is about possibility, and they need each other. Without the reckoning, the possibility feels like fantasy. Without the possibility, the reckoning just feels heavy.

So let yourself see the next two years. Don't just picture the vague 'I want a better life' version. Get specific. What does Tuesday morning feel like? What does the dinner table look like? What energy are you bringing to your work, your relationships and yourself? That picture isn't fiction, it's a blueprint.

Why must I?

Finally, ask yourself, 'Why *must* I? What makes this non-negotiable?' Should is polite and could is theoretical. Must is where commitment lives. This is the moment you stop negotiating with yourself, when 'maybe tomorrow' becomes 'this has to be today'. You can always find a reason not to do something; today is your time to start committing.

When someone says, 'I should eat better', they might. But when someone says, 'I must eat better, because my father had a heart attack at 52 and I'm 48 looking at my children', that person changes. Your 'must' might be fierce or it might be quiet. It might bring tears. Whatever it is, let it be the truth.

Go back over these six questions. They provide six anchors holding you to this work. On the hard days, and they're coming, you won't need all six. You'll just need one. One answer that pulls you back to what's true.

> *Knowing your why gives you direction; reckoning with your why gives you fire.*

Now, with all of that in your hands, let's turn it into something you can carry every day.

The why clarification exercise

Let's put the ideas in this chapter into practice. Uncover (or clarify) your deeper why through the following exercise.

The life audit question

Imagine you're at the end of your life, looking back. Ask yourself, 'What would I most regret not having done, experienced or become?'

Write down everything that comes to mind. Don't censor or judge, just let it flow.

The 'five whys dig'

Choose one thing from your list that feels most charged — the one that creates the strongest emotional response. Write it down.

Now dig by asking 'why does that matter' five times. Your final answer is your deep why.

The 'why now?' reckoning

Write down your responses to the 'why now?' reckoning questions:

- Why me?
- Why now?
- What's the cost of another year?
- Who else is affected?
- What becomes possible?
- Why must I?

The why statement

Using what you've uncovered, complete this sentence:

'I am committed to *[xxx]* because *[xxx]*, and this matters more than my comfort, my fear or my excuses.'

This why statement is your anchor. Write it somewhere you'll see it daily. Where you put it matters: stick it on your bathroom mirror, set it as your phone wallpaper, or write it on the first blank page of this book so it's the first thing you see every time you pick it up. My statement lives on a sticky note inside my wardrobe door and it's the first thing I see when I get dressed every morning. Find the spot where your eyes land naturally and let your why meet you there.

(continued)

The connection test

Read your why statement out loud and notice what happens in your body.

If you feel something, such as a tightening in your chest, a surge of emotion and tears behind your eyes, you've found something real.

If you feel nothing, if it sounds true but doesn't feel true, dig some more. You haven't hit your deep why just yet. Try this exercise as many times as you need till your why statement feels right for you.

My why, now

You know my why from the hospital: the woman I hadn't met, the children I hadn't held and the man I hadn't become. So, what's my why now, 13 years later? I met her. Her name is Jules. She's everything the voice promised and more. I'm building that family, two little legends I'm grateful for every day. And I'm living that life I couldn't see in the darkness. But my why has evolved. It's no longer just about what I want for myself. It's also about what I want to create for others.

Every week, I hear from people who are where I was, people who are counting ceiling tiles at 3 am, holding choices in their hands that feel like endings, and who have lost the ability to see any path forward. My why now includes them. It includes you.

I want to reach into whatever darkness you might find yourself in and remind you: you don't have to feel ready. You just have to be willing. You will find the path out of this. I've walked it. You can too.

When I get tired, and I do get tired (having two boys to run me ragged), I think about the message I got last month from a woman in Perth who said my work saved her life. I think about the father in Brisbane who said he's present with his kids for the first time in years. I think about all the people I'll never meet who might stumble across something I've created on their darkest night, like the couple we randomly met in the backstreets of Santorini, Italy, who recognised me from my Instagram stories. One of them told me these were the first stories they watched every morning, for years. They said, 'They always seem to land perfectly for me at that moment in my life to help me to keep going and reassure me that everything is alright. I just wanted to say thank you, please never stop, not just for me but for so many more'. Stories like this are my why.

This why gets me out of bed on mornings when I don't feel like it. It pushes me to keep sharing even when I'd rather stay private or when I doubt it will be helpful. It sustains me when the work is hard or when I feel like an imposter. As one of my mentors reassured me, 'If just one person sees your thoughts, words and inspiration and it helps them, it's all worth it'.

Letting go of the ego and tapping into my why helps me present the world with my gift. If it helps even just one person, it's worth it.

> *Your why will evolve as you do. What matters is that it's always connected to something real.*

Willingness Pillar summary

Pillar 1: Willingness is the foundation of my entire Clarity Method. Here's what to take forward:

- *Readiness is a myth:* You start and then get ready, not the other way around. The Willingness Equation is Willingness + Small action = Motivation. This means the motivation you're waiting for follows action rather than preceding it. Willingness is a choice rather than a feeling, and you can make that choice right now.
- *Willingness alone depletes:* To sustain transformation, you need a deep why — an anchor that holds you in every storm. Viktor Frankl's insight from the concentration camps remains true: your why gives you something to live for and can help you survive any suffering. Your deep why lives in your chest, not your head. You can use the 'five whys dig' to find it.
- *Purpose changes your biology:* People with a strong sense of purpose live an average of seven years longer, with lower rates of disease, better sleep and reduced anxiety. Your why doesn't just help you endure hardship. It literally keeps you alive.
- *The daily practice is showing up:* Rather than performing at your best or waiting to feel inspired, just showing up is the whole point.
- *Your why is your anchor in every storm:* Willingness depletes. When the old voices return and comfort calls you back, a deep why is the only thing that holds you, living in your chest and becoming unshakeable.

- *Knowing your why isn't the same as owning it:* The 'why now?' reckoning closes that gap. The shift from *should* to *must* is where commitment begins.
- *Your why will evolve as you do:* What matters isn't that it stays fixed. What matters is that it's always connected to something real.
- *Willingness is the door:* Everything else is on the other side.

Chapter Five

Pillar 2: Awareness

> The moment you can observe the storm, you are no longer inside it.

You might have heard the ancient Zen story about two monks walking along a muddy road. They come to a river crossing and see a young woman, beautifully dressed, unable to cross without ruining her clothes. Without hesitation, the older monk lifts her onto his back, carries her across the river and sets her down on the other side. She thanks him and goes on her way.

The two monks continue walking in silence. Miles and hours pass. The younger monk grows increasingly agitated, his face tight, his steps heavy. Finally, he can't contain himself any longer. 'How could you do that?' he bursts out. 'We are monks! We have taken vows! We are not supposed to touch women, let alone carry them. How could you pick her up like that?'

The older monk looks at him calmly and says, 'I put her down at the river. Why are you still carrying her?'

I first heard this story in therapy, about a month after leaving the hospital. My therapist told it to me after I'd spent 45 minutes rehashing a conversation from three years earlier, raving about something someone had said to me, how unfair it was and how I couldn't believe they'd treated me that way. For 45 minutes I went on about something from three years ago, which the other person had probably forgotten within a week.

'Cam', my therapist said gently after sharing the Zen story, 'you put that conversation down three years ago. Why are you still carrying it?'

That question cracked something open in me and it wasn't just realising I'd spent more than $200 to talk about something that did not serve me at all (I could have just told the neighbour's cat and saved the cash).

My bigger realisation was that I wasn't just having thoughts about that old conversation. I was those thoughts. I had fused with them so completely that I couldn't see where the memory ended and I began. The story was running me, and I didn't even know it was a story. That's the moment I began to understand awareness.

You need to decide what to pursue and what to walk away from. You need to become transparent to truly free yourself.

The autopilot problem

How much of your life are you actually present for? I don't mean physically present—I'm sure you show up to most of the places you're supposed to be. I mean genuinely present, aware and conscious of what you're doing while you're doing it. If you're like most people, your honest answer is likely, 'Not much'.

Too often, we sleepwalk through our lives. We wake up, go through our routines, react to emails, have conversations, make decisions, eat meals and go to bed, often without ever really being there for any of it.

Researchers call this 'mindlessness' or 'autopilot mode'. And the data is staggering.

As mentioned in chapter 1, a landmark study from researchers at Harvard University found that people spend nearly 47 per cent of their waking hours thinking about something other than what they're currently doing and that this mind-wandering is directly correlated with unhappiness. The more your mind wanders, the less happy you are. You could be on a tropical beach but if your mind is replaying an argument from last week, you're miserable. You could be stuck in traffic but if your mind is genuinely present, you're at peace.

Happiness isn't about *where* you are; it's about whether you're actually *there*.

> *Awareness is the first step to freedom. You cannot change what you refuse to see.*

This is the problem that Pillar 2 addresses. Before you can change your patterns, you have to see them. Before you can choose a different response, you have to notice that you're responding at all. Before you can step off autopilot, you have to realise you're on it. Most people never do. They go through their entire lives fused with their thoughts, identified with their emotions, running programs that were installed decades ago and never once stepping back to ask, 'Is this actually me? Or is this just a pattern I've never examined?'

You are not your thoughts

This insight transformed my understanding of my own mind: 'You are not your thoughts. You are the one observing your thoughts'.

I know that sounds strange and perhaps even sounds wrong. After all, your thoughts feel like you. When a thought arises—whether it's a worry, a judgement, a memory or a plan—it doesn't feel like something separate from you. It feels like your own voice, your own perspective and your own self. But if you can observe a thought, you can't be that thought.

Think about it. Right now, you might have a thought arise: 'This is confusing' or 'I'm not sure I agree' or 'I wonder what's for dinner'. Notice there is the thought, and then there's you, noticing the thought. The thought is an object of awareness. You are the awareness itself.

This is the distinction that contemplatives have been pointing to for thousands of years. It's what Eckhart Tolle means when he talks about 'the watcher'. It's what Buddhists call 'witness consciousness'. It's what psychologists call 'metacognition', the ability to think about thinking.

And this isn't just an idea for philosophy or psychological theory. It's a skill and a capacity that can be developed.

> *You are the sky. Your thoughts are just weather.*

I love this metaphor because it captures something essential. The sky doesn't become a storm. Clouds pass through it, rain falls and lightning flashes but, through it all, the sky remains the sky: vast, unchanging and unharmed by the weather moving through it.

You are like that. Thoughts can arise, such as worries, fears, judgements and desires, and emotions move through, including anger, sadness, joy and shame. Through it all, a part of you remains untouched. This part is the observer or witness. It is the awareness that watches everything come and go.

When you learn to access this observer, everything changes. You're no longer trapped inside your thoughts or controlled by your emotions. You have space, perspective and choice.

The neuroscience of observation

Dr Dan Siegel, clinical professor of psychiatry at UCLA School of Medicine, has spent decades studying what happens in the brain when this observing capacity is developed. His research has led to a simple but profound insight: 'name it to tame it'.

When you're caught up in an emotion, let's say anxiety, your amygdala is firing and you're in reactive mode. The feeling consumes you because you are the feeling. No separation exists between you and the anxiety. But when you step back and name the emotion, 'I notice I'm feeling anxious', something remarkable happens in the brain. The act of labelling activates your prefrontal cortex, which then sends inhibitory signals to your amygdala, literally calming the emotional response. The simple act of observing and naming your experience changes your brain state.

This has been verified through fMRI studies. Participants who practiced labelling their emotions showed reduced amygdala activation and increased prefrontal activity. They weren't suppressing the emotion or pretending it wasn't there. They were simply observing it, and that observation changed everything.

The moment you observe a thought, you're no longer controlled by it. It's almost paradoxical. You'd think that paying attention to a difficult emotion would make it stronger, but the opposite is true. Attention that's observational—curious, non-judgemental, spacious—actually reduces the power of the emotion over you.

The thought you try to suppress gains power. The thought you observe with awareness loses power.

Living the examined life

Almost 2500 years ago, in a courtroom in Athens, Socrates faced a choice: renounce his teachings or die. He chose death. And in his final defence, he spoke the words that have echoed through millennia: 'The unexamined life is not worth living'. While those words might sound dramatic, they're not.

Socrates understood what we're only now proving scientifically: a life lived on autopilot, without self-examination, without awareness of your own patterns and assumptions, is not really living. That's sleepwalking. That's being lived by your conditioning rather than choosing your path.

In the examined life, you turn your attention inward and ask, 'Why do I believe what I believe? Why do I react the way I react? What patterns am I repeating? What stories am I telling myself?' This isn't navel-gazing or self-indulgent introspection. It's the foundation of freedom.

When you don't examine your life, you risk repeating the same patterns forever. The same relationships, conflicts, self-sabotage and coping mechanisms. It may be with different faces and in different circumstances, but the same fundamental dynamics will play out over and over because you've never stepped back to see them.

> *Where you are now is a result of what you repeat. Change the pattern, and you change the outcome.*

My repeated behaviour and patterns led to the same outcomes, and that's exactly how I ended up in hospital. This time, I was at rock bottom but I had been given signs for years. Consider the following:

- The woman who keeps choosing unavailable partners isn't unlucky. She's running a pattern she hasn't examined.
- The man who sabotages every opportunity isn't cursed. He's enacting a script he hasn't seen.
- The person who 'always' ends up in the same situations isn't a victim of fate. They're responding from autopilot, making the same unconscious choices and getting the same predictable results.

Awareness breaks the cycle. When you can see the patterns in your life, you can choose differently. When you can observe the script, you can rewrite it.

What I learned to see

When I started actually paying attention to my thoughts—not believing or fighting them, just watching them—I was shocked by what I found. I realised I had a running commentary in my head that was almost entirely negative. *You're not good enough,* it told me. *You'll never recover. Everyone can see what a mess you are. You're a burden. You don't deserve to be happy. Something is fundamentally wrong with you.*

This commentary had been playing for years and maybe decades. I'd never heard it before because I'd never stepped back to listen. I was so fused with the voice that I thought it was reality. It was just how things were and just the truth about me.

Awareness showed me what I'd taken for the truth was instead a voice and a pattern. It was a set of sentences that my mind had learned to repeat, probably as a protection mechanism that had long outlived its usefulness. The voice wasn't trying to hurt me. It was trying to protect me, by keeping me small, keeping me safe, keeping me prepared for the worst so I wouldn't be caught off guard. But that protection was destroying me.

Once I could see the voice—really see it, as something separate from myself—I had options I'd never had before. I could ask, 'Is this thought true? Is it helpful? Do I want to keep believing it?' Sometimes the answer was yes, and I really did need to change something. But most of the time, the answer was no. The thought was a distortion, and a habit. It was a ghost from the past that I could let go of. Not by fighting it or suppressing it, but by seeing it clearly and choosing not to follow it.

> *You cannot change what you refuse to see. But once you see it, you can change anything.*

The observer practice

Here's a simple practice for developing the observer within. This is something you can do right now, anywhere, for just a few minutes.

Pause

Whatever you're doing, stop. Close your eyes if you can. Take a breath.

Notice

Ask yourself, 'What am I experiencing right now?' Your body has been collecting data your entire life. The tightness before a hard conversation, the heaviness when you're dreading something, the lightness around someone safe: these aren't random.

They're information. So, pause for 30 seconds and ask, 'Where in my body am I feeling something right now?' Just locate the sensation — jaw, chest, stomach, shoulders. Then ask, 'What might this be trying to tell me?'

Notice:

- *Physical sensations:* Do you notice tension in your shoulders? Tightness in your chest? Settling in your stomach?
- *Emotions:* Do you feel anxious? Bored? Curious? Resistant?
- *Thoughts:* What is your mind saying? What's the commentary track?

Label

Give a simple label to what you notice. Don't create a story, just give a label. For example:

- 'I notice tightness in my chest.'
- 'I notice I'm feeling anxious.'
- 'I notice my mind is planning.'
- 'I notice a judgement.'

The words 'I notice' are important here. They create distance. They put you in the observer position rather than the experiencer position. Over time, you'll build a vocabulary between you and your body. You'll notice patterns — your shoulders climb around that person, for example, or your stomach settles near the ocean or your jaw clenches when you're not being honest. This intelligence arrives faster than thought and it's almost always right.

(continued)

Allow

Whatever you're experiencing, let it be there. Don't try to fix it, change it or make it go away. Just allow it.

Say to yourself, 'This is here. I can observe it. It won't destroy me'.

Return

Open your eyes. Continue with your day.

That's it. You might need 30 seconds to two minutes, but in those moments, you've practised dis-identification. You've stepped out of the thought stream and onto the bank of the river. You've remembered that you are the sky, not the weather.

Do this throughout your day. When you feel stressed, pause and observe. When you feel triggered, pause and observe. When you feel overwhelmed, pause and observe.

You're building the muscle of awareness and, like any muscle, it gets stronger with use.

Awareness as compassion

Before we move on, I want to address something important: how you observe matters. One kind of observation is harsh, critical and judgemental. It watches your thoughts and says, 'You're so stupid for thinking that'. It notices your patterns and says, 'What's wrong with you?' It sees your emotions and says, 'You shouldn't feel that way'. This isn't awareness. This is just more thinking, more noise, more judgement and more of the inner critic that got you into trouble in the first place.

You might not be able to control that first thought, but you can control the second thought and the way you respond to it. True awareness is compassionate. It watches without judging and notices without criticising. It observes with the gentle curiosity of a scientist studying something interesting, rather than the harsh evaluation of a judge looking for faults.

When you observe a negative thought, you don't have to condemn yourself for having it. You can simply note, 'There's that thought again. How interesting'. When you observe a difficult emotion, you don't have to punish yourself for feeling it. You can simply note, 'Ah, here's sadness. It's visiting again'.

This compassionate observation doesn't mean you approve of everything you see or won't work to change patterns that aren't serving you. It just means you're watching from a place of kindness rather than cruelty.

> *Awareness without compassion is just another form of violence against yourself.*

You've probably been violent with yourself long enough. Awareness invites a different way.

Mapping your inner landscape

If you were a child in the 1980s and 1990s and lucky enough to have flown somewhere, you may also have been lucky enough to have been invited to sit in the cockpit with the pilots and see the view up ahead and down below. Unfortunately, 9/11 in 2001 changed many things, and this was one of them. Maybe you've never heard of such an experience but, trust me, it used to be a thing and if you were lucky enough to be invited it was incredible. I remember being 12 years old and heading up the front of the plane with the captain. The cockpit had so many buttons and levers but the real sight to behold was outside the windows.

I'd always loved flying and was so curious about how it all worked. I wanted to know how the planes even got in the air and to their destination: the physics of it, the freedom of it, the idea of navigating vast distances with precision and skill. I had so many questions that I think the captain would have loved to land the plane then and there. Instead, he shared a lesson that I'll never forget (and probably only fully understood many years later).

He said the first thing they taught at pilot school wasn't how to fly but how to read aeronautical charts. These charts show everything a pilot needs to know: terrain, elevation, airspace boundaries, radio frequencies, navigation aids, obstacles and restricted zones. They're dense with information because in aviation, what you don't see can kill you. He then said something I've never forgotten: 'The aircraft doesn't care about your confidence. It doesn't care about your intentions. It only responds to reality. Your job is to know the reality before you're in it'. He was talking about flight planning, but now I know he could have been talking about life.

Most people try to navigate their lives without a map. They have vague ideas about where they are and where they want to go. But they're flying blind, making decisions based on feelings, assumptions and guesses. They then wonder why they keep crashing into mountains they didn't see coming.

Awareness isn't just about observing your thoughts. It's also about seeing your life clearly, honestly and completely. It's about mapping the terrain so you can navigate it intentionally rather than stumbling through it reactively.

The following sections give you the tools to create that map.

Gaining the bird's-eye view

When you're lost in the forest, everything looks the same. Trees seem to extend in every direction and landmarks are hard to spot. You have no perspective and could walk in circles for hours without knowing it. But climb a hill, get above the canopy, and suddenly everything changes. You can see the river to the east, the mountain to the north and the clearing where you entered. From above, the path becomes obvious.

This is what awareness tools provide: a bird's-eye view of your own life. They give you a chance to fly above and so see yourself clearly and what is really going on.

When you're inside your problems, they consume your entire field of vision. The relationship issue feels like everything. The work stress feels permanent. The health concern feels defining. You can't see past the immediate crisis because you're too deep inside it.

But step back, way back, and you start to see patterns. You can see that the relationship issue is connected to the work stress, which is connected to the sleep problems, which is connected to the exercise you stopped doing six months ago. You see how one area of neglect ripples into others. You see where you're thriving and where you're just surviving.

You can't navigate what you haven't mapped. Awareness exercises give you that map. They show you where you are across every domain of your life, not where you think you are or wish you were, but where you actually are.

This might be uncomfortable. Maps don't lie. They show the terrain as it is, including the parts you've been avoiding.

But that discomfort is the price of clarity. And it's a price worth paying.

Rating your Wheel of Life

The Wheel of Life is one of the most powerful self-assessment tools ever created. Coaches and therapists have used versions of it for decades because it works—it gives you an instant visual snapshot of your life's balance (or imbalance).

Imagine your life as a wheel with ten spokes. Each spoke represents a different domain of your existence:

1. *Physical health and fitness:* Your body, energy, sleep, nutrition, movement and physical vitality.
2. *Mental and emotional wellbeing:* Your psychological health, stress levels, emotional regulation and inner peace.
3. *Love and relationships:* Your intimate partnership, romantic connection, self love and sense of being deeply known by another person.
4. *Social, family and friendships:* Your family relationships, friendships, social connections and sense of belonging among the people in your life.
5. *Career and work:* Your professional life, job satisfaction, sense of purpose at work and career trajectory.
6. *Finances and wealth:* Your money situation, financial security and relationship with wealth.
7. *Personal growth and learning:* Your development, education, self-improvement and commitment to becoming more of who you want to be.
8. *Fun and adventure:* Your hobbies, play, leisure, new experiences and genuine enjoyment of life.

9. *Spirituality and faith:* Your connection to something greater than yourself: whether that's God, the universe, nature, a sense of meaning or simply the feeling that life has a purpose beyond what you can see and touch.
10. *Community and contribution:* Your involvement in something beyond your own life: your neighbourhood, causes you care about and the ways you give back to the world around you.

For each domain, you rate your current satisfaction from 1 (completely dissatisfied) to 10 (completely fulfilled).

Then you plot those numbers on the wheel, connect the dots and look at the shape, and how smoothly the wheel would roll. A wheel with all eights and nines rolls smoothly. A wheel with a nine in Career but a two in Health is lopsided: it lurches and stumbles rather than gliding. And a wheel with all ones and two is flat: it struggles to move at all.

When most people do this exercise honestly, they are surprised by what they see. The successful executive discovers her Career is a nine but her Love and relationships are a three. The devoted parent realises Social, family and friendships a ten but Personal growth and learning is a two. The person who 'has it all together' sees that three or four areas are quietly falling apart.

Your daily behaviour reflects your deepest beliefs. The Wheel of Life reveals what you actually believe, not what you say you believe, but what you demonstrate through your choices. If Health is a three, you believe (at a behavioural level) that health doesn't matter that much. If Fun is a two, you believe that enjoyment isn't important. Your actions have spoken, even if your words say otherwise.

You also need to be aiming for some kind of balance on your wheel. However, when I say 'balance' what I really mean is 'blend'. I don't really believe balance exists. There is only a 'blend' of things you need in that season or moment of your life.

The Wheel of Life exercise

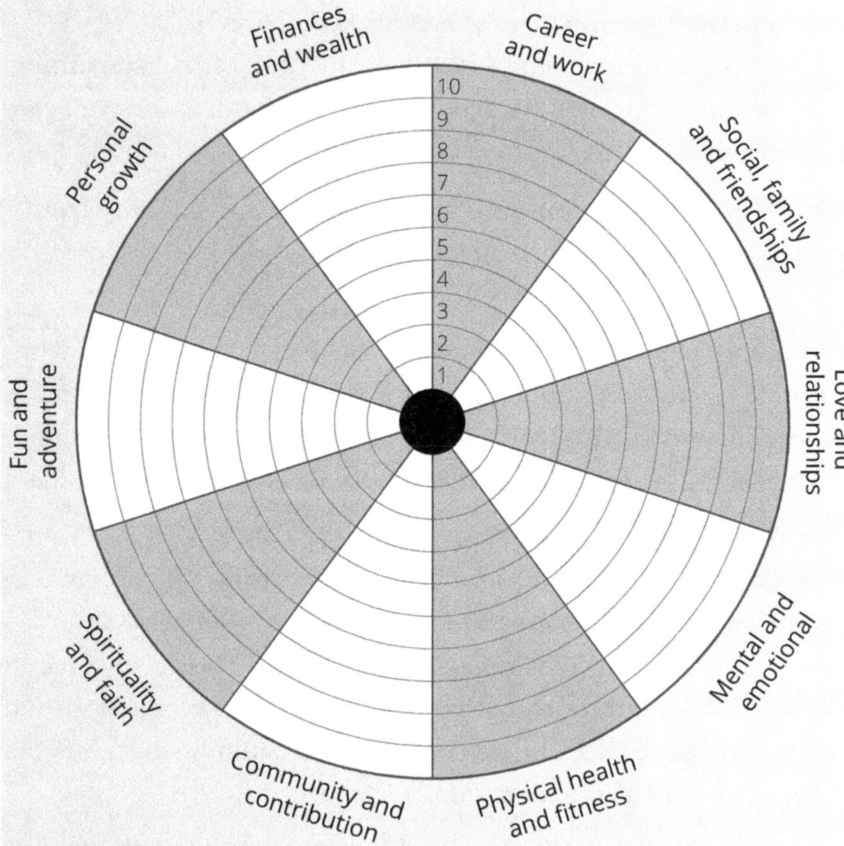

Go to the blank Wheel of Life in the Clarity Workbook or simply draw a circle in your journal. Divide the circle into ten equal sections like a pizza. Label each section with one of the ten life domains.

Now, for each domain, ask yourself, 'How satisfied am I with this area of my life right now, on a scale of one to ten?'

Be honest. No-one else will see this. The only person you hurt by inflating your numbers is yourself.

Rate yourself out of ten on the following:

- *Physical health and fitness:* How is your physical energy? Your sleep? Your nutrition? Your fitness level? Your relationship with your body?
- *Mental and emotional wellbeing:* How is your psychological wellbeing? Your stress levels? Your emotional regulation? Your sense of inner peace?
- *Love and relationships:* How is your intimate relationship? If single, how is your dating life? Do you feel loved and deeply known by another person?
- *Social, family and friendships:* How are your friendships? Your family relationships? Do you feel socially supported and connected? Do you have people you can call at 2 am?
- *Career and work:* How is your job satisfaction? Your sense of purpose at work? Your professional growth and trajectory?
- *Finances and wealth:* How is your financial situation? Your relationship with money? Your sense of security and abundance?
- *Personal growth and learning:* Are you growing? Learning? Developing? Becoming more of who you want to be?
- *Fun and adventure:* When did you last have genuine fun? Do you have hobbies? Do you seek out new experiences? Do you enjoy your life?

(continued)

- *Spirituality and faith:* Do you feel connected to something greater than yourself? Do you have practices, beliefs or moments that ground you in meaning beyond the day-to-day?
- *Community and contribution:* Are you involved in something beyond your own life? Do you give back? Do you feel part of a community that matters to you?

Now plot these numbers on your wheel, with ratings of one in the centre out to ratings of ten at the edge of the circle. Connect the dots and look at the shape.

The shape matters more than any individual number. A perfectly round wheel, even if every score is a five, rolls smoothly. A lopsided wheel with a nine in Career and a two in Health lurches and stumbles no matter how fast you push it. You're not aiming for tens everywhere. You're aiming for a shape that can actually roll. If your wheel looks more like a starburst than a circle, that's not failure — that's information. The pointy bits show you exactly where the imbalance lives.

Now reflect on the following:

1. What do you notice about the shape of your wheel?
2. Which area scored lowest? Are you surprised?
3. Which area scored highest? What's working there that isn't working elsewhere?
4. If you could only improve one area, which would have the biggest ripple effect on the others?
5. What has this exercise revealed that you've been avoiding?

Discovering hidden connections

The areas of your wheel are not independent. They're interconnected in ways that aren't always obvious.

When I was at my lowest but back in the real world after my stint in rehab, I came back to a reality that smashed me in the face. Once again, I was faced with all the same questions and pressures that society will throw at you, along with the pressure I put on myself.

I felt I was so far behind in life compared to all my friends, who had houses, families, corporate careers and all looked to be 'flourishing' and 'succeeding' at life. They all seemed to be handing out business cards with their names and job titles on them. At the time, I didn't have an impressive job title (let alone business cards) so I thought I needed to focus entirely on my career. I thought success here would make everything better, or at least I'd have a card with my name on it that I could hand to people and look like I was doing okay in life.

I wanted career strategies, tactics and productivity hacks — anything to accelerate my professional success and help me look the part (and feel important).

But when I did the Wheel of Life, a different picture emerged:

- *My Health was a three:* I was sleeping four or five hours a night, running on caffeine, rarely exercising and eating poorly (or whatever I could find in the cupboard).
- *My Mental was a four:* I was anxious, overwhelmed, and constantly stressed. Even post-rehab, I was still struggling because I was now forced to do the work on my own in the real world and not in a facility that provided everything for me.
- *My Fun was a two:* I couldn't remember the last time I'd done something purely for enjoyment.

My wheel gave me an amazing birds-eye's view of what was really going on. Yes, my Career was a two, but what if this had nothing to do with better work strategies? What if it was because I was trying to pretend to perform at a high level and create a job for myself on a body that was exhausted, a mind that was depleted and a spirit that was starved of joy?

I stared at the ceiling for a long moment. This time I was in my own room and I wasn't counting tiles, but I did feel like I wanted to be back in rehab. It felt a lot safer there compared to where I was right now. But I knew that the first step towards recovery always feels uncomfortable and like a step back. I also knew fear always screams loudest when your magic is closest, which is why giving yourself grace and continuing to be open with things that are trying to tell you something is so important. Lean in, listen and face it.

I realised I didn't need to work on my Career. I needed to work on my Health, my Mental and my Fun. Just from that revelation and taking the pressure off myself, I started sleeping seven hours. I began walking every morning, taking in the fresh morning air and being grateful for the surroundings and things I did have, as opposed to focusing on what I didn't. I scheduled one fun activity per week and made this non-negotiable. I found the joy in the things I used to love and which I knew helped make me smile.

At the time, my job was coaching kids at cricket. Within three months, my Career score had jumped and I had developed new relationships and opportunities. This didn't happen because I'd developed new professional skills, but because I now had the energy, clarity and emotional resilience to perform better and be at my best for the youngsters who were with me. The energy I now had said so much more about me than a business card with my name on it and a fancy title I was trying to kid someone with. Rather than soulless, this felt soul fulfilling.

> *Sometimes the area you need to work on isn't the one that's bothering you most. It's the one that's secretly sabotaging everything else.*

This is why the map provided by the Wheel of Life matters. Without it, I would have kept grinding, thinking that Career was everything, while my real problem areas, Health, Mental and Joy, continued to drain my capacity. The map showed me what I couldn't see from inside the problem and what really was important.

Finding your special ingredients

Think about your family's famous cake. Perhaps it's made by your mum or your dad, but let's say it's made by your mum. The first time she made it, she followed a recipe step by step. Over time, though, she didn't need the recipe anymore. She just knew. A little more of this. A touch less of that. She understood the ingredients that made it taste just right—the ones that made everyone come back for another slice.

Now imagine if, out of nowhere, she decided to throw in something bizarre—tuna, say, or soy sauce. Something that didn't belong. The cake would no longer make sense. That one ingredient would ruin what was already working.

Your life is no different. When you know the ingredients that make you feel energised, calm, focused and connected, the things that make your life taste good, why would you randomly swap them out for habits, environments or expectations that don't fit?

Clarity begins when you recognise what works for you *and* have the courage to not only keep it and own it but also be honestly aware when it's not serving you and needs a change. Ego or stubbornness doesn't help anyone.

Your ‘special ingredients’ are the specific activities, practices, environments and conditions that support your wellbeing. I don’t mean what supports wellbeing in general, but what supports yours.

Having a great day and feeling outstanding doesn’t happen by accident. You have done something—indulged in something, somehow and someway—that has gone into you and has made you feel that way. That’s your special ingredient. Be aware of it and do it consistently on a day-to-day basis.

The same applies if you’ve had a poor day and are not feeling great. It’s not a coincidence either. You have done something, seen someone, felt something that didn’t serve you and has set you up to feel the way you are feeling. Again, be aware of it and replace it with something that does serve you.

The self-help industry often seems to sell the idea that one formula will work for everyone: wake up at 5 am, meditate for an hour, take cold showers, journal every day. If that doesn’t work for you, you’re doing it wrong. But that’s nonsense. The practices that support human flourishing vary dramatically from person to person. Your job isn’t to copy someone else’s formula. Your job is to discover your own. Remember: success leaves clues. What are your special ingredients?

> “*Stop guessing what you need and start understanding what works for you.*”

The special ingredients inventory

Take some time now to reflect on when you felt your best: energised, clear, capable and alive. What was present during those times?

What fills you up?

List activities, practices or conditions that genuinely fill you up. Don't write down what you think should fill you up, write down what actually does.

If you're not sure what 'fills you up' feels like, think about it this way. When I go for an ocean swim, for the first few laps my brain is screaming, *Why are you doing this to yourself?* My lungs burn, my goggles fog up and every stroke feels like a bad decision. But the moment I finish — standing on the sand, slightly out of breath, skin tingling — something clicks. I feel alive. Not just 'fine' or 'okay' but genuinely, physically alive. That tingle, that quiet buzz of *I did it and I'd do it again*: that's what 'fills you up' feels like. It's the things that make you feel more like yourself afterward, even if they're uncomfortable during.

Consider movement and exercise, social connection, the environment, creative expression, learning, spiritual practices, and routine versus spontaneity.

Write down at least ten things that genuinely fill you up.

What drains you?

List activities, practices or conditions that drain you. Again, don't write down what you think is expected, write down what actually depletes you.

(continued)

Write down at least ten things that drain you.

The reality check

Look at your 'fill you up' list. In the past week, how many of these did you actually do?

Now look at your 'drain you' list. In the past week, how many of these did you experience?

If your week was heavy on drains and light on fills, you now know why you're exhausted.

The prescription

Choose three items from your 'fill you up' list that you will commit to this week — no matter what. These are your non-negotiable special ingredients.

Next, choose one item from your 'drain you' list that you will reduce or eliminate this week.

Doing a habit audit

The last map I want you to create in this chapter is a map of your habits.

You are what you repeatedly do, not what you intend to do or what you believe you should do, but what you actually do, every day, on autopilot.

Your habits are the invisible architecture of your existence. They shape your health, relationships, career, wealth and happiness—everything. And most of them are running without your conscious awareness. The habit audit brings them into the light.

This exercise can be confronting, because when you list what you actually do every day, you see what you actually believe.

If you say health matters but your habits include skipping breakfast, sitting all day and scrolling until midnight, your actions reveal what you really believe about health.

If you say your relationship matters but your habits include checking your phone during dinner, prioritising work over connection and never scheduling quality time, your actions reveal what you really believe about your relationship.

The habit audit isn't about judgement but truth. And truth is where change becomes possible.

The habit audit exercise

Take some time now to consider your current habits.

Morning habits (first two hours after waking)

What do you usually do in the first two hours of your day? Answer this honestly. Write down every action, in order.

Next, mark each habit with one of the following:

- + for habits that serve who you want to become
- – for habits that don't serve who you want to become
- ? for habits you're unsure about.

Evening habits (last two hours before sleep)

Now think about what you actually do in the last two hours of your day. Write down every action, in order.

Mark each of these habits with +, –, or ?

(continued)

The hidden habits

Some habits are so automatic you barely notice them. Ask yourself:

- What do I do when I feel stressed?
- What do I do when I feel bored?
- What do I do when I feel lonely?
- What do I do when I feel overwhelmed?
- What do I do when I first wake up?
- What do I do when I can't sleep?
- What do I reach for when I want comfort?
- What do I avoid when I should act?

Write down your answers — honestly.

Pattern recognition

Look at your audit. What patterns do you see? Consider:

- How many + (positive) habits versus – (negative) habits do you see?
- What triggers your – habits?
- What's the first – habit in your day? (This often sets the tone for everything that follows.)
- What's missing? What habits would serve you that aren't present at all?

The one change

Based on this audit, identify *one* habit you want to change — just one.

Pick either:

- one – habit you want to reduce or eliminate
- one + habit you want to add or strengthen.

Write it down.

Also think about why you picked this habit. What impact would changing this one habit have on the rest of your life? (I talk about habits, and how to change them, in much more detail in chapter 9.)

What my map revealed

Back when I was just out of rehab and I combined all the tools provided in this chapter—the Wheel of Life, my special ingredient inventory and my habit audit—my overall map became pretty clear. I've already mentioned my ratings in some of the sectors when I did the Wheel of Life honestly, not the version I wanted others to see, but the real one. Here's the full rundown of what I found:

- *Health and fitness:* Two. I'd completely neglected my body.
- *Mental and emotional:* Two. Obviously, I had just got out of a psychiatric facility.
- *Love and relationships:* Three. I felt isolated and disconnected, and was pushing people away.
- *Social, family and friendships:* Four. I was present but not really present.
- *Career and work:* One. I was going through the motions and my energy was non-existent.
- *Finances:* One. This was at its lowest. I didn't know how I was going to survive.
- *Personal growth:* Two. I'd stopped growing years ago.
- *Fun and adventure:* One. I couldn't remember the last time I'd had genuine fun, or even smiled or laughed. I believe it was when my beloved rugby league team, the Manly Sea Eagles, made the Grand Final in 2013. I was at my worst. I can't remember it. I was numb.

- *Spirituality and faith:* Two. I've always talked to a higher power but through this time I had lost hope and this part of me, which is so full today, had completely lost its way.
- *Community and contribution:* Three. I knew I still loved connecting but I had isolated and retreated and felt I couldn't physically do it. It became about my hurt and pain as opposed to helping others. I wasn't part of anything.

My wheel was barely a wheel at all. It was a flat mess. No wonder my life felt like it was constantly lurching from crisis to crisis. I was trying to roll on something that wasn't actually a wheel at all.

My special ingredients inventory revealed that the things that genuinely filled me up—the beach, being in nature, cricket, sport, music, meaningful conversations, creative expression and physical challenge—had all been absent from my life for years. I'd replaced them with numbing habits: staring at screens, scrolling, surface-level socialising, drinking and staying busy to avoid feeling.

My habit audit was even worse. My first action every morning was checking my phone. My last action every night was checking my phone. In between, I was running on autopilot, reacting to whatever demanded attention and never once asking if any of it was serving who I wanted to become.

My overall map was brutal but liberating.

Once I could see my life with this bird's-eye view, I knew exactly what needed to change: not vaguely or theoretically, but specifically. I needed to rebuild my Health from a two. I needed to rediscover Fun. I needed to reintroduce my special ingredients. I needed to replace my – habits with + habits, starting with that phone in the morning.

The map doesn't judge you. It just shows you where you are. And once you can see where you are, you can choose where to go.

Cartography as an annual practice

Once a year, I create a new map for myself, running through all the exercises in this chapter. I do it around my birthday. (This is 4 January, which Jules insists I should change to 4 June because she clearly feels an early January birthday is just too hard with Christmas and New Years so close. If you're also a Capricorn, I feel you. Keep celebrating your birthday. You matter and don't let anyone else tell you any different.)

Back to my fresh Wheel of Life, special ingredients inventory and habit audit. I do this because the terrain changes. What filled you up last year might not fill you up this year. The habits that served you in one season might not serve you in the next. The areas of your life that were strong might have weakened, and the areas that were weak might have grown. And so, your map needs to be regularly updated.

I also do a mini map update quarterly. I just look at my Wheel of Life and check where I am now, what's shifted and what needs attention. This practice keeps me from drifting too far off course and catches the slow slides before they become crises. It helps me maintain the bird's-eye view even as I'm down in the forest doing the daily work.

So, pick some markers in your own life—perhaps your birthday, and perhaps each new season—for your own annual and mini map updates.

> *"Awareness isn't a one-time event but an ongoing practice. Your map needs to be redrawn as the territory changes."*

Awareness Pillar summary

Pillar 2: Awareness is about learning to see — first your thoughts and then your life. Here's what to keep in mind:

- *You are not your thoughts:* You are the awareness that observes them. This distinction is the foundation of psychological freedom. When you can name an emotion, 'I notice I'm feeling anxious', you activate your prefrontal cortex and calm the amygdala. Observation changes your brain state. You are the sky. Your thoughts are just weather.
- *Awareness isn't only about observing thoughts:* Awareness is also about seeing your life clearly. The Wheel of Life exercise shows you where you're thriving and where you're lurching. Your special ingredients reveal what fills you up and what drains you. The habit audit shows what you actually believe through what you actually do. Sometimes the area you need to work on isn't the one bothering you most, but the one secretly sabotaging everything else.
- *When you are having a great day, it's not a coincidence:* Certain things, people and environments have showed up for you and helped you to feel your best. What are they?
- *Understanding your special ingredients is a great way to know what best works for you:* Pay close attention to these ingredients and double-down on them.
- *Awareness without compassion is just another form of violence against yourself:* Watch with curiosity, not judgement.
- *The map doesn't judge you:* Your map just shows you where you are. Once you can see where you are, you can choose where to go.

Chapter Six

Pillar 3: Accountability

> The heaviest thing you will ever carry is the story about why it's not your fault.

By about four weeks into my stay at the mental facility, the acute crisis had passed. The medication was stabilising and the therapy sessions were happening daily. By all external measures, I was 'doing the work'. But inside, I was running a different program entirely. I was building a case—not for recovery but for why none of this was my fault.

'It's the sporting industry', I told myself. The pressure of being a professional sportsman and the support I didn't have during my time was at fault. I should still be playing. I was a better player than most still in the game. The expectations were impossible. The system chews people up and spits them out.

'It's the trauma', I argued. No-one could go through an experience like the tsunami and be okay. Anyone would struggle after seeing what I saw.

'It's my parents' fault', I concluded. They took me out of school in Sydney when I was in year 11 and life was great, and moved us all up to the Gold Coast because of my mother's health. I had to start at a new school and find new friends, when I'd just wanted to stay happy where I was. They did this to me.

I had an explanation for everything and a reason for every failure. I could justify every broken relationship, every missed opportunity and every way my life had fallen short of what I'd hoped. My mind was a courtroom, and I was both prosecutor and judge, building an airtight case for why I was a victim of circumstances beyond my control.

And then, somewhere between ceiling tile 43 and 44, something cracked. Maybe this was caused by exhaustion. Maybe it was grace. Maybe it was the accumulated weight of all those therapy sessions finally breaking through. But in that moment, lying in that bed, staring at that ceiling, a question popped up that I couldn't push away: 'Cam, what if *you* are the common denominator in everything that isn't working?'

The question hit me like ice water. The issue wasn't the circumstances, the sporting industry, the trauma or my family dynamics. It was me. I was the through-line in all of it. The relationships that failed: I was there. The opportunities that slipped away: I was there. The health that deteriorated: I was there. The choices that led to this hospital bed: I made them.

For a moment, I wanted to reject the question entirely. It felt like blame and shame. It felt like adding insult to injury—here I was, already broken, and now I was supposed to take responsibility for breaking myself? But something in me knew the question wasn't an attack but an invitation.

If I was just a victim, if everything that had gone wrong was truly beyond my control, then I was powerless. I was at the mercy of forces I couldn't influence. My future was as predetermined as my past.

But if I was the common denominator, if my choices, my patterns, my responses had played a role in creating this mess, then something extraordinary followed. I also had the power to create something different.

In that realisation, I stopped building the case and started taking inventory. And in that moment of radical, painful, liberating honesty, something shifted in the fabric of my existence.

I remember saying to myself, as tears continued to stream down my face and hit the bed sheets, 'Okay, if I'm doing this then I'm going to take complete ownership of my life—full accountability and responsibility for everything I've done, every decision, the good, the bad, the ugly that has led me to this exact moment in my life right now. No more casting blame; I'm here because of one person and that person is me'.

As I told myself this, I remember feeling something truly liberating. I can only describe it as the universe exhaling. My shoulders felt lighter, my mind felt clearer, and I felt more at ease and calmer.

'Oh', that force seemed to say. 'Thank you, Cameron. We've been waiting for you to say this and take ownership for a long time. Thank you. You're ready now. You're finally ready to stop being a victim and start being the author of your life. Get ready to watch some really cool shit happen for you now.'

I could breathe fully again, and I smiled. That moment, that shift from blame to ownership, was the turning point of my entire recovery. My circumstances and my past were the same, but my relationship to all of it transformed completely. I went from passenger to driver, from spectator to participant and from victim to architect.

> *No-one is coming to save you. That's the bad news. The good news is you don't need saving. You need ownership.*

Introducing the Accountability Equation

The framework that changed everything for me, and for thousands of others who've applied it, is called the Accountability Equation. It looks like this:

Event + Response = Outcome

In this equation, the Event is what happens to you. It could be a diagnosis, breakup, job loss or betrayal. It could even be the economy, your childhood, trauma, the global pandemic, an accident or a death. You cannot control these events. They happen, and often without your permission or input.

The Response is how you choose to react: your thoughts, emotions, actions, mindset and interpretation. Essentially, your response is your next move. This is the only part of the equation you have complete control over.

The Outcome is where you end up in your relationships, health, peace, clarity and your life.

Where most people get stuck is trying to change their Outcomes by complaining about their Events. 'If only that hadn't happened to me', they might say. 'If only they had treated me differently. If only I'd had better opportunities. If only the timing had been better. If only I'd been born into different circumstances…' This was most certainly me on every occasion, and in every chapter of my life. The events weren't fair and the outcomes weren't my fault, that's for sure.

But look at the equation again. You cannot change the Event; it has already occurred. The past is fixed. The only variable you can control is your Response. Change your response and you change your outcome, every single time.

This isn't simply positive thinking and it certainly isn't toxic optimism. This isn't pretending bad things don't happen or that pain isn't real. I'm definitely not an advocate of that; however, I do believe that you get to choose the thing that you go looking for. If you can get up and say, 'I'm going to take responsibility and go out and find some evidence of a good day', the likelihood of you having one is that little bit higher.

> *You are not responsible for everything that happened to you. You are responsible for who you become because of it.*

I'm not asking you to take responsibility for what others did to you or pretend that injustice didn't happen. I'm not asking you to forgive the unforgivable or minimise your pain. You might have been through something that should never have happened. You might have had things done to you, not by you, which wounded you in ways that still ache. I'm sorry for that. I honour that and I see it. I've sat with people and heard some heartbreaking stories.

And, still, the equation holds. You are not responsible for the Event, but you are responsible for your Response. And your Response determines your Outcome.

This is liberation. The moment you truly understand this equation, you take back the power that the event stole from you. You may need to sit with it for a while and that's okay. When you are truly ready you will be able to see that the equation holds. More importantly, you will be able to see how it can serve you.

Victims versus victors

Before we go much further, I'd like to add a quick word on the labels I'm using. When I use the word 'victim' here, I'm not using it the way society often does, as a judgement or a weakness. If something painful happened to you, you were a victim of that event. That's not a character flaw; it's a fact. The distinction I'm drawing is between staying in the victim story, letting it define your future, and choosing to rewrite it as a victor story. You're not always responsible for what happened to you. But you can always choose what you do with it next.

Victims live in the event. They replay it, retell it and let it define them. Their identity becomes fused with what happened to them. When they think about their lives, they think first about the bad things that occurred. Their past has become their prison. I know, because I lived here for a long time. I know how much energy is used here, along with the amount of pain and unnecessary suffering.

Victors, on the other hand, acknowledge the event and then pour their energy into the response. They take ownership by asking different questions:

- Given what happened, what am I going to do now?
- Who am I going to become?
- What response will I choose today?

Same event, but with a different focus and radically different outcomes. For me, as I write this chapter sitting at Dee Why Beach in Sydney, my different outcomes are obvious. I sit here with a smile on my face, appreciative that Jules is looking after both boys and I can get away to write. I'm overlooking the ocean, with blue skies and a glistening sun. Happy couples are walking hand in hand, families are creating memorable moments and I'm so grateful to be writing this for you. I know that if I hadn't chosen the victor outlook and instead leant into the victim mentality, my story would not have had a happy ending and this book wouldn't even exist. But here I am, typing (slowly) to capture my story and everything I've learned. My radically different outcome is proof this approach works.

I spent years as a victim, not because I was weak but because I was human, doing what humans do when they're hurt. But every year I spent prosecuting my past was a year I didn't spend building my future.

The tsunami happened. I couldn't control that event, but how I responded to the trauma in the decade that followed was my choice. And for a long time, I chose numbing over healing, performing over processing, and running over facing. My response created my outcome. And my outcome was a hospital bed.

The victim mentality felt good in a way. It protected me. If nothing was my fault, I didn't have to change. I didn't have to face the uncomfortable truth that some of my choices had made things worse. I could stay righteous in my pain. But the cost of that protection was my life.

> *Victims wait for the world to change. Victors take ownership and change their response to the world.*

The moment I stopped waiting for someone to rescue me—stopped waiting for an apology, for circumstances to improve or for the universe to acknowledge the injustice—was the moment everything started to shift.

I wasn't rescued. I rescued myself through the quality of my response.

The neuroscience of ownership

Your brain operates differently in victim mode versus ownership mode. Here's how:

- When you're in victim mode—blaming, complaining, feeling helpless—your amygdala lights up. Cortisol and adrenaline flood your system. You enter survival mode and your prefrontal cortex goes offline. You literally cannot think straight. Zero clarity is available.
- When you shift into ownership by accepting responsibility, focusing on what you can control, asking empowering questions, your prefrontal cortex activates. The stress hormones decrease. Creativity returns and solutions become visible. The future opens up. Yes, your future! Love neuroscience yet? It lights me up! (It is Valentine's Day as I write this, so maybe Cupid is in the air somewhere.)

Blame keeps you in survival mode while accountability activates your potential.

Dr Julian Rotter developed his 'locus of control' theory back in the 1950s and 1960s, and his findings have been replicated many times since. People with an internal locus of control, who believe they have agency over their lives, achieve more professionally, maintain healthier relationships, experience lower rates of anxiety and depression, recover faster from setbacks and live longer.

Taking ownership of your life isn't just noble. It's literally life-extending. And a life extension was exactly what I was fortunate enough to get.

> *Your circumstances are not your sentence unless you keep pleading guilty to victimhood.*

The parable of the two arrows

The parable of the two arrows is a Buddhist teaching I return to often. When something painful happens, this teaching tells us, it's like being struck by an arrow. The event itself—the loss, the rejection, the failure or the betrayal—causes pain. That first arrow is unavoidable. It's part of being alive.

But then, we shoot a second arrow into ourselves. This second arrow is our response to the event. It's the story we tell ourselves about why it shouldn't have happened. It's the rumination about who's to blame. It's the resistance to accepting what is. It's the narrative of victimhood that we construct and then inhabit.

The first arrow causes pain. The second arrow, the one we shoot ourselves, causes suffering. And I don't want anyone to suffer anymore; it's why I do what I do, including writing this book.

Pain is inevitable but suffering is optional. And the second arrow often hurts more than the first:

- The break-up hurts, but the six months of asking, 'Why did they do this to me?', 'What's wrong with me?' and 'Why is life so unfair?' is the second arrow. That's the suffering we add to the pain. (Along with an incredibly unhealthy number of messages and missed calls. Just stop sending the messages, they received them.)

- The job loss hurts, but the year of bitterness about how the company mistreated you, the resentment that poisons every subsequent interview, the identity crisis of seeing yourself as someone who 'got screwed' is the second arrow.
- The trauma hurts, but the decade (perhaps even more) of building your entire identity around being damaged, of using the trauma as an explanation for every failure, of letting the event become the defining feature of your existence is the second arrow.

The first arrow is unavoidable but the second arrow is optional. Accountability is learning to stop shooting yourself.

When I lay in that hospital bed, I finally saw all the second arrows I'd put into myself over the years. My experiences with cricket, the tsunami, my relationships were all the first arrow. Everything I'd done to myself in the decade since—the numbing, the avoiding, the victim story I'd constructed—those were second arrows. I'd shot myself with dozens of them, and my self-inflicted wounds hurt more than the original trauma.

Accountability isn't about denying the first arrow; it's about putting down the bow.

The resistance to ownership

If accountability is so powerful, why do we resist it? In a similar way to unwillingness (from chapter 4), victimhood has benefits we don't like to admit. For example:

- *Victimhood provides sympathy:* When you're a victim, people feel sorry for you. They validate your pain and agree that you've been treated unfairly. A social reward comes with being wronged.

- *Victimhood provides protection:* If it's not your fault, you don't have to face the uncomfortable truth that you had power you didn't use. You don't have to grieve for the time you lost. You don't have to confront your own role in your suffering.
- *Victimhood provides an excuse:* Nobody expects much from the person who 'couldn't help it'. Your failures are pre-explained and your lack of progress pre-justified. The bar is conveniently lowered.
- *Victimhood provides identity:* Strangely, many people don't know who they'd be without their victim story. The trauma, injustice and wounds have become so central to their sense of self that releasing them feels like a kind of death.

I'm not judging these benefits. I claimed every single one of them myself, for years. They're human and they're understandable. They're the natural response to pain. But they're also expensive.

> *Blame is a cage. Accountability is the key you've been holding all along.*

The comfort of victimhood comes at the cost of your clarity. Every day you spend explaining why you can't is a day you don't spend building what you could. Every ounce of energy you pour into your case against life is energy you're not investing in your future.

Here's the question that broke me open: what would become possible if you let go of your need to be right about why you're stuck?

This isn't about forgetting what happened, excusing anyone's behaviour or pretending it didn't hurt. It's about releasing your grip on the story long enough to ask, 'What now? What's my move? What response am I going to choose today?'

The Accountability Equation in action

Nelson Mandela spent 27 years in prison for fighting against the apartheid government in South Africa. After 27 years, he had every reason to emerge bitter, vengeful and consumed by blame. The injustice was real, the suffering was real and the event was monstrous. But Mandela chose a different response. He walked out of prison and chose reconciliation over revenge. He chose nation-building over score-settling. He became president and led the country that had imprisoned him.

Same equation; Event + Response = Outcome. A brutal Event plus a transcendent Response equals an Outcome that changed the world.

Bethany Hamilton is an American surfer and writer who was attacked by a shark at 13 years old. Already a professional surfer, she lost her arm. The event seemed career-ending; life-defining in the worst possible way. One month later, she was back in the water and surfing again. She didn't pretend the event didn't happen or suppress her grief, but she refused to let the event become her identity. Her response—getting back on the board, adapting her technique, choosing courage over comfort—changed her outcome entirely. She went on to become one of the most accomplished surfers in the world.

My own story is smaller than these, but the principle is identical. The tsunami happened. The cricket profession was lost. The relationship ended. The mental breakdown occurred. The decade of struggling happened. The hospital bed happened. But the moment I took ownership, the moment I stopped building my case and started building my life, everything changed. It might not have happened overnight or easily, but the eventual change was complete.

Here's the thing: life throws you curveballs, or in-swingers and slower balls, in cricketing terms. You've had to face them in the past, but it's time to let go of what no longer serves you and move forward. Taking ownership is also about forgiving yourself, because you did the best you could with the information you had at the time.

If you're going to move forward, you have to let go of the past. I know that's scary. You're never going to forget whatever you have been through, and that's okay and normal—you are human. However, letting go of the past means you don't allow your scars to hold you back anymore, and stop you from considering the endless possibilities that are available to you. Your scars are also evidence of a life fully lived. Be proud of that. But also forgive yourself and face up to the choice you now have: stay stuck or go make some new scars with new opportunities. Choose wisely.

Ten years later, I have the relationship I dreamed of in that dark room. I have the career that's built on turning my pain into purpose to help others. I have the peace I thought was impossible. This inner peace is bliss, and it is available to you also.

The equation is the same, but a different response creates a different outcome.

> *The event doesn't determine the outcome; the response does.*

The ownership questions

The questions in this exercise can help you shift from victim to owner. They're not comfortable and they're not meant to be. Growth rarely happens in comfort.

(continued)

This works better on paper, so grab a pen and write down your responses as you ask yourself the following.

'Where am I stuck?'

List three areas of your life where you feel stuck or frustrated, or like things aren't working.

'Who or what have I been blaming?'

For each area you just identified, write down who or what you've been blaming. Be honest. Let the victim voice speak freely.

'What's *my* part?'

This is the hard one. For each area, ask yourself, 'What is my role in this? What choices have I made that contributed? What patterns am I running? What response have I been choosing?'

'What response would change the outcome?'

If you stopped focusing on the event and focused entirely on your response, what would you do differently? What new choice could you make?

'What's one action I can take in the next 24 hours?'

For each area, identify *one* small action that demonstrates ownership. This isn't a complete solution; it's just a first step that proves you're no longer waiting.

The language of ownership

One of the fastest ways to shift from victim to owner—without a journal, without a therapist and without even leaving your chair—is to change your language, because the words you use shape the reality you experience. Language sounds small but it's the operating system your mind runs on. Let me show you what I mean. The following table provides some examples of victim versus owner language.

Victim versus owner language

Victim language	Owner language
'I have to.'	'I choose to,' 'I get to.'
'I can't.'	'I haven't yet.'
'They made me.'	'I allowed it.'
'That's just how I am.'	'That's how I've been.'
'Why does this always happen to me?'	'What is this teaching me?'
'It's not fair.'	'What can I do about it?'
'I don't have time.'	'It's not my priority.'
'You make me so angry.'	'I feel angry when ... '

These different word choices might seem like small changes, but they're anything but. Language is the operating system of your mind. Every time you say something like, 'I have to', you reinforce powerlessness. Every time you instead say, 'I choose to', you reinforce agency.

Try it for one day. Catch yourself using victim language and consciously replace it with owner language. Notice how it feels and how it changes your relationship to your circumstances.

Rewriting the story you tell yourself

The phone call that would help me rewrite my story came on a Friday afternoon. I was eight months out of the hospital and still fragile. I was still rebuilding but I was making real progress: the kind you can feel in your bones even when you can't see it from the outside. I was coaching youth cricket, helping youngsters with their technique, mindset and confidence, and I was showing up three afternoons a week. It wasn't a career. It was a lifeline that got me out of bed and reminded me I had value beyond my wounds.

On this particular afternoon, I had just finished a session in the nets when my phone rang, showing a number I didn't recognise. When I answered, I was asked, 'How much do you love cricket mate?'

'I love cricket that much that it's a Friday afternoon and everyone's finished work and headed to the pub and I'm here coaching cricket', I said.

'Wow, Cameron! What an answer', came the response from someone who turned out to be the owner of a successful cricket equipment brand. He was looking for a new product development manager and someone who could manage some of the best cricketing athletes in the world. 'When can we meet mate?' he asked. 'I'd like to talk to you about the role.'

I almost laughed. I was a broken former cricketer who'd just spent six weeks in a psychiatric facility. What could he possibly want in me? But I listened. And what he described was an opportunity I never saw coming: a chance to be part of something that would change the trajectory of my life entirely.

After I hung up, I sat in my car in the cricket club parking lot for a long time. My hands were shaking and my mind was racing, but not with anxiety this time. I was excited by the possibility. And then the old voice showed up, right on cue. 'Who do you think you are? You can't do this. You're damaged goods. They'll find out what a mess you are. You'll fail publicly and humiliate yourself. You should call back and say no. Stay small. Stay safe. Don't risk it.'

Even six months earlier, I would have listened to that voice. I would have called back, made an excuse, and retreated to the familiar comfort of my limitations. The victim story would have won. But something had shifted in me since the hospital. The ownership work I'd been doing, the daily practice of catching my victim patterns and choosing different responses, had started to rewire something fundamental.

So instead of obeying the voice, I observed it. *There you are,* I thought. *There's the victim story. There's the part of me that wants to stay stuck because stuck feels safe.* And then I asked a different question. Instead of 'Why can't I do this?', I asked 'What if I can?' I asked:

- What if the breakdown wasn't the end of my story but the middle of it?
- What if the hospital wasn't my lowest point but my turning point?
- What if everything I'd been through—the trauma, the struggle, the recovery—was preparing me for something I couldn't have handled before?

So, I called back and I said yes. That decision led to experiences I couldn't have imagined. I travelled around the world, developing equipment and working alongside some of the best cricketers who have ever played the sport, from Michael Clarke, Chris Gayle, Kevin Pietersen and Sachin Tendulkar, to David Warner, Steve Smith, Holly Ferling, MS Dhoni and Phoebe Litchfield.

For the next five years, I learnt so much about business, relationships, athletes and myself. I was given the chance to not only lean into something I have so much passion and interest in and build a career around it but also grow my confidence and worth in the real world. I had time to heal and forgive myself, and learn a new road that still had elements of the old one I knew. This role both brought me back to me and helped me meet a new version I was constantly growing into—a version I was proud of which. It eventually helped me lead my life to meeting Jules and to the platform I now have to help others. It led to the life I'm living today.

But, importantly, the external opportunity didn't change my life. My response to the opportunity did.

Six months earlier, the same phone call would have led to the same retreat. The same event with a different response led to a completely different outcome.

> *Your story isn't written yet — and you're holding the pen.*

The science of story

The story you tell yourself about your life has measurable physiological effects and much research supports this.

Dr James Pennebaker at the University of Texas has spent decades researching the relationship between narrative and health. His studies show people who reframe traumatic experiences into coherent, meaningful narratives show measurable improvements in immune function, fewer doctor visits, better mental health outcomes and even faster wound healing. The story doesn't change the facts, but it can change the body's response to those facts.

Dr Martin Seligman, the father of positive psychology, has demonstrated that your 'explanatory style', how you explain events to yourself, influences depression, achievement and even longevity. And this style can be changed through deliberate practice.

The story you tell yourself becomes the life you live.

Moving along the victim–victor spectrum

Most people aren't pure victims or pure victors in their internal narrative. They slide along the victim–victor spectrum depending on the day, the domain and the trigger. You might be a victor at work but a victim in your relationships. You might own your health completely but blame everyone else for your financial situation.

Your goal isn't perfection but an awareness of where you are on the spectrum and consistent movement toward the victor end.

If you're closer to the victim end of the spectrum, you:

- blame others for your problems
- focus on what happened (the event)
- ask, 'Why me?'
- see obstacles as permanent
- wait to be rescued
- use your past as an excuse
- use language such as, 'I can't', 'They made me' and 'It's not fair'
- feel depleted, resentful and stuck.

If you're closer to the victor end, you:

- take ownership of your response
- focus on what to do next
- ask, 'What now?'
- see obstacles as temporary
- act despite fear
- use your past as fuel
- use language such as, 'I choose', 'I will' and 'What can I learn?'
- feel activated, determined and in motion.

Victims ask, 'Why is this happening to me?' Victors ask, 'What is this teaching me?'

Where do you typically live on this spectrum? I don't mean where you'd like to live or where you think you should live. Where do you actually live, most of the time, when you're honest with yourself? And more specifically, in which areas of your life do you slide toward victim? What triggers the slide?

For me, the trigger was rejection. Any time I felt rejected—by a person, an opportunity or an outcome—I would slide hard toward victim. I'd catastrophise and globalise ('this always happens'). I'd blame anyone but myself.

Knowing your triggers is half the battle. Once you know what pushes you toward victim, you can catch yourself faster and you can interrupt the pattern before it takes over.

The story rewrite

While the facts of your life don't change, your relationship to those facts can change completely. Every event in your history can be told as a victim story or a victor story. The facts remain identical, but the framing transforms everything.

To give you an example of this, here's my victim story (the one I told for years):

> I was traumatised by the tsunami at 20 years old. It destroyed my sense of safety and gave me PTSD that I didn't know how to handle. I tried to push through, but the mental health system failed me. No-one understood what I was going through. The pressure of my career made everything worse. I had no support. Eventually, I broke down completely and ended up in a psychiatric hospital. I lost years of my life to a trauma that wasn't my fault.

Every word of that story is factually true. And it kept me stuck for a decade.

And here's my victor story (the one I tell now):

> At 20 years old, I survived one of the worst natural disasters in human history. That experience showed me the fragility of life and planted a seed that would eventually become my purpose. I struggled for years because I didn't have the tools to process what happened and that struggle taught me what works and what doesn't. When I finally hit rock bottom, I was forced to rebuild from the ground up. That hospital stay became the foundation of everything good in my life. My wound became my wisdom. My breakdown became my breakthrough. Everything I went through prepared me to help others who are going through the same thing.

This has the same facts and events but it's a completely different story. It indicates a completely different relationship to my past and completely different energy moving forward.

The facts don't change, but your relationship to them does. The victim story made me feel powerless. The victor story makes me feel purposeful. The victim story used my past as an anchor, holding me in place. The victor story uses my past as a sail, propelling me forward.

The story you choose to tell—to yourself, about yourself—shapes everything.

The story rewrite exercise

Now it's your turn to rewrite one of your victim stories as a victor story. Grab a pen and your journal (or the Clarity Workbook) and get started.

(continued)

Identify your victim story

Think of a situation, period of your life or ongoing circumstance where you've been telling a victim story. Write this victim version without censoring yourself. Let the hurt and resentment flow. Get it all on paper.

Extract the facts

Now strip away the interpretation. What are the bare facts? Remove the emotions, judgements and 'should haves' and write down what actually happened.

Find the gifts

This is the hard part. Ask yourself, 'What did this experience teach me? How did it make me stronger? What skills, wisdom or empathy did I develop because of it? What would I not have if this hadn't happened?'

Write down those gifts.

Write the victor story

Now rewrite the same events as a victor story. Use the same facts but frame them as part of your hero's journey. You're not denying the pain — you're transcending it.

Read both aloud

Read your victim story aloud and notice how it feels in your body. Now read your victor story aloud. Notice the difference.

Which story do you want to keep telling?

Holding yourself accountable

A victim story generates more victim experiences. A victor story generates more victor experiences through the way story shapes perception, which shapes interpretation, which shapes response, which shapes outcome. In the following sections, I outline some tools to shift your thinking towards the victor story and hold yourself accountable.

Taking the 1 per cent accountability challenge

Changing your thinking can start with small steps. Every day, take 1 per cent more ownership than you took yesterday—that's it. You don't need to attempt a complete overhaul or a dramatic transformation. Just aim for 1 per cent more ownership and accountability. But what does 1 per cent more look like? Here are some examples:

- Yesterday you blamed traffic for being late. Today you acknowledge you could have left earlier.
- Yesterday you complained about your boss. Today you ask what you could do differently.
- Yesterday you said, 'I can't' about the workout. Today you say, 'I'm choosing not to' and feel the difference.
- Yesterday you rehearsed why your ex was wrong. Today you spend five minutes honestly examining your part.

None of these is a huge shift. All of them are 1 per cent movements toward the victor end of the spectrum.

You can also make small changes in your daily practice. Every evening, before bed, ask yourself two questions:

1. Where did I play victim today?
    - What did I blame on others or circumstances?
    - Where did I avoid responsibility?
    - What excuses did I make?
2. Where did I take ownership today?
    - What did I own even though I could have blamed?
    - Where did I focus on my response instead of the event?
    - What action did I take despite wanting to wait?

Write down your answers in just a few sentences. This practice takes less than five minutes but, over time, it can transform the way you move through the world.

The key is consistency, not intensity. A 1 per cent daily change, compounded over a year, produces exponential change.

> *You don't become a victor in one dramatic moment. You become a victor in a thousand small choices.*

Finding an accountability partner

How far you can go alone is limited. Self-reflection is powerful but it has blind spots, and you can convince yourself of almost anything. You can find justifications that sound reasonable to you but wouldn't survive outside scrutiny, and stay stuck in patterns you can't see because you're inside them.

This is why accountability partners matter. I love nothing more than that friend who is genuinely honest, sometimes almost too honest. They love you dearly but aren't a 'yes person'. They tell you how it really is with raw, unfiltered and brutal honesty. Do you know such a person? We all need one of them in our lives.

When I was at my lowest and in the middle of my six-week rehabilitation stint, still trying to find answers and just before I decided to take complete accountability for my life, a huge turning point came in the form of my Aunty Verna. It happened on a weekend when we were allowed out into the 'wild' for an hour or two, like a pet being let out to do its business before being called back in.

I'm forever grateful for this moment in my life, but I very rarely talk about it because of the enormity of what I was contemplating. I know a lot of people who have unfortunately been touched by suicide and this story does come with a trigger warning. If you have lost a loved one, my heart goes out to you. I know how hard it is and for that I am so sorry.

On that fateful weekend, I got a smack in the face from my aunt that changed everything for me. Sometimes we need that friend or relative who tells it like it is. If you are in the right place to hear it in that moment, their straight-talking can change everything for you. This moment changed everything for me and I'm so grateful for it.

At the time, my late great and dearest Aunty Verna was battling stage 3 cancer. She had always told it as it was and certainly didn't have time to sugar-coat anything now. Still, I sat next to her on the couch, in full victim mode and hoping for some sympathy. 'I'm hurting', I told her. 'I'm thinking of taking my own life.'

Her response: 'How dare you! Do you know what that would do to your mother! It would destroy her. How could you be so selfish?! She carried you for nine months and raised you for 29 years and this is how you repay her? It would completely destroy her'.

I was jolted, and in that moment it was exactly what I needed. I'm not saying this is always the right response to someone who is having suicidal ideations, but for me, in that moment, it was.

Even though I'd been hoping for a very different response, something within me changed in that moment.

At first, I was flabbergasted. I'd wanted comfort and empathy; a bit of, 'It's okay. There, there. You'll be okay. Oh no, don't think like that'. Instead, I got some harsh truths and honesty that saved my life. I was able to see beyond myself to the damage I would leave behind.

I realised I needed to do something fast if I wanted to change my life and not continue to hurt the people I loved. This was my chance and I'm forever thankful for Aunty Verna and her honest ways. We all need someone like her in our lives, so maybe at your next family gathering, seek out that aunty or uncle you tend to stay clear of. They might just have a little bit of life-changing dust to sprinkle all over you. It might not be what you want, but it might be just what you need.

You also need an accountability partner in your day-to-day life. This is someone who has permission to tell you the truth, to call out your victim patterns when you can't see them (and even when it feels uncomfortable), to celebrate your ownership when you downplay it and to ask the hard questions you're avoiding. They won't sugar-coat their questions or insights, or let you stay comfortable in the way you're feeling because change is scary and seems too hard.

Not everyone is qualified for this role. You need someone who:

- *Has done their own work:* They can't help you see your patterns if they're blind to their own.
- *Genuinely cares about your growth:* You don't want someone who will validate your victim stories to make you feel better.

- *Will be honest, not nice:* Kindness and honesty aren't opposites, but someone who only tells you what you want to hear isn't helping.
- *Is committed to the relationship:* Accountability requires consistency. A partner who disappears isn't a partner.

I have had three such people in my life since Aunty Verna passed, who had explicit permission to call me on my bullshit. Jules is one of them. She knows my victim patterns better than I do and she loves me enough to tell me when I'm sliding.

When she says, 'Cam, that sounds like a victim story', I don't get defensive anymore. I get curious, because she's usually right. She's my biggest critic and yet my biggest fan, which makes for a pretty good accountability partner. Sometimes she doesn't even need to say anything, just gives me that look. (Maybe you know the look I'm talking about?)

Noticing the victim voice versus the victor voice

One more focus for your daily practice is learning to distinguish the victim voice from the victor voice in your own head. Both voices live inside you, and both will speak up when challenges arise. The question is which one you listen to and which one you let drive.

I talk about the language of ownership, and provide some examples of victim versus ownership language, earlier in this chapter. The victim versus victor voice is similar, as shown in the following table (overleaf).

Victim versus victor voice

Victim	Victor
'This isn't fair.'	'This is hard, and I can handle hard.'
'I can't believe they did this to me.'	'What's my next move?'
'Why does this always happen?'	'What can I learn from this?'
'There's nothing I can do.'	'What's within my control right now?'
'If only they would change.'	'How can I grow from this?'
'I'm not strong enough for this.'	'I've survived difficult things before.'
'It's too late for me.'	'It's not too late to start.'
'I've always been this way.'	'I'm becoming someone different.'

When you notice the victim voice speaking, don't fight it or try to suppress it. Just notice it: 'Ah, there's the victim voice'. Then consciously choose to give the microphone to the victor voice. Ask yourself, 'What would the victor voice say right now?'

You're not pretending the victim voice doesn't exist. You're choosing which voice gets to narrate your life.

> *You can't stop the victim voice from speaking, but you can stop giving it the microphone.*

The self-forgiveness letter

You may have read the Accountability Equation and felt power, allowing you to shift from passenger to driver. That's beautiful. But you may have felt a different weight. You may have felt not liberation but 'it's all my fault'. If that's you, hear this: accountability is not the same as blame. You did the best you could with what you had at the time. That's not an excuse. It's the truth. When I finally forgave myself, I created an acceptance that allowed me to really start moving forward with my life, without blame. I allowed myself to heal and start becoming my own best friend.

Write a letter to the version of yourself who made the choices you're most ashamed of. Start with what happened, don't soften it. Then draw a line. Above that line, write what happened to you. The events you couldn't control. Below it, write the responses you chose. Both sides can be true simultaneously.

Now write the letter. Start with: 'Dear *[your name at that age]*, I want you to know something…' Tell them what you understand now that they couldn't have known then. Tell them you see why they made those choices.

Close with this: 'I forgive you. Not because what happened doesn't matter, but because carrying this weight no longer serves either of us. I'm choosing ownership now. And ownership starts with letting you off the hook'.

Accountability without forgiveness is just a more sophisticated way of staying stuck. Take ownership of your future and give grace to your past. Know that you deserve that.

The accountability declaration

I'm closing this chapter with something I invite you to declare, out loud, if possible. Declarations have power. They take internal commitments and make them external and real.

The following is my accountability declaration. Read it slowly and with intention. If it resonates, claim it as your own. Real 'owning your fucking story' energy is liberating.

Make your accountability declaration:

> I am done waiting for life to be fair. I am done blaming others for my circumstances. I am done telling victim stories that keep me stuck.

I acknowledge that painful things have happened to me. I make peace with my past, forgive myself and move forward. I do not deny my wounds. But I refuse to let my wounds become my identity. I refuse to let my past author my future. I refuse to give away my power to people and events that are no longer here.

From this day forward, I choose ownership.

I accept that my response is always within my control and my response determines my outcome.

I will ask, 'What can I do?' instead of, 'Why did this happen?'

I will focus on the next step, not the last step.

I will use my past as fuel, not as an anchor.

I will surround myself with people who hold me accountable to this commitment.

I will slip and I will fall back into victim mode. That's okay. When I do, I will notice it, own it and choose again.

I am not a victim of my story. I am the author of it. Starting today, I'm writing a different ending.

Let's go!

Accountability Pillar summary

Pillar 3: Accountability is where everything pivots. Here's what to carry forward:

- *The Accountability Equation is Event + Response = Outcome:* You can't control the event, but you always control your response. Your response determines your outcome. You are not responsible for everything that happened to you, you *are* responsible for who you become because of it.
- *You can avoid the second arrow:* In the parable of the two arrows, the first arrow (the event) causes pain. The second arrow (your story about it) causes suffering. Pain is inevitable but suffering is optional. Accountability is learning to stop shooting yourself.
- *You live on a victim–victor spectrum:* Know your triggers and know where you slide towards the victim end of the spectrum. The story rewrite shows that the same facts can be told as a victim story (keeping you stuck) or a victor story (propelling you forward). The 1 per cent accountability challenge compounds daily ownership into transformation. Find an accountability partner who loves you enough to tell you the truth.
- *No-one is coming to save you:* This is okay because you don't need saving. You need ownership.

Chapter Seven

Pillar 4: Regulation

> Your body was never the enemy. It was the messenger you refused to hear.

The storm started brewing long before I knew I was standing in it. From the outside, everything looked magnificent. I was 25 years of age and for the past four years, I had built not only a life in Toronto, Canada, but also a foundation. I had a relationship and a family who felt like home; a coaching and professional playing career; a broadcasting role on TV and radio; travel. I had purpose and momentum.

But I'd always felt this pull back to Sydney, due to the story I'd been telling myself since I was 16. The story that said, 'Home is where life happens; real life is waiting for you there. You need to go back'. So, I did what strong, decisive men do—I burned everything I had down. I ended the relationship and let go of the family I cherished. I walked away from the broadcasting contracts and the coaching commitments. I packed my life into a few bags and left for the airport, ready to board a flight back to Australia to 'start fresh'. I thought I was choosing freedom, but I was walking into collapse.

When my body stopped listening to my mind

I felt the first tightening at the airport in Toronto. It started subtly, and felt like someone had wrapped a belt around my ribs and was slowly pulling it tighter. I tried to breathe deeper but the air wouldn't come. The belt tightened. My heart was pounding, violently. I could feel it in my throat, my temples and my fingertips. Each beat felt like it might be the one that tipped me over the edge.

The boarding call for my flight came over the PA but I couldn't move. They ended up calling my name and I was the last to board, on legs that felt like they didn't belong to me. My body was screaming something but I couldn't translate the language. I walked onto that plane because my mind had made the decision and I had always trusted my mind.

The moment the plane took off, my breathing became shallow and sharp. I needed a paper bag. I needed to stand up. I needed to get off. But we were already 11 000 feet in the air with no exit possible.

Somewhere above the clouds, the truth hit me: I'd made the wrong decision. I wanted Toronto. I wanted my life back. I wanted safety and certainty. But there is no emergency landing for regret.

We landed in Vancouver for a stopover before flying on to Australia. It was freezing winter and snowing; the cold and bleak surrounds were exactly what my mind and body were feeling. They seemed to be telling me this was what my future would look like if I didn't make a decision fast.

A small wave of calm came over me. *This is it,* I thought. *Go back.* But when it came time to act, I froze. It was late. I had nowhere to go. I had about a hundred dollars in my bank account. I stood there staring at the departure board like it was written in another language. I couldn't think. I couldn't decide. I couldn't move.

In the end, I spent the night in a cheap hotel room in Vancouver, alone with the silence and my thoughts. My body wouldn't stop trembling. Pain pulsed through my muscles. My chest burned and my head throbbed. Every cell felt like it was firing distress signals. Something was terribly wrong, my nervous system was in full shutdown, and I couldn't logic my way out of it.

The next morning, I scraped together enough coins for breakfast and to get myself back to the airport. I was still unsure and still stuck. In that moment I realised something I had never understood before. In life, we stand on certain supports: home, family, work, purpose, identity. If one support shakes, the others hold you up. But if they all collapse at once, you don't just fall; you disintegrate. That's exactly what had happened to me.

I had voluntarily removed every stabilising structure in my life at the same time. My relationship, career, community and my future plan were all gone. I had nothing to stand on and so I collapsed. For four days, I stayed in the Vancouver departure lounge—yes, four days. I couldn't call anyone because I couldn't explain it. I couldn't move forward or backward. My brain felt like it had melted. I wasn't depressed or weak or playing victim. My body had hijacked me.

Like Tom Hanks in *The Terminal*, I existed in limbo, except this wasn't a movie. This was my nervous system in collapse, and it was the lesson that broke me open. What I didn't understand at the time, but know now, is this: you cannot think your way out of a nervous system response.

When your body perceives threat—even if that threat is uncertainty, loss of identity or destabilisation—it doesn't ask your permission.

It moves into survival mode, quickly choosing between fight, flight or freeze. And I was frozen. My body wasn't broken. It was protecting me. It had assessed that every anchor in my world had disappeared, and it pulled the emergency brake to save me. It was the most humbling lesson of my life.

Throughout my life and career, I had built strength in discipline, performance, resilience and mindset. But I had never learned regulation. That was the missing skill that opens up everything. I didn't know how to calm my nervous system. I didn't know how to stabilise my physiology. I didn't know how to create internal safety when external safety collapsed.

And without regulation, clarity disappears. You can't access logic, vision or courage. When the body feels unsafe, it will always override the mind, every time.

Looking back, that storm wasn't a breakdown but a wake-up call. It taught me that clarity is not a mindset skill. It is a regulated nervous system skill. When your body feels safe, you can choose wisely. When your body is calm, you can see clearly. When your system is stable, you can move forward.

But when your nervous system is in chaos, you can have all the motivation in the world and still be stuck in an airport lounge for four days. I had no idea what I was dealing with during those four days and what I felt still terrifies me all these years later, especially as I write about it here now. As I said, the experience broke me open. I did make it home to Australia and to sleeping on my friend's couch, but I would soon be booking myself a one-way ticket into a mental rehab facility. Those times show how life can change so quickly, when you least expect it and when you haven't kept up the work.

If your body is not regulated, your life will feel chaotic, no matter how strong your mind is. Strength is not pushing through.

Strength is knowing how to come back to safety inside yourself. When your body can listen to your mind again, your life starts to move again.

The gap between knowing and embodying

The gap between knowing and embodying can ruin people. They may have read the books and understood the concepts. They may be able to explain the psychology perfectly and outline what they're supposed to do. But then they get triggered and all of it disappears. This might happen to:

- the business executive who knows she needs to stay calm in high-stakes meetings but freezes the moment the CEO asks her a direct question
- the father who has committed to being patient with his kids but explodes in rage when they push his buttons and then hates himself afterward
- the person in recovery who has all the tools and knows all the strategies, but relapses anyway when the craving hits.

The gap between knowing and embodying is the gap between your prefrontal cortex (where knowledge lives) and your nervous system (where survival responses live). And when those two are in conflict, the nervous system wins every time.

This isn't weakness; it's biology.

> *You can't think your way out of a nervous system response. You have to breathe your way through it.*

Awareness and accountability give you the map. Regulation gives you the ability to actually use it.

Your nervous system: A user's guide

Your autonomic nervous system, the part that operates below conscious awareness, has two main branches:

1. *The sympathetic nervous system is your accelerator:* It activates the 'fight or freeze' response. When it fires, your heart rate increases, your breathing quickens, your muscles tense and stress hormones flood your system. You're preparing to fight a threat or run from it. (This response is actually a bit more complicated, and I'll get to that shortly.)
2. *The parasympathetic nervous system is your brake:* It activates the 'rest and digest' response. When it's dominant, your heart rate slows, your breathing deepens, your muscles relax, and your body focuses on healing, digestion and restoration.

In a healthy system, these two branches work together in balance. You activate during a genuine threat and then return to rest when the threat passes.

But for many of us, and especially those who've experienced trauma, chronic stress or prolonged overwhelm, the system gets stuck in the sympathetic nervous system response. The accelerator stays pressed down even when no real danger is present. The nervous system remains hypervigilant, constantly scanning for threats and constantly ready for disaster.

Dr Stephen Porges, who developed polyvagal theory, proposed that the nervous system responses are actually more complex than just 'fight or flight'. Instead, Porges highlighted the role of the vagus nerve (which runs from the brainstem to the abdomen and regulates functions such as heart rate and digestion) in a three-stage hierarchy of responses:

1. *Social engagement (ventral vagal):* When we feel safe, we're able to connect, communicate and be present with others. This is our optimal state—calm but alert, and relaxed but engaged.
2. *Fight or flight (sympathetic):* When we perceive danger, we mobilise to address it—heart racing, muscles ready and heightened awareness. This is appropriate for real threats but devastating when chronically activated.
3. *Freeze or shutdown (dorsal vagal):* When the threat seems overwhelming—when we can't fight or flee—the system shuts down. This is the collapse response, and includes numbness, dissociation, depression and the sense of being 'checked out' from your own life.

You are not weak when you are in shutdown. Your system is overwhelmed. Understanding this removes the shame. If you've been stuck in anxiety (sympathetic overdrive) or depression (dorsal shutdown), it's not because you're broken. Your nervous system is doing what it has evolved to do: protect you from perceived threats. The problems emerge when the threats it's responding to aren't real, and are instead echoes, memories and patterns from the past that have been encoded in the body.

The body keeps the score

Dutch psychiatrist and author Dr Bessel van der Kolk wrote the landmark book *The Body Keeps the Score.* The title says everything. Your body keeps score of everything that's ever happened to you. Every trauma, every wound and every moment of feeling unsafe is stored somewhere in your tissues, muscles and nervous system.

This is why you can 'know' something is safe and still feel terrified. Your mind knows the situation isn't dangerous but your body remembers something—a smell, a sound, a sensation—that's linked to an older experience of danger. It responds to that memory as if it's happening now.

Van der Kolk's research showed that trauma isn't a story in the mind but a state in the body. You can't heal from the trauma just by changing your thoughts. You also have to change your body's relationship to safety.

This was revolutionary when I first learned it. At the time, sleep felt like the safest place for me to be, but I'd often wake with my heart pounding and my chest tight. (Not a pleasurable way at all to start the day.) I had been trying to think my way out of anxiety and argue with my panic attacks. I had been trying to reason with my nervous system and convince myself I was safe. It didn't work because my nervous system doesn't speak the language of logic. It speaks the language of sensation, breath, movement and nervous system state.

> *The body keeps the score. It's time to change the game.*

Regulation isn't about controlling your body through force of will. It's about learning to communicate with your nervous system in its own language and building a felt sense of safety that's deeper than any thought.

Understanding your window of tolerance

Developed by clinical professor of psychiatry Dr Dan Siegel, the 'window of tolerance' describes the zone in which you can function optimally. Here's how it works:

- Inside the window, you can think clearly, feel your emotions without being overwhelmed, and respond rather than react.
- Above the window is hyperarousal, where you feel anxiety, panic, rage and overwhelm. Your sympathetic system is in overdrive, with too much activation and not enough brake.
- Below the window is hypoarousal, where you feel numbness, depression, dissociation and shutdown. Your dorsal vagal system has taken over, with too much brake and not enough activation.

The goal of regulation isn't to never leave your window of tolerance—that's impossible and would make you less human. Your goal is to widen the window (so you can handle more without getting dysregulated) and to develop the skills to return to the window when you leave it.

Most people have no idea what their window looks like. They don't know what pushes them into hyperarousal or drops them into hypoarousal. They don't recognise the early warning signs of dysregulation. And they have few tools for returning to their window when they leave it. (I certainly didn't, that's for sure.)

Through understanding your window of tolerance, calm becomes accessible rather than conditional. That's the promise of regulation work. You will still get triggered and life will still throw challenges at you. But calm will become something you can access and create within yourself. It won't depend on everything going perfectly.

Why regulation must come before change

You cannot sustainably change your behaviour from a dysregulated state. Think back to every New Year's resolution that died by February, every diet that lasted two weeks, and every commitment to be more patient, present and disciplined that collapsed the moment stress hit. Those weren't failures of willpower. They were failures of regulation.

When your nervous system is dysregulated, your prefrontal cortex goes offline. Your body's resources get redirected to survival. This is why you can make a commitment with complete sincerity and then break it an hour later. The you who made the commitment was regulated. The you who broke it was dysregulated. You're operating from different brain states with different capacities.

Lasting change requires a regulated foundation, similar to when you're building a house. You can have the most beautiful architectural plans, the finest materials and the most skilled craftsmen, but if you try to build on an unstable foundation—on shifting sand, on a swamp or on ground that won't hold weight—the house will fall.

Your nervous system is the foundation for your health. All the external aspects covered in the next part that you're trying to build—your identity, habits, connection and contribution—rest on it. If the foundation is unstable, everything wobbles.

Signals, not sentences

Your symptoms are signals, not sentences. This means:

- The anxiety isn't a verdict that you're broken. It's a signal that your nervous system needs attention.
- The panic isn't proof that you can't cope. It's information that something is overwhelming your current capacity.
- The numbness isn't evidence that you're damaged beyond repair. It's your system's attempt to protect you from what feels like too much.

For years, I made my symptoms into identity, telling myself, 'I'm an anxious person', 'I have panic disorder', 'There's something wrong with me'. Those sentences turned temporary states into permanent identities. They made me feel hopeless and they were backwards. The more accurate framing is, 'My nervous system is sending me signals. My job isn't to fight the signals or shame myself for having them. My job is to understand them and respond in ways that help my system feel safe'.

When you feel anxiety rising, instead of saying, 'Oh no, here we go again; I'm so broken', try, 'Ah, my nervous system is activating. It's trying to protect me from something. What might it be responding to? And what does it need right now?'

This shift from judgement to curiosity is massive. One keeps you stuck in shame while the other opens the door to change.

> *Your nervous system isn't your enemy. It's a frightened guardian that needs to learn you're safe.*

My regulation journey

After that panic attack mental breakdown in the Vancouver airport and my eventual admission to mental rehab, I became obsessed with understanding what was happening in my body. I read everything I could find to work out why my body was shutting down in panic and responding to certain circumstances. I found out about the neuroscience of trauma, and learnt more about the vagus nerve and how to regulate it.

More importantly, I started practising ways to calm my body:

- *I began with breathwork:* It's amazing what breathing can actually do. (Who'd have thunk it, right?) At first, I focused on simple stuff: learning to take slow, deep breaths into my belly instead of shallow gasps into my chest. I practised when I wasn't triggered, building the skill so it would be available when I needed it.
- *I learned to recognise my early warning signs:* For me, dysregulation starts in my shoulders, they creep up toward my ears when stress is building. If I catch it there, I can intervene before it cascades into full activation.
- *I discovered what regulates me specifically:* This includes cold water on my face and walking, especially in nature or down to our local beach to just sit and be. Certain music also helps, as does a five-minute affirmation meditation. I also lie on the floor with my legs up the wall and talk to Jules, even if I don't want to talk. I use vigorous exercise when I'm hyper, and gentle movement when I'm hypo.
- *I also learned what dysregulates me:* This includes too much caffeine, not enough sleep and scrolling news on my phone. It can also include certain people who leave me feeling drained, and overcommitting and then feeling trapped by my own calendar.

Knowing what worked for me took time. I needed months of practice before I could stop a trigger turning into a full hijack, and a year before I felt like I had genuine tools instead of just concepts. But I got there, and you can too.

The anxiety and moments of panic still happen occasionally. But they're rarer now, and they don't terrify me in the same way. When one comes, I know what it is, I know it will pass and I know what to do. And that knowledge, that felt sense of competence in the face of my own nervous system, is priceless.

> *Once you befriend your nervous system instead of battling it, you change everything.*

The regulation foundation assessment

Before we move to regulation tools in the remainder of this chapter, take some time now to assess where you are.

Your current state

On a scale of one to ten, rate your typical nervous system state over the past month. Base your rating on the following:

- One = Completely shut down — numb, depressed and dissociated.
- Five = Regulated — calm but alert; able to function well.
- Ten = Completely activated — anxious, panicked and unable to settle.

Your hyperarousal triggers

What pushes you above your window of tolerance? Think about what makes you anxious, panicked or overwhelmed, and write down your top five triggers.

Your hypoarousal triggers

What pushes you below your window? Consider what makes you shut down, numb out or feel depressed, and write down your top five triggers.

(continued)

Your early warning signs

How does your body tell you that you're leaving your window? What are your early signals of dysregulation? Consider your hyperarousal early signs (before full anxiety/panic) and write them down. Next, think about your hypoarousal early signs (before full shutdown) and write them down.

What currently helps

What already helps you regulate? What brings you back to your window when you leave it? List anything that works, even partially.

This assessment gives you a baseline. Keep it somewhere you can reference, because we're about to build on it through the rest of this chapter.

Regulation practices that calm the storm

The moment I knew these tools actually worked wasn't in a meditation retreat or a therapy session but in a shopping centre car park, two days out from Christmas. (I know, I'm sorry to take you there. I apologise if this scene brings up some stressful memories you would rather forget.)

Jules and I had been together for about a year and were doing the last-minute gift run—the frantic kind in which every store is packed, every parking spot is contested and the holiday cheer has curdled into something closer to holiday combat.

I was circling the car park for the third time, watching people cut in front of me and spots disappear the moment I approached them. The pressure of the season was already high. We had family commitments, travel logistics, the weight of making everything perfect. And then someone stole my spot. You know that feeling, don't you? *Are you kidding me!?*

I'm not talking about some confusion about who got there first. I'm talking about me, indicator on, clearly waiting, and this guy just deciding to take my park. He didn't even look at me. Just slid in like I didn't exist. I felt the surge of rage instantly, heat rising up my chest into my neck. My hands tightened on the steering wheel and my jaw clenched. Every cell in my body wanted to do something—get out of the car, confront him, scream, pound the horn—anything to discharge this sudden volcanic pressure.

The old me would have—in fact the old me had, many times. I'd had road rage incidents I'm not proud of and confrontations that escalated. They were all moments when I let my nervous system drive and dealt with the consequences later. I once let a guy in on the road in Wellington, New Zealand, near the Basin Reserve where I played cricket for the Wellington Firebirds. He didn't give me a wave. His lack of courtesy made me so mad I drove around the Basin Reserve (which if you don't know it, also acts as one of the biggest one-way roundabouts in New Zealand), honking from behind the whole way. Unfortunately, this was just before a training session and some of my fellow teammates saw the incident and proceeded to call me 'Rage' for the remainder of the season. It didn't stick long term, thank goodness, but most of them still couldn't comprehend how my usually calm nature could, on occasion, be hijacked so quickly by a ferocious rage.

But in that car park just before Christmas, something different happened: I noticed. I don't mean the anger, I had definitely noticed feeling that. I mean I noticed the process. I noticed my body activating. I noticed my breath getting shallow. I noticed the heat, the tension and the tunnel vision starting to form.

And because I noticed, I had a choice. I took one deep breath into my belly and slowly exhaled. I said to myself, 'I notice I'm feeling rage. My nervous system is activated. This is a response to feeling disrespected. The threat isn't real. I'm safe'. (I also notice this guy is a dick, but that's not a part of the scientific recovery work).

I took another breath. The volcanic pressure dropped maybe 10 per cent. I asked myself, 'What do I want here? Do I want to confront a stranger two days before Christmas? Do I want to ruin the afternoon with Jules over a parking spot? Do I want to let this random person determine my emotional state?' No. I wanted to find a spot, buy some gifts and have a nice day with the woman I loved.

I drove on, found another spot three rows over, and walked into the shops with Jules, who had no idea anything had happened.

The whole intervention took maybe 45 seconds. But those 45 seconds represented years of practice and years of building tools. It came from years of training my nervous system to respond differently from how it had been programmed to respond.

Between stimulus and response there is a space. The tools outlined in the following sections help you find it.

The Clarity Pause

The Clarity Pause is the foundational regulation practice. Everything else builds on it. The Clarity Pause gives you the moment between stimulus and response—the space where freedom lives. It's the practice of interrupting your automatic reactions long enough to choose something different.

The following sections run through how it works.

Step 1: Stop

The moment you notice activation—anger, anxiety, overwhelm or whatever form it takes—stop. Physically stop (if possible) and interrupt the momentum.

This isn't as simple as it sounds simple. When your nervous system is activated, it wants to do something, whether that be fight, flee, freeze, fix, argue or escape. Stopping goes against every survival instinct, but it is essential. As long as you're in motion, you're in reaction. Only in stillness can you access choice.

If you can't physically stop. If you're in a meeting, a conversation or driving, for example, you can still create an internal pause. Take a moment of stepping back even while life continues.

Step 2: Breathe

Take three conscious breaths. Not shallow chest breaths—deep, slow, belly breaths. Practise the following:

- Inhale through your nose for four counts.
- Hold for four counts.
- Exhale slowly through your mouth for six counts.

Exhaling through your nose keeps the breath slow and controlled, which is exactly what your nervous system needs to downshift. If nasal exhale feels uncomfortable at first, breathe out gently through your mouth. The key is making the exhale longer than the inhale.

Taking three breaths like this can shift your physiology in under a minute.

Step 3: Notice

Observe what's happening without judgement. Use the 'I notice' language from chapter 5, for example:

- 'I notice my heart is racing.'
- 'I notice tension in my jaw.'
- 'I notice I'm feeling defensive.'
- 'I notice the urge to attack.'
- 'I notice fear underneath the anger.'

You're not trying to change anything yet. You're just seeing clearly. Awareness creates distance and distance creates choice.

Step 4: Ask

Ask yourself one question: 'What do I actually want here?'

This isn't about what your reactive nervous system wants or what would feel satisfying in the moment. What do you actually want in alignment with your values, your relationships and your long-term wellbeing?

Step 5: Respond

Act from choice rather than reaction. Your response might look exactly the same as what you would have done anyway. Or it might look completely different. The point isn't that the action changes but that the quality of the action changes. It comes from clarity instead of chaos.

> *"The Clarity Pause is the practice; everything else is just reaction."*

I use the Clarity Pause dozens of times a day, for both major triggers and small ones. I use it before I respond to a frustrating email, before

I address something with Jules, before I make a decision when I'm tired and even before I eat something I might regret.

Each time I use it, I'm building the 'regulation muscle' and strengthening neural pathways. Each time I choose response over reaction, I'm rewiring my nervous system's default patterns.

Your regulation tools

When was the last time you took a really deep breath in, held it and sighed it out? Maybe a while? Well, I can tell you it is one of the greatest regulation tools you have. Breath is the master key to regulation and is the one autonomic function that you can consciously control. You can't directly slow your heart rate or lower your blood pressure, but you can change your breathing and the rest follows from there.

Here are the tools I use regularly. Full step-by-step instructions are in the companion Clarity Workbook, but you can use the following to get started:

- *Box breathing (4–4–4–4):* My go-to when pressure builds. Breathe in for four counts, hold for four, breathe out for four and hold for four. I also love to use a visual with my hands, especially when I'm teaching a workshop. I use one hand to draw the box in the air on each count of four, while my other hand is on my belly, feeling the rise and fall. This technique is used by Navy SEALs to stay calm under extreme pressure. If it works in combat, it can work in your life. (You might not want to use your hands while out front in a meeting, that might look and seem odd, but you get the idea.)
- *The physiological sigh:* The fastest known way to reduce anxiety in real-time, researched by Dr Andrew Huberman at Stanford. Take a deep inhale through the nose, then a second short inhale

to top up the lungs, and then a long slow exhale through the mouth. One to three of these can shift your state in 30 seconds. I use them mid-panic when nothing else cuts through.

- *Extended exhale breathing:* Use this when you're above your window of tolerance: anxious, agitated and activated. Inhale for four counts and then exhale for six to eight counts. The longer exhale stimulates the vagus nerve and activates your calming system. I use this technique before sleep and during any extended period where I need to downregulate.
- *Energising breath:* Use this when the problem isn't anxiety but shutdown—you're feeling sluggish, numb and collapsed. Take quick sharp inhales and exhales through the nose for 20 to 30 cycles, and then rest. In a similar way to the 'breath of fire' yoga practice or Wim Hof's breathing techniques, this exercise helps bring your energy back online. Caution: only use this technique when you're in the numb zone, not when you're already activated.
- *5-4-3-2-1 sensory grounding:* In this grounding technique, name five things you can see, four you can touch, three you can hear, two you can smell and one you can taste. This engages your sensory cortex, pulls resources away from fear centres and forces present-moment attention. It's more difficult to catastrophise about the future while counting textures.
- *Feet on floor:* In the simplest grounding technique of all, feel your feet on the ground, press them down deliberately and notice the sensation of support. Say to yourself, 'I am here. The ground is holding me. I am safe in this moment'. Sometimes the simplest tools are the best.
- *Cold exposure:* Splash cold water on your face, hold ice cubes or stand for an extra 30 seconds under cold water at the end of your shower. Cold activates the 'dive reflex'—an ancient

survival mechanism that immediately slows the heart rate and calms the nervous system. It's jarring, but its effects are faster than almost anything else.

- *Physical movement:* Push against a wall, do jumping jacks, shake your body vigorously or stomp your feet. If your nervous system is mobilising energy to fight or flee and you don't use that energy, it stays stuck in your body. I get Ollie to do this kind of movement after a day at school and before bedtime. (He often still has a lot of energy needing to be used up.) I also do this when I'm about to speak on stage and it allows my nervous energy and stress to shift. Movement completes the stress cycle. Animals do this naturally—after a threat, they literally shake it off. We've lost that instinct, but we can reclaim it.
- *Emotional labelling:* In chapter 5, I talk about the 'name it to tame it' technique. When you notice a difficult emotion, pause, locate it in your body and label it with specificity—'I notice I'm feeling anxious about the meeting', for example, rather than 'I feel bad'. The more precisely you name it, the more your prefrontal cortex calms your amygdala. Emotions are not facts. They're information. Label them, learn from them, but don't let them drive.

The daily regulation practice

Individual tools are powerful, but they're most powerful when embedded in daily practice. Morning sets the direction. Evening captures the meaning.

Start with some morning regulation (10 to 15 minutes):

- Take three conscious breaths before getting out of bed.
- Set an intention for the day, and then smile and say, 'Thank you!'

- Be grateful for what is in your life currently, whether this be family, your health or a roof over your head.
- Visualise who you want to be for the day. What values do you want to possess and what energy do you want to bring to the day.
- Practise five to ten minutes of light movement (stretching, yoga or walking).
- Follow with three to five minutes of box breathing. (Or perhaps just one minute to start and build from there. Deal?)
- Ask yourself, 'What's most important today?' Write it down.

Most importantly, do not touch your phone for at least the first 15 minutes after waking up. Going straight to your phone disturbs everything—including your dopamine levels that set you up for your day. I know how hard it is to resist, but if you can get in the habit of not checking your phone first thing, your future self and mental health will thank you, I promise.

Next, implement a midday reset (two to three minutes):

- Take a Clarity Pause—stop, breathe, notice, ask and respond.
- Do a quick body scan—where are you holding tension? What does your body need?
- Check your progress—are you on track with what matters most today?

Finally, make time for an evening release (five to ten minutes):

- Review your day—where did you get triggered today? Where did you stay regulated?
- If you can feel some residual stress, use movement or extended exhale breathing to release it.
- Write down three things you're grateful for or that went well for you today.

To get ready for sleep, ensure you have no screens for 30 to 60 minutes before bed. Let your nervous system know it's safe to rest. Also try some quick gratitudes and affirmations to allow your nervous system to be calm overnight. This helps you wake up in the morning with a fresh and vitalised inner self, ready for the day. Try the following:

1. 'Thank you for everything in my life, seen or unseen, big or small.'
2. 'I let go of anything negative that happened to me today and I welcome peace into my mind and body.'
3. 'I'm ready to wake up aligned with peace, clarity and abundance.'

And to really lock in some easy ways to implement gratitude throughout your day, try setting three gratitude alarms:

- *First alarm (between 5.30 and 7.30 am):* Say and feel what you love. Tap into a moment so you feel it.
- *Second alarm (between 12.30 and 2.30 pm):* Stop for a moment, breathe, look around or go outside. What are you grateful for?
- *Third alarm (between 5.30 and 7.30 pm):* What was the best thing that happened today?

Create action around these alarms when they go off to train your brain into really appreciating and seeing the good that surrounds you. (For more on my overall daily clarity rituals, see chapter 9.)

Sleep: your overnight regulation reset

One regulation tool can be used every night that most people undervalue: sleep. When you sleep fewer than six hours, your prefrontal cortex loses up to 60 per cent of its function. Your amygdala becomes up to 60 per cent more reactive. Sleep deprivation does the exact opposite of everything this chapter teaches—it takes the rational brain offline and hands the keys to the fear centre.

During my worst periods, sleep was the first thing to go. I'd lie awake at 3 am with my heart pounding, and then drag myself through the next day on cortisol and caffeine. I thought my anxiety was causing the poor sleep. What I didn't realise was the poor sleep was causing my anxiety, or at least making it dramatically worse. It was a cycle feeding itself.

Three practices made the biggest difference for me. First, be consistent with your timing, go to bed and wake within the same 30-minute window every day, weekends included, because your body wants predictability. Second, sleep in a cool and dark room, because your core temperature needs to drop for sleep to initiate. Third, run a 'worry download' and before bed, spend two minutes writing down anything circling in your mind. Get it out of your head and onto paper. Tell your brain, 'I've captured this. You don't need to hold it overnight'. This alone cut my 3-am wake-ups in half.

Protect your sleep the way you protect your morning ritual. Without sleep, every other tool in this chapter is fighting with one hand tied behind its back.

The room on level three

Let's look at this idea of gratitude in a little more detail, because it really is one of the fastest ways to calm the mind and bring clarity back into your life. I don't like the forced kind of gratitude or the 'pretend everything is perfect' kind. I mean real gratitude, the kind that shifts how you see the moment you're in.

I learned this lesson in a way I will never forget. Many years ago, I was organising a Christmas trip to Phuket, Thailand, for my family to say thank you for the support they had given me over the years with cricket. At the time, I was just starting to make inroads in the sport and move up the ranks towards achieving my dream of becoming a professional cricketer.

I wanted the trip to be special, so when I booked the resort, I made sure my parents had the best room available—a beautiful poolside room right by the beach. The kind of room where you wake up, open the door and almost step straight onto the sand.

When we arrived, however, the receptionist looked at the computer screen and hesitated. 'I'm sorry, Mr Merchant', she said. 'Your room has been double-booked. We can't give you the poolside room tonight. We do have another room available for you. It's on level three. We're very sorry, and we promise we'll make it up to you tomorrow.'

You kick stones for a moment but there's nothing you can do. So, we accepted it and went up to the room on level three, and you know what? We still had a wonderful Christmas Day. The sun was shining. The beach was beautiful. Tourists were swimming and laughing. Our family spent the day enjoying each other's company and creating memories.

At the time, the room change felt like a minor inconvenience; just one of those travel hiccups. But 24 hours later, that inconvenience would take on an entirely different meaning.

The morning everything changed

The next morning, a staff member from reception called. 'Mr Merchant, your poolside room is ready now.' Perfect. We packed our bags and began getting ready to move downstairs.

And that's when it happened. A sound I will never forget: a thunderous clap followed by a deep, violent thump. It echoed through the entire hotel and, within, seconds people were shouting and running. The tsunami had arrived. A giant wave surged across the beach, over the road and straight into the resort.

In the chaos that followed, I was separated from my parents. For a moment, I had no idea where they were. My mind immediately went to the worst possible place: the poolside room we were supposed to have. The room that had been double-booked.

When I eventually made my way down there, the entire room was filled to the ceiling with water. Furniture was floating around and the doors were blown open. In that moment, perspective arrived with absolute clarity. The inconvenience from the day before had protected us.

When the woman at reception said they would make it up to me, she had no idea how true that statement would be. The room on level three had just saved our lives.

Over 12 hours later, exhausted after searching through the chaos and devastation, I finally found my parents. They were alive and safe. In that moment, I felt something deeper than relief. I felt overwhelming gratitude and I know they did too.

The room that saved us

We were grateful for our lives. If things had gone the way I originally planned, that Christmas could have ended very differently. Sometimes the detour is the deliverance. For us, the inconvenience was protection and the disappointment was grace. The room I didn't want was the room that saved us.

Gratitude is not about ignoring pain. It's about recognising protection and honouring what remains. It's about choosing to see that even when life feels unfair, it is often unfolding in ways we cannot yet understand.

So, the next time something doesn't go your way, instead of asking, 'Why is this happening to me?' try asking, 'What might this moment be protecting me from?' or 'Is this happening to me or is this happening for me?'

Those questions don't eliminate the challenge, but they change the lens through which you see it. And when your perspective changes, your mind settles, your body relaxes and your thinking becomes clearer.

Remember: you can't be grateful and anxious at the same time because being grateful simply is the quickest way to bring you into the present.

The compound effect of regulation

The tools outlined in this chapter don't just help in the moment. They also change your baseline over time:

- Every time you practise box breathing, you're strengthening the neural pathways that support calm.
- Every time you use the Clarity Pause, you're building the habit of response over reaction.
- Every time you complete a stress cycle through movement, you're teaching your nervous system that it can return to safety.
- Every time you express gratitude, you're regulating the mind and bringing yourself to the present moment.

Breathing to support calm even helped in my cricket career, and it is now something I coach in my mindset sessions with cricketers all over the world.

When you are at the crease and about to face an extremely hard cricket ball coming towards you at 130+ kilometres per hour, you want to be pretty clear on your decision-making, right? Otherwise, it could end badly.

I learned that when you are breathing correctly and all neural pathways are clear, from the eyes to the brain to the body, you're better able to decide what you want to do with the ball and how you want to hit it. You simply make better decisions in that split second between the ball leaving the bowler's hand and hitting your bat. And this allows you to trust all the hours of work you have done prior to the game, in the nets and elsewhere.

This kind of clarity is how you become one of the best in the world in your area of expertise, whether that's sport or something else. When you can access that clarity, you have the opportunity to make world-class decisions in your life.

> “*When you can regulate and create clarity, calm becomes accessible rather than conditional.*”

That's been my experience. Moments of anxiety still come over me occasionally, but my baseline is different now. I wake up more regulated. I stay regulated through stressors that would have destroyed me years ago. And when I do get triggered, I come back faster.

This is the compound effect of regulation—and it's available to you.

So please, just remember to breathe.

Building your personal regulation toolkit

Not every tool in this chapter works equally well for everyone and part of the regulation journey is discovering what works specifically for you. So, grab a pen and your journal (or the Clarity Workbook). This works better on paper.

Ask yourself:

- 'When I'm in hyperarousal (anxious, panicked and agitated), what are the tools that help me most?'
- 'When I'm in hypoarousal (numb, shut down and depressed), what are the tools that help me most?'
- 'What are my early warning signs that I'm leaving my window of tolerance?'
- 'What is the first thing I will do when I notice those signs?'
- 'What will my non-negotiable daily regulation practice be for the morning, midday and evening?'

Write down your responses, and work out the tools and daily practices you are going to implement.

Regulation Pillar summary

Pillar 4: Regulation is the foundation everything external rests on. Without it, clarity is impossible. When you can regulate and create clarity, calm becomes accessible rather than conditional. Here's what to keep in mind:

- *You cannot think your way out of a nervous system response:* When your body perceives threat, it overrides your rational mind. This is biology, not weakness. Your 'window of tolerance' is the zone where you can function optimally. Above it is hyperarousal (anxiety and panic); below it is hypoarousal (numbness and shutdown). The goal is to widen your window and develop skills to help you return to it.
- *The Clarity Pause is your flagship regulation tool:* Stop, breathe, notice, ask and respond. This 45-second pause can change everything. Your breathing toolkit gives you practices for different states — calming when activated, energising when shut down. Grounding techniques anchor you in the present. Emotional labelling activates the prefrontal cortex and calms the amygdala. Gratitude shifts perspective, multiplies your blessings and brings you into the present; you can't be grateful and anxious at the same time.
- *Regular practice changes your baseline over time:* Calm becomes accessible, not conditional. Your symptoms are signals, not sentences. Your nervous system isn't your enemy. It's a frightened guardian that needs to learn you're safe.

Part III

Living your clarity with pillars five to eight

Chapter Eight

Pillar 5: Identity

> You were somebody long before you became someone.

When I was 23 years old, I knew exactly who I was — or so I thought.

I was a cricketer. I wasn't just someone who played cricket; I was a cricketer. It was my identity, my purpose, and my answer to every question about who I was and what I was doing with my life. When people asked what I did, I said, 'I'm a cricketer' with the kind of certainty that left no room for follow-up questions.

I was also a survivor. After the tsunami, that became part of how I defined myself. I was the guy who lived through the Boxing Day disaster. The one with the story. People would ask about it at parties, and I'd tell a practised version — dramatic enough to be interesting; sanitised enough to be bearable.

I was an achiever. I got good grades at school, played in representative teams and had the trajectory of someone going somewhere. I collected accomplishments like other people collected stamps, each one a brick in the wall of who I believed myself to be.

I was a performer. I was the life of the party. The one who could make people laugh, could hold a room, and seemed confident and capable and like he had it all figured out.

Cricketer. Survivor. Achiever. Performer. That was me. That was my identity. Those were the answers to 'Who is Cameron Merchant?'

And then, piece by piece, all of my identity was taken away.

Uncovering the self beneath the story

The cricket career didn't end in glory. It faded in self-doubt, setbacks and the gradual realisation that the dream I'd built my entire self-concept around wasn't going to materialise the way I'd imagined. I wasn't going to be a professional cricketer. I was going to be someone who used to play cricket—past tense; former; was.

The survivor identity curdled as what had felt like strength became a weight. The story I told at parties started to feel hollow, performed and disconnected from the actual experience that still haunted my nights. I wasn't heroically surviving, I was barely coping, and the gap between the story and the reality had grown unbearable.

The achiever had nothing left to achieve. Without cricket, without a clear path, I was drifting. The accomplishments I'd stacked so carefully felt meaningless. Who cares about under-19 representative honours when you're 29 and lost?

The performer kept performing, but the performance was exhausting. I was smiling when I wanted to scream and entertaining when I wanted to disappear. I kept trying to be 'on' when everything inside me had switched off. I felt hollow.

By the time I reached that hospital bed, I had no idea who I was — in a terrifying, existential, groundless sense. Every identity I'd constructed had either collapsed or been revealed as a costume I was wearing rather than a skin I was living in. Who was I without cricket? Who was I without the survivor story? Who was I without accomplishments to point to? Who was I when I stopped performing?

I remember lying in that bed in the early days, and a therapist asking me to describe myself without using my job, my relationships or my achievements. I couldn't do it, maybe because I was ashamed of burning that life down not so long ago, which had brought me to where I was.

I could not find words for who I was beneath the labels. There was just nothing, a void where a self should be, and an emptiness that terrified me more than the depression, anxiety and any of my other symptoms.

'I don't know who I am', I told her. 'Worst of all, whoever I am, I despise them. I don't like me at all.' I started to cry the wracking sobs of someone confronting a truth they've been running from for years.

My therapist nodded like this was exactly what she expected. 'Good', she said softly. 'Now we can begin.'

The identity crisis nobody talks about

My experience wasn't unusual; it was just unusually visible. Most people are walking around with identities built on sand. They've constructed a sense of self from external materials—job titles, relationship status, achievements, roles, possessions and other people's opinions—and they've never stopped to ask what would remain if all of it disappeared.

As long as life cooperates, this works fine. The job provides meaning. The relationship provides validation. The achievements provide worth. The roles provide structure. But life doesn't always cooperate. The job gets eliminated. The relationship ends. The achievement stops mattering. The role changes, kids grow up, parents pass away and careers shift. And, suddenly, you're confronted with the question you've been avoiding your whole life: 'Who am I beneath all of this?'

This is the identity crisis that nobody talks about. It's not the dramatic kind of the teenager finding themselves or the midlife crisis with the sports car. It's the quiet kind; the kind that happens when the labels you've been hiding behind are stripped away and you're left alone with a self you've never met.

> *You are not your job title. You are not your relationship status. You are not your accomplishments or your failures. You are not the roles you play. Who are you beneath all the labels?*

I've worked with hundreds of people in this crisis:

- The executive who built her entire identity around her career, then got laid off at 52 and didn't know who she was without her title.
- The mother whose children left for university, leaving her with an empty nest and an emptier sense of self.
- The athlete whose body gave out, taking his purpose with it.
- The person who got divorced after 30 years and realised they had no idea who they were outside that relationship.

It's the same pattern, just with different details. The external identity props get kicked out, and the person discovers nothing is holding them up from the inside.

The layers of identity

Think of your identity as layers. From outermost to innermost, you have:

- *Labels:* These are the words you use to describe yourself to others. They include your job titles, roles and demographics. Labels are useful for social navigation, but the shallowest form of identity.
- *Roles:* These are the functions you perform, such as parent, partner, employee and friend. Roles are deeper than labels, but still external, defined by your relationship to others, not by your intrinsic nature.
- *Stories:* These are the narratives you tell about yourself. 'I'm the one who overcame adversity.' 'I'm the black sheep.' These feel more real because they're personal, but they're still constructed—interpretations of events, not objective truths.
- *The self beneath:* This is the awareness that exists prior to labels, roles and stories. It's the 'I' that was present before you had any identity at all. Most people never access this layer. They live entirely in layers one to three, and when those layers get disrupted, they feel annihilated.

You are not your labels. You are not your roles. You are not your stories. You are something more fundamental—and when you discover that, nothing external can shake you again.

Why identity is Pillar 5

You might wonder why Identity comes after the Willingness, Awareness, Accountability and Regulation Pillars. It's because you can't do this work from a dysregulated state. Exploring who you are beneath your identities is destabilising. It requires you to loosen your grip on the very things you've been using to hold yourself together.

Willingness gives you the courage to look beneath the surface. Awareness gives you the capacity to observe yourself without being consumed. Accountability ensures you're not using identity confusion as an excuse for victimhood. Regulation gives you the stability to tolerate the groundlessness of not knowing who you are.

Without that foundation, identity work becomes either an intellectual exercise or an emotional crisis. But with the foundation in place, identity work becomes the doorway to freedom.

The gift of losing everything

I didn't understand it at the time, but lying in that hospital bed with no identity was a gift—a brutal, unwanted and excruciating gift, but a gift nonetheless. When everything was stripped away, I finally had the opportunity to ask who I was without these labels and stories. I couldn't hide behind 'cricketer' anymore. I couldn't perform my way through with charm and humour. I couldn't point to achievements or roles or relationships.

I was just… there. A human being in a bed; awareness without labels. And in that emptiness, something began to emerge. It wasn't a new set of labels to replace the old ones, although, trust me, I thought of taking the easy path on that one many times. Instead, I chose something different: a sense of self that didn't depend on what I did or what had happened to me and an identity that was prior to all the identities I'd constructed.

I discovered that I am the one who experiences, not the experiences themselves but the awareness in which experiences arise. I am the one who has thoughts, not the thoughts themselves. I am the one who plays roles, not is the roles; the one who lives through stories, not becomes the stories.

Because when your identity is grounded in awareness itself rather than in any particular content of awareness, you become unshakeable. Jobs can come and go. Relationships can form and dissolve. Achievements can rise and fade. None of it touches who you fundamentally are.

> *You are not your worst moments or your best moments. You are the presence that witnesses all moments.*

The prison of fixed identity

Fixed identities become prisons. When you believe 'I am *x*', you become trapped by that belief. You can only act in ways consistent with *x*. You filter reality through the lens of *x*, missing everything that doesn't fit. For example:

- *'I'm not a creative person.'* Now you can't write, paint or innovate—that's not who you are.
- *'I'm bad with money.'* Now you can't build wealth, that would contradict your identity.
- *'I'm someone who struggles with relationships.'* Now every relationship must struggle—to prove you are right about yourself.

These identity statements feel like facts but they're not. They're stories that became beliefs that became self-fulfilling prophecies. Who you've been is not who you have to be. Identity is not fixed. It's a story you tell and you can tell a different one.

What I discovered beneath the labels

I was 20 years old when the ocean tore some labels off my life. It was the morning of the 2004 Indian Ocean earthquake and tsunami. But in that moment, it wasn't a headline. It was a wall of water. It was noise and confusion. It was the sudden, sickening realisation that the world as I knew it could disappear in seconds.

When the first wave hit, instinct screamed at me to run, to find my parents and secure my own safety. I couldn't see my parents. I didn't know where they were and, for a split second, fear tried to own me. But then something else rose faster than fear.

All around me were people almost frozen in shock. They were injured and crying, searching for loved ones. In that moment, I was confronted with a simple but defining question: 'What is actually in my control right now?'

I couldn't control the ocean or whether another wave was coming. I couldn't control where my parents were. But I could control what I did next. So instead of fleeing, I stayed.

I helped lift debris. I helped steady people who couldn't stand. I moved toward the chaos rather than away from it. I wasn't fearless as I did this. My heart was pounding and my mind was racing. But clarity arrived in the middle of catastrophe: if I was here and I was able, I would help. Pressure didn't paralyse me; it focused me.

The next day, when we returned to what felt like Ground Zero to retrieve whatever belongings hadn't been claimed by the sea, the fear was still alive in everyone's bodies. No-one felt safe. And, again, I noticed the same thing within myself. While others were overwhelmed, my mind moved toward structure and stability. It moved toward how I could help.

'We take 15 minutes', I told the others. 'We go in together. We come out together. No-one lingers.'

Over those 48 hours, something was revealed to me that no sporting arena, title or applause ever had. Beneath the labels—cricketer, athlete, young man chasing a dream—was something more fundamental. When the highest pressure was catapulted onto my shoulders, I didn't collapse. I leaned in. I organised. I protected. I served.

All I wanted to do was help and I see now that at the time my values were service and kindness. I leant into those then and I continue to lean into them today. At my core, beneath ambition and identity and expectation, I discovered this:

- I am someone who moves toward responsibility when others step back.
- I am someone who seeks calm inside chaos.
- I am someone who finds purpose in protecting and guiding others.

The tsunami stripped away the noise. What remained was not a label but character. It was identity.

Over time, I've also discovered some deeper truths:

- *I am someone who loves deeply:* I don't mean the performed love of trying to be seen as loving, but real love—the kind that wants nothing back and that shows up even when it's inconvenient. I also mean the kind of love that includes myself (which was the hardest part to learn).
- *I am someone who needs nature:* My soul requires time in wild places, in and around water especially. Something about being near the ocean puts me back together in ways I can't explain.

- *I am someone who values truth over comfort:* I'd rather know the hard thing than believe the easy lie.
- *I am someone with a deep capacity for darkness and light:* I'm not just the bright, entertaining performer. I'm also someone who has visited very dark places. Both are me; wholeness includes shadow.

None of these discoveries are achievements. They're not things I did but things I found when I stopped doing. They're not roles I play but qualities that exist regardless of what role I'm in.

> *Identity is not something you build but something you uncover.*

The identity excavation

Take some time now to strip away the layers to get to your identity.

The label inventory

List all the labels you use to describe yourself including job titles, relationship roles, identity groups, personality labels and story-based labels.

The stripping question

For each major label, ask yourself, 'If this were taken away tomorrow, who would I be?'

Notice which labels feel most threatening to lose. Those are the ones you've most confused with your actual self.

The constant question

Think back across your entire life, through all the changes, all the different phases. What has remained constant? What qualities, values or ways of being have been present throughout?

The essence question

Complete this sentence without using roles, achievements or labels: 'At my core, I am someone who ... '

It's also okay to not know who you are right now. 'I don't know' might be the most honest and liberating answer to the identity question, because the moment you say, 'I am *x*', you've limited yourself. What if you're more than any boundary can contain?

The greatest freedom is having nothing to prove. When you no longer need to be someone, you can finally discover who you are. When you can develop your values and understand your personalised strengths as a human, you start to create some powerful clarity within.

Values: The foundation of a true identity

Clarity doesn't come from having more options, but from knowing what matters most.

Identity without values is performance. Identity built on values, on the other hand, is integrity. Values are what anchor you when your labels change. They are the internal standards that guide your decisions when no-one is watching.

If your labels were stripped away tomorrow—job title, relationship status, achievements, everything external—what would remain? I don't mean what you do, but what you stand for. That's what values are: the non-negotiable principles that define who you are when nobody's watching.

You know what's crazy? I didn't really learn about and understand values till I was in my 30s. I had to reach absolute rock bottom before I could connect the dots. Now I understand that knowing your values is one of the most important aspects of knowing who you are and being comfortable with your identity.

Trying to figure out your values isn't easy; however, here's a quick cheat. If you go back and have a think about your 'why' from Pillar 1 (outlined in chapter 4), it may just give you an idea of what is important to you. A big part of my why is my kids. When I dig a bit deeper on this, and consider what I want to ensure when I'm with my kids, I realise it is simply energy, being present and being healthy. When Jules was pregnant with our second child, Carter, I remember thinking, *I need more energy because keeping up with one was hard enough. Two and I'm going to be in trouble.* It was then and there that 'health' as a value went from in my top five to my number-one value, because I knew it would provide solutions for everything in our life at that point.

The values you choose over life aren't locked in for good. They are constantly changing and adapting with you as you go. You just need to figure out what values are important to you in your current season of life and allow them to guide you.

> *You don't rise to your goals. You default to your values.*

The most simplest of examples I teach the young kids at my cricket mindset academies when talking about values is this: if one of your values is 'honesty' and your so-called friends ask you to come and steal a chocolate bar from the local supermarket, what do you think your value of honesty will guide you to do? It will guide you to say no because it doesn't align with being honest. Like I said, this is a pretty simple way of describing values, but if ten-year-olds can understand the principle then hopefully you do too.

This is where values become more than words—they become a decision-making filter for your entire life. External identities can be stripped away, but values are yours forever.

Discovering your values

Before you start this exercise, think back to the personal glossary at the beginning of this book. How did you define words like 'trust', 'courage' and 'purpose'? Those definitions were yours and they're already pointing you toward your values. What you chose to define, and how you defined it, reveals what matters most to you.

Keep those definitions in mind as you work through the following to discover your values:

1. Look at your proud moments. When have you felt most proud of yourself? I don't mean successful; proud. What value was being honoured?
2. Look at your anger. What frustrates you the most? Often, violated values live there.
3. Look at your admiration. Who do you respect deeply? What qualities are you actually respecting?

(continued)

4. Narrow it down. You're aiming for five, maybe seven core values. Clarity lives in constraint. From the following table, select ten values that resonate most strongly. Go with your instinct.

Example values

Adventure	Autonomy	Belonging
Creativity	Compassion	Contribution
Courage	Curiosity	Family
Freedom	Fun	Grace
Growth	Health	Honesty
Inner harmony	Integrity	Kindness
Love	Loyalty	Resilience
Responsibility	Security	Self-respect
Spirituality	Stability	Wealth

Add your own value if it's missing from the table.

5. Reduce your selection to your five core values.
6. For each value, write what it means to you personally. Values without definitions become vague ideals. Your definitions give them power.
7. Now stress-test your values. Think of a recent decision that didn't sit right with you. This could be a conversation you walked away from feeling off, a commitment you made that drained you or a moment when you compromised something that mattered. Hold that decision against your five values. Which one did you betray? That tension you feel, the discomfort in your chest when you see the mismatch, is your compass recalibrating. It's telling you exactly where you drifted. Values aren't just

words on paper. They're a filter for every decision you make. When a decision aligns with your values, it feels clear. When it doesn't, your body knows before your mind catches up

Once you have your values, you can also use a simple check-in for any decision: 'Does this align with what matters most to me?'

Knowing your strengths

Most people spend their life trying to become well-rounded—often ending up a 'Jack of all trades, master of none'. That was certainly me at one stage. But excellence rarely comes from being average at everything. It comes from understanding where your natural strengths already exist.

When you focus your time and energy on your strengths, confidence grows, momentum builds and impact increases. While weaknesses should be managed, strengths should be maximised. Here's a reframe worth sitting with: you don't actually have strengths and weaknesses, you have attributes and characteristics that show up differently depending on your situation. The real skill isn't fixing your weaknesses. It's knowing which situations bring out your best, and putting yourself there as often as possible.

At some of my previous jobs, I've sat in front of a computer and tried my best to master an Excel spreadsheet. I now know that's not my thing, and I wasted hours of energy and time. Getting out and meeting people and clients, however, chatting, getting to know them and connecting—that's me any day of the week. Again, though, sometimes it takes time to figure out what is for you and what's not. There are no wrong answers and everything is leaving clues for your success.

Strengths exercise

Ask yourself:

- 'When do people naturally come to me for help?'
- 'What activities give me energy rather than drain me?'
- 'When do I feel most confident?
- 'What do others consistently say I'm good at?'

Based on your answers, write down five strengths that consistently show up in your life.

Your strengths plus your values equals clarity on your identity. When your strengths align with your values, work begins to feel meaningful, decisions become easier and confidence grows naturally. You don't build a meaningful life by becoming good at everything. You build it by becoming exceptional at what you're naturally built for.

Finding yourself in your best essence

A version of you is possible that feels unmistakably right. This version isn't trying to prove something or perform for approval. This version of you feels calm, clear, capable and connected. It's the real you.

You have already experienced this version of yourself, perhaps during a moment of deep flow, a meaningful conversation or a time when life simply felt aligned.

Recall these moments to help you recall your identity. Remember who you are when you are living in alignment with your values, your strengths and your natural energy. Once you remember this, you can return to it.

The best essence practice

Find a comfortable seat, close your eyes and go back to a time when you were at your best. I don't mean your most impressive. I mean your most you. Notice what it feels like. What are you doing? Where are you? What is your energy like? Now step into that version of you. Feel it in your chest, your stomach and your shoulders. Name the emotions present. Now choose a simple anchor — a word, a gesture or a breath — and connect it to this feeling. This version of you is not far away. You can return to it.

A full guided practice on finding your best essence is available in the Clarity Workbook.

Declaring your essence

Now that you've reconnected with your best essence, I want to give you a way to carry it into your day, not as a memory but as a decision.

Most people wake up and let the day decide who they're going to be — the emails decide, or the traffic, the kids' mood or the first thing that goes wrong decides. And by 9 am, you're already reacting instead of leading.

The essence declaration flips that. Before the world gets a say, you get yours first.

This declaration is one of the first things I do each morning before the phone and all the other noise. I sit with two questions and I answer them honestly. This practice takes less than two minutes but it sets the tone for everything. It's the difference between walking into your day on autopilot and walking in on purpose.

The two questions are as follows:

1. *Who are you choosing to be today?* This question is about you—not who you hope to be or who you'll try to be if everything goes well. Who are you being today, regardless of what happens?
2. *How do you want people to feel after being around you today?* This second question is about your impact. You are an experience for other people. In every room you walk into, every conversation you have and every interaction, you leave something behind. The question is whether you're leaving it by accident or by design.

I saw the power of this practice in a session I did with Laura, a friend of mine. I guided her through the declaration, the same one I'm about to give you. She closed her eyes. She paused. She breathed. And for a moment, everything around us went still. Then she calmly spoke—and I don't think I'd ever heard her speak like this before and with so much conviction.

She said, 'At my core, my best essence is that I know I have an aura around me. I have an energy that radiates and sparks, and that energises and inspires people, and makes others feel good when they're around me'.

She didn't whisper it. She didn't say it like a question. She said it with a conviction that made time seem to stand still. It was as if she was meeting a version of herself she'd always known was there but had never given permission to speak.

The experience was emotional for both of us. I don't think she'd ever gone that deep and been that honest with herself before, yet she had known the truth all along. I don't think anyone had ever asked her the question (it's not the type of question you get asked every day), but when she finally asked it of herself, the answer was already there, waiting.

Laura now steps into her best essence every day and I'm so proud of her. Does she forget sometimes? Of course. We're human. But when she remembers, when she chooses to show up as that version of herself, it moves mountains, not just for her but also for everyone around her. That's what happens when someone steps into who they actually are. It ignites something in them that ignites something in others and the world is simply a better place.

That's what's available to you too, right now.

Creating your essence declaration

Each morning, complete these two declarations:

- I want to be the essence of [list three to four attributes].
- I want others to experience me as an expression of [list three to four attributes].

Here's my declaration from this morning: 'I want to be the essence of happiness, calm, present and assertive in all that I do. I want others to experience me as an expression of energy, presence, inspiration and fun'.

Notice the difference between the two sentences. The first is about your inner state — how you want to feel inside your own

(continued)

skin. The second is about your outer expression — the energy you want to put into the world. One is for you and the other is for everyone you'll meet today. Together, they create alignment between who you are and how you show up.

Your answers to the two questions that form your essence declaration will change. Some days you need calm while other days you need fire. Some days you need patience more than anything else on the planet. That's the point, it's not a fixed formula. It's a daily check-in with the version of you who already knows how to live well.

When you name something, you claim it. And when you claim it before the day begins, you're no longer hoping to show up as your best self. You're choosing to, from first thing in the morning and then throughout the whole day. You get the opportunity to reconnect back to it whenever you need to.

> *You are not just having an experience. You are the experience. Choose who you're being and show up as that person always, before the world chooses for you.*

A moment in the dressing room

I witnessed the power of finding your true identity long before I had a name for it.

When I was playing cricket in New Zealand, I was part of the Black Caps team who were playing a game against the West Indies. One of New Zealand's greatest batsmen was in the team and, at the time, was under enormous pressure. The media had been relentless, and commentators and fans were questioning his place in the team. Everyone knew the reality: if he didn't score runs that day, it could be his last game.

He was tight and rigid. You could see the tension sitting in his shoulders, the kind of tension that makes even the best athletes forget how to do what they've done for almost their whole lives.

He walked out to bat with the weight of all of that sitting on him and then something unexpected happened. It started to rain. The covers came out, and both teams walked back into the dressing room for a rain delay. I grabbed him a drink and handed it to him while we waited in the sheds.

The television in the corner of the room was replaying highlights from a match about 12 months earlier. And there he was on the screen, the same player, but a completely different version of him.

He looked relaxed and free. His movements were flowing and he was batting beautifully, timing the ball, moving effortlessly, enjoying himself. The commentators were praising him. The crowd was cheering.

As he sat in front of the screen and watched, something interesting happened. He closed his eyes. For a moment the room went quiet around him. We all could see he wasn't watching the highlights anymore but reliving them. His breathing slowed and his shoulders dropped. His face softened with a sudden slight smile.

The anxious, rigid player who had walked out to bat 15 minutes earlier began to disappear. In his place was the version of him from the highlight reel—calm, present, confident and happy.

Eventually the rain stopped and the players walked back onto the field and something about him was different. He looked lighter and looser. He walked to the crease like someone who had remembered who he was, and what happened next was incredible to watch. More than just surviving the innings, he dominated it.

Shot after shot flowed from the middle of his bat. The same player who had looked trapped by pressure earlier was now smiling between overs, enjoying the contest and doing what he did best. By the end of the innings, he had scored a century and was back to his best. His return to form hadn't come from trying harder. It came from remembering who he was when he was at his best.

That moment in the Black Caps dressing room taught me something I've carried with me ever since. When people lose their way, they rarely need to become someone new. They just need to remember themselves.

Sometimes the breakthrough we're searching for isn't ahead of us. It's behind us—waiting to be remembered.

The identity excavation (continued)

Pay attention to who and what brings out the best version of you. Ask yourself:

- 'Who brings out my best?'
- 'Where do I feel like me?'
- 'What actions return me to myself?'

Use your responses to determine what essence these people, places and actions are bringing out. Choose to live more in that essence.

Tell yourself, 'This is who I'm being for the day. This is my direction. This is my intention'.

You get to create the experience that you are having in every moment. It's not happening to you; you are happening. You can choose the experience and to show up as your best self.

Clarity begins when you remember who you are at your best. Do you trust that version of you enough to build your life from it? That's where belief comes and that's where we go next.

The five cardinals of belief

The night before I proposed to Jules, I almost didn't. This wasn't because I didn't love her. I loved her more than I'd ever loved anyone. And it wasn't because I wasn't sure she'd say yes. I was as certain as you can be about another person's heart. And it definitely wasn't because the ring wasn't right or the plan wasn't ready. I almost didn't propose because a voice in my head told me I didn't deserve her.

I was lying awake at 2 am, the ring hidden in my sock drawer, the moment I'd been planning just hours away. And instead of excitement, I felt terror, not nervous butterflies but existential dread.

'Who do you think you are?' the voice whispered. 'You're the guy who ended up in a psychiatric hospital. You're the one who couldn't hold it together. You're damaged goods. She deserves someone whole, someone stable, someone who doesn't have your baggage.' The old voice had returned and this was all going to go down on national television.

'What happens when she sees the real you? The dark parts. The broken parts. The parts that still wake up at 3 am counting ceiling tiles. She'll realise she made a mistake. And you'll have dragged her into your mess. You should let her go. Let her find someone easier so she doesn't have to deal with you. This whole "experiment" for the last three months has just been a facade.'

I lay there in the dark as the voice made a compelling case. It had evidence and history. It pointed to every failure, every breakdown and every time I'd let someone or myself down. It built a prosecutor's argument for why I wasn't worthy of this love, this woman and this future.

And then I did something I'd learned to do through years of practice. I questioned the voice. I didn't argue with it, that gives it too much power, I just questioned it and examined it. I held its 'evidence' up to the light.

'Is this true?' I asked. 'Am I actually unworthy of love? Or is this an old story that's afraid of something new?'

'What's the evidence on the other side?' I continued. 'I've done years of work. I've rebuilt myself from the ground up. I'm not the same person who checked into that hospital. Jules has seen my darkness, I've shown her, and she chose me anyway, not despite who I am but because of who I am.'

'And what does "deserve" even mean?' I asked. 'Do I have to be perfect to deserve love? Does anyone? Or is worthiness something I claim, not something I earn?'

By 4 am, something had shifted. (Thank goodness, because the film crew was rolling into my room at 7 am.) The voice hadn't disappeared, but I was no longer controlled by it. I could see it for what it was: fear dressed up as truth. It was an old identity trying to protect me from disappointment by keeping me small.

I proposed that day. She said yes. We built a life together.

That moment at 2 am wasn't won by willpower. It was won by belief. I don't mean blind belief or wishful thinking; I mean a structured, examined, hard-won belief in my own worthiness.

Few pieces of advice are worse than someone telling you (with conviction as well) to just 'believe in yourself'. Have you ever had that? 'Go for it. Go on, just believe in yourself!' When dispensing this advice, few people tell you how. They act like belief is a switch you flip, either you have it or you don't; you're confident or you're not. But belief isn't binary. It's architectural, built from specific components. When you understand those components, you can construct unshakeable self-trust deliberately, brick by brick.

These components make up the framework I call the Five Cardinals of Belief.

> *Belief isn't magical thinking; it's strategic building.*

Introducing the Five Cardinals of Belief framework

The following table outlines the components that make up the Five Cardinals of Belief framework, the core question for each and the beliefs each unlocks.

Cardinal	Core question	What it unlocks
Ability	'Can I do this?'	Competence belief
Capacity	'Can I do this at the level required?'	Bandwidth belief
Value	'Will this create value for others?'	Contribution belief
Worth	'Do I deserve this?'	Worthiness belief
Proof	'Have I done hard things before?'	Evidence belief

When you're struggling to believe in yourself—when doubt has you paralysed, imposter syndrome is screaming and you can't take the leap—one or more of these cardinals is compromised.

The gift of this framework is diagnosis. Instead of a vague 'I don't believe in myself', you can pinpoint exactly which belief is shaky.

And once you know which cardinal is weak, you know exactly what to address.

The following sections run through each of the five cardinals.

Ability: 'Can I do this?'

Believing in your competence is the most basic belief: do you have the skills, knowledge and capability to accomplish what you're attempting?

Most ability gaps are solvable. You can learn or practice. You can get training, find mentors and acquire skills. An ability gap simply provides information about what you need to develop. The question isn't, 'Do I have this ability right now?' but, 'Can I develop this ability if I commit to it?'

You can strengthen this cardinal by identifying any specific skill gaps. Find evidence that the skill is learnable and take one step toward acquiring it. Reframe 'I can't' as 'I can't yet'.

Capacity: 'Can I do this at the level required?'

You might believe you can do something but doubt you can do it well enough or at the level the situation demands.

This doubt is often based in imposter syndrome—the feeling that you've somehow fooled everyone and you're about to be exposed. Dr Pauline Clance and Dr Suzanne Imes first defined imposter syndrome (or what they called the 'imposter phenomenon') back in 1978 when studying high-achieving women. Further research has since found that it affects an estimated 70 per cent of people at some point in their lives. And it's most common among those who are highly competent. In what's known as the Dunning–Kruger effect, the truly incompetent rarely doubt themselves, and instead give overly positive assessments of their ability. As competence grows, people are more likely to underestimate their skills.

If you're feeling like you're not good enough for this level, that feeling might actually be evidence that you are good enough. Here's the secret: we all have these doubts. It's okay and you're not alone.

To strengthen this cardinal, reality-test your doubt with objective feedback. Remember that everyone is figuring it out. Focus on preparation, not comparison. Ask, 'What would I do if I knew I was capable?' Then do that.

Value: 'Will this create value for others?'

You might be doubting whether what you're doing is actually worth doing. Will it matter? Will it help someone?

We often underestimate our value because we're too close to it. The things that come naturally to us seem ordinary, but what's obvious to you may be transformative for someone else.

I was once a professional cricketer who looked like he had it all figured out but then fell into a heap and rebuilt his life from scratch. I'm now so proud and happy in life, as I use social media to spread joy, hope and inspiration. I've written this book and have conversations to help others see what is genuinely possible. If I can do it, anyone can. Together, we can create a ripple effect, allowing others to tell their story and inspire someone else to do the same. So much value comes from that.

Your mess becomes your message. Your struggle becomes your service.

> *"Your presence might be the answer to someone's prayer."*

Strengthen this cardinal by asking who benefits from your actions—if even one person's life is better, your actions have value. Focus on contribution, not validation.

Worth: 'Do I deserve this?'

This is the deepest cardinal. The first three—ability, capacity and value—are about what you can do. Worth is about who you are.

This was my 2 am demon before proposing to Jules. I could believe in my ability to be a good partner. I could believe in my capacity. I could believe in the value of the relationship. But worthiness—did I deserve this love?—that's where the voice attacked.

Worthiness is not earned, however; it's claimed. You don't become worthy through achievements. You don't prove yourself into deservingness. Worthiness is your birthright. You were born worthy of love, worthy of belonging, worthy of good things, and nothing you've done or failed to do has changed that fundamental fact.

The voice that says you're unworthy is lying. It might be using real events as evidence, but it's constructing a false conclusion from selective data.

> *"You don't earn worthiness. You claim it. It was always yours."*

To strengthen this cardinal, separate behaviour from being. Challenge the inner critic's evidence. Practice self-compassion. Tell yourself, 'I am worthy of this'. Say it until you believe it (and just know I believe in you, too).

Proof: 'Have I done hard things before?'

The final cardinal is about evidence, not theoretical belief but demonstrated history.

You have survived 100 per cent of your worst days so far; every single one. You have faced challenges you didn't think you could face. You have endured pain you didn't think you could endure. You have found resources you didn't know you had, again and again, whenever life demanded it.

That's not luck but data. That's proof of something fundamental about you: you figure it out. You find a way. You survive, adapt and often grow.

> *The proof is in your past: you've survived 100 per cent of your worst days.*

Strengthen this last cardinal by making a list of all the hard things you've overcome. Recognise transferable evidence from this list. When doubt says, 'What if I can't?' answer with evidence: 'I've faced hard things before. I've figured it out before. I will again'. Sometimes, as humans, we tend to forget about the incredible things we've done and instead focus on the things that haven't gone to plan. They are just lessons; start focusing on the good stuff.

The five cardinals in action

When I was preparing to share my mental health story publicly for the first time, all five cardinals were under attack:

- *Ability:* Can I even articulate this? Do I have the communication skills to do this well?
- *Capacity:* Can I do this at the level required for a public platform? Millions of people could potentially be watching.
- *Value:* Will this actually help anyone? Or is it just self-indulgent oversharing?

- *Worth:* Do I deserve this platform? Other people have suffered and achieved more, and have more expertise.
- *Proof:* I've never done anything like this before. What if I freeze? What if I break down?

Every single cardinal was compromised. If I'd tried to address my doubt with a vague 'just believe in yourself', I would have failed. The doubt was too specific; it needed specific answers.

So, I worked through each cardinal:

- *Ability:* I prepared extensively. I rehearsed. I got coaching. I built the skill I needed.
- *Capacity:* I reminded myself that the bar wasn't perfection. It was authenticity.
- *Value:* I thought about one person who might be watching from their own dark place. If my story helped even that one person feel less alone, there was value.
- *Worth:* I did the inner work. My worthiness wasn't contingent on being the most qualified. I had a story worth telling. That was enough.
- *Proof:* I listed every hard thing I'd ever done: the tsunami, the recovery, hospital, rebuilding my life. I'd survived all of it. I could survive this too.

By the time I walked onto that platform, the doubt wasn't gone. But I had specific answers to its specific attacks. I had rebuilt each cardinal, brick by brick.

And I delivered.

The Five Cardinals of Belief audit

Think of something you want to do, be or achieve but doubt is holding you back. Write it down.

Now audit which cardinals need attention:

1. *Ability:* On a scale of one to ten, how much do you believe you have the ability? If your rating is below seven, what specific skill gap is creating this doubt? What's one step to address it?
2. *Capacity:* On a scale of one to ten, can you do this at the level required? If your rating is below seven, is this based on evidence or fear?
3. *Value:* On a scale of one to ten, will this create value for others? If your rating is below seven, who specifically might benefit?
4. *Worth:* On a scale of one to ten, do you believe you deserve this? If your rating is below seven, what story are you telling yourself about your unworthiness? Is it true?
5. *Proof:* On a scale of one to ten, how much evidence do you have that you can do hard things? If your rating is below seven, list three hard things you've overcome.

What cardinal did you give your lowest rating to? This is where you need to focus. What's one action you could take this week to strengthen it?

The confidence paradox

Confidence isn't feeling certain. It's trusting yourself to handle uncertainty.

We think confident people don't feel doubt or fear, but they do. We think they have some quality we lack, some inner certainty that makes hard things easy, but they don't.

Confident people feel all the same doubt and fear you do. The difference is their relationship to those feelings. They've learned that they can feel afraid and act anyway. They've learned that doubt is just a thought, not a command. They've learned that the proof of their past gives them reason to trust their future—it doesn't guarantee it, but they can trust it.

> *Confidence isn't feeling certain; it's believing you'll figure it out.*

You don't need to feel confident to act with confidence. You just need to trust that whatever happens, you'll handle it. Because you always have.

The daily belief practice

Morning (two minutes)

Before you start your day, ask yourself:

- 'What's one thing I'm doing today that requires belief?'
- 'Which cardinal might be challenged?'
- 'What's one sentence I can tell myself to strengthen that cardinal?'

Evening (two minutes)

Before you sleep, reflect on the day by asking yourself the following:

- 'Where did I act with belief today despite doubt?'
- 'What did I learn about my capabilities?'
- 'What evidence did today provide for my proof cardinal?'

This practice takes four minutes total. However, compounded over weeks and months, it fundamentally rewires your relationship with self-belief.

Remember: your beliefs are not facts. They're stories you've told yourself so many times you forgot you made them up.

Identity Pillar summary

Pillar 5: Identity is about discovering who you are beneath everything and learning to trust that self. Here's what to take away:

- *Most identities are built on external foundations:* When external foundations such as job titles, relationships, achievements and roles shift, most people crumble because they've never discovered who they are beneath the labels. Identity is not something you build but something you uncover. The excavation activities in this chapter help you find what has always been constant, at your core.
- *Values anchor your identity when labels change:* Strengths show you where you naturally contribute. Your best essence reconnects you with the version of you that already knows how to live well.
- *Step into your best essence and declare, 'This is who I'm being for the day; this is my direction and these are my intentions':* You get to choose, and you can connect to your best essence at any time.
- *The Five Cardinals of Belief diagnose doubt:* They ask you to consider your ability ('Can I do this?'), capacity ('At the level required?'), value ('Will this matter?'), worth ('Do I deserve this?') and proof ('Have I done hard things before?'). Worthiness is not earned but claimed. Confidence isn't feeling certain but trusting you'll figure it out. You've survived 100 per cent of your worst days. That's your proof.

Chapter Nine

Pillar 6: Habits and discipline

> Who you are tomorrow is being built by what you repeat today.

Six months after leaving the hospital, I fell apart again. It didn't happen all at once or dramatically. It happened slowly, silently, like a house settling into bad foundations, a crack here and a shift there, until one morning I woke up and realised I was nearly back where I'd started.

It began with the small things:

- The morning meditation I'd practised religiously in the facility but then skipped one day because I was running late. I then skipped it again because I was tired. And then I quietly abandoned it altogether.
- The journaling that had helped me process my days but then skipped one day because I was 'too exhausted'. I told myself, 'I'll catch up tomorrow'. Tomorrow became next

week and next week became a notebook gathering dust on my nightstand.

- The exercise routine that had been my anchor but then I missed one session and then two. Then I stopped pretending I was going to the gym at all.
- The evening wind-down ritual that was replaced by scrolling.
- The meal preparation that was replaced by takeaway.
- The sleep schedule I'd fought so hard to establish that was eroded by 'just one more episode' until 2 am became my normal bedtime again.

None of this happened because of a moment of crisis. I didn't go through a relapse event or have a dramatic collapse. It was just a slow, insidious slide—one skipped practice at a time, one small compromise at a time, one 'just this once' at a time—until I woke up one grey morning and could not get out of bed. The depression had crept back in through the gaps I'd left unguarded.

You are what you repeatedly do

I lay there, staring at the ceiling. I wasn't counting tiles this time, but I was doing something worse: wondering if any of the work I'd done had been real at all. Maybe I was just broken. Maybe the hospital had been a temporary fix rather than a genuine transformation. Maybe some people just weren't capable of lasting change. Maybe this was just what I was destined for.

And then, somewhere in the fog, a question surfaced: 'What changed?' This wasn't about what had changed emotionally or psychologically, so what changed behaviourally? What was I doing differently now compared to what I had been doing when things were working? The answer was devastating in its simplicity: everything.

I had stopped doing everything that had stabilised me. I didn't do this intentionally or because the practices weren't working. Instead, I'd made the fatal error of believing that transformation was something that happened once and then you were all set, rather than something that happens daily. I had changed my mind without changing my life.

All that therapy, all those insights, all that beautiful understanding of my patterns and wounds and potential; none of it had been embedded into my daily existence. It had stayed in my head while my habits stayed the same. When the insights faded, as insights always do, nothing was left to hold me up.

> *Clarity without consistency is just entertainment.*

That morning when I couldn't get out of bed was the second major turning point of my recovery. The first was deciding to get help. The second was understanding that getting help wasn't enough. I had to become the kind of person who didn't need that level of help anymore. And becoming is not a one-time event. Becoming is what you do every single day.

I realised constant becoming—consistent transformation, motivation and happiness—was like taking a bath. You need to take it daily (or shower or whatever you're into). You don't just get clean from one bath and never have to wash yourself again. Change and transformation and staying mentally fit was always going to be an everlasting and ongoing process for me, and I was okay with that because I was committed to it. I'd had a taste of what inner peace and clarity looks and feels like, and knew it was much better than the alternative.

So, I got out of bed. I didn't feel like it. I didn't have the motivation or inspiration or any of the things we think we need before we can act. I just got out of bed and did one thing: I sat on the floor and breathed for five minutes. That's it. That was the entire victory for that day; five minutes of conscious breathing. The next day, I did it again and the next and the next.

From those five minutes, everything else eventually rebuilt. Remember your special ingredients from chapter 5, part of the recipe for when you have a quality day compared to when you don't? Yep, this is why knowing yourself and what they are is so important now.

You are not transformed by what you do once. You are transformed by what you do consistently.

> “*Show me your habits and I'll show you your future.*”

The identity–habit loop

Identity without action is just philosophy. You can believe you're the kind of person who values health but if you eat junk food every night and never move your body, your actions are telling a different story. You can believe you're someone committed to growth but if you have no growth practices, no daily disciplines and no consistent investment in becoming better, then 'committed to growth' is just a nice thing you tell yourself.

This works in both directions:

- *Identity → habits:* Who you believe yourself to be shapes what you do. If you identify as a runner, running feels natural. If you identify as a non-runner, every run is a battle against your self-concept.

- *Habits → identity:* What you do shapes who you believe yourself to be. Run enough times, and eventually you start thinking of yourself as a runner. The evidence becomes undeniable.

In *Atomic Habits*, James Clear captures this perfectly: 'Every action you take is a vote for the type of person you wish to become'. Every time you meditate, you cast a vote for being a mindful person. Every time you choose patience over reaction, you cast a vote for being calm. Every time you show up for your practice, you cast a vote for being disciplined.

No single vote determines the election. But if you accumulate enough votes in one direction, you win.

> *Every action is a vote for the person you're becoming. Who are you voting for today?*

The compound effect

If you get 1 per cent better at something every day, how much better are you after a year? While your intuitive answer might be 365 per cent better, the actual answer is 3700 per cent better. That's 37 times your starting point.

This is due to the power of compounding. Small improvements don't add but multiply. The reverse is equally true. If you get 1 per cent worse every day, you decline to nearly zero.

A single meditation session doesn't transform your mind, but after a year of meditation your baseline anxiety, emotional reactivity and capacity for presence will all be fundamentally altered. After my second turning point, I stayed with my daily meditation and, over time, have realised the incredible difference it has made to my life. I'm so glad that I stuck with it.

The changes that matter are almost never visible in the moment. They're only visible in the accumulation. And because they're not visible in the moment, most people quit before the compound effect has time to work.

The most powerful outcomes are built not by dramatic actions but by boring consistency.

Discipline reconsidered

For many people, discipline feels like a dirty word, conjuring images of punishment, restriction and joyless grinding. Discipline is not punishment, however; it's care for your future self.

When you go to bed on time instead of scrolling until midnight, you're giving a gift to tomorrow-you. When you exercise even though you don't feel like it, you're giving a gift to future-you. When you get up to do your morning practice even though the bed is warm and the resistance is strong, you're giving a gift to the version of yourself who will move through the day regulated instead of reactive, grounded instead of scattered and clear instead of confused.

Discipline, properly understood, is an act of love—love for the person you're becoming, love for the future you're building and love for the life that's waiting on the other side of consistent action.

I remember thinking for so long how stupid my daily morning routine felt—waking up, running through my practices and morning gratitude over and over again, just expecting life to be suddenly great. Over time, however, the automatic thought process that would take place as soon as I opened my eyes was incredible.

Now, as my mind awakens and my eyes open, my thought process focuses on 'thank you'. *Thank you for being here.* I'm grateful for my children, my wife, my health, my home, my family and my friends. After years of practice and intentional devotion to what I am truly grateful for — boom. My brain has found a short cut and open door to just know, as soon as I wake, this is what we do now. The feeling is incredibly peaceful and fulfilling, and it's such a special way to start the day. All the early feelings of discomfort and doubt were (and are) worth it. Trust the process and stick with it, because it works.

Perhaps you're also feeling this is 'so cliché'. Perhaps you're embarrassed by what others may think about your 'cringe' morning routine. Don't let this stop you in your tracks of actually doing something that has huge benefits for you and your health. Stand tall, stick the chest out and say, 'I don't give a fuck what they think!' They are not you and they are not living your life. If you have found something in your 'special ingredients' that works specifically for you, continue it. I often get a little embarrassed when someone asks me about my morning routine and they seem a little taken aback by it. Some people even judge me or ask if I'm trying to be some kind of Buddhist monk. What I am doing is trying to keep myself out of hospital, because I know what can potentially happen if I don't do my morning routine. I'm staying healthy for my kids and you too can connect your discipline back to your why. Don't worry about what anyone thinks; if it works for you, do it!

The neuroscience of habit

Habits live in your basal ganglia, an ancient brain structure that evolved long before your conscious mind. When a behaviour becomes habitual, your basal ganglia allows it to run on autopilot, freeing your prefrontal cortex for other tasks. This is why, for example, you can drive a familiar route while having a complex conversation.

The habit formation loop is cue → routine → reward. Your brain is constantly running this loop, looking for patterns. When it finds a reliable sequence, it encodes it as a habit to conserve cognitive energy.

The crucial insight here is that you can't delete habits, but you can overwrite them. Once a habit loop is encoded, the neural pathway doesn't disappear; however, you can build a new routine that uses the same cue and delivers a similar reward. Don't just try to stop stress-eating, for example; instead, replace it with a different response to stress (such as going for a walk, breathwork or calling a friend) that delivers emotional regulation through a healthier mechanism.

> *Habits are not your enemy. They're your infrastructure. The question is what you're building.*

Why new habits fail

New, healthier habits tend not to stick due to two main failure modes: too much, too fast, and waiting for motivation.

Too much, too fast

Otherwise known as the 'New Year's resolution' pattern, this is where you decide on a new diet, new exercise routine, new morning ritual, new evening practice, new everything, starting Monday. Gym owners rub their hands together but, by Wednesday, you're exhausted. Change is cognitively expensive. Try to change ten things at once, and you bankrupt your cognitive budget.

To fight against this kind of failure, start smaller rather than what feels meaningful. Don't aim to start meditating for 30 minutes a day. Start with two minutes. Don't aim to get up at 5 am from now on when you usually get up at 8 am. Start with 7.55 am and go in increments of five minutes every day until you reach that elusive 5 am club; otherwise, you'll just burn yourself out. Give yourself a chance. And remember: if the 5 am trend isn't for you, that's fine too.

The goal at first isn't impact but consistency. For now, you're building the neural pathway. Impact comes later.

Waiting for motivation

As discussed back in chapter 4, motivation is not the cause of action but the result of it. You don't get motivated and then act. You act and motivation follows, sometimes. But action comes first.

To fight this kind of habit fail, make the decision once and then stop deciding. You don't decide each morning whether to brush your teeth. Your clarity practices need to reach the same level of automaticity.

> *Consistency beats intensity — every single time.*

The truth about willpower

When researchers studied people who score high on self-control measures, they found these people don't actually resist more temptations than others. They just experience fewer temptations through environment design and habit formation. They've structured their lives so that willpower is rarely necessary. They've made the good behaviours automatic and eliminated the cues for bad ones.

So, instead of trying to find superhuman willpower to transform your life, you need to implement smart systems. You need habits that run on autopilot and environments designed for success.

Getting to the gym in the morning is important to me, so I lay my gym clothes out in the kitchen the night before. In part, this is so I'm not fluffing around in the morning, waking the whole family up. But it also locks in my intentions that I will be going. When my gym clothes are already laid out, I don't have an excuse not to get dressed. I can't start telling myself, 'I don't know what to wear to the gym. It's too hard. I'll go later'. I won't go later and I know it. Laying my clothes out means I have one less reason to find and create bullshit excuses that let myself down.

Don't rely on willpower; instead, design systems where willpower isn't required.

My non-negotiables

The habits that form my non-negotiable foundation — the practices I do every day regardless of circumstances, mood or convenience— aren't impressive. They're not complicated or time-consuming, and that's the point. I go into these habits in more detail later in this chapter, but I've provided a quick rundown here to get you thinking about your own habits and your own non-negotiables.

In life, we have a million different circumstances, challenges and scenarios that come at us each and every day. Before you decide to present yourself to them, you need to be armoured and that's why I like to create my 'force field' first. When I'm home, I know my wife and kids will be coming at me, as will emails, work, social media, negative comments and just everyday life. The same will show up for you and you need to have your force field on so that you can respond as best as you can to all of it. I know if I haven't done my non-negotiables first thing in the morning, and created my force field, I respond in completely different, and unhealthy, ways to when I do and that's not healthy at all.

Let's dive into this a little deeper. For your brain, dopamine is your motivation fuel. You wake up each morning with a full tank, replenished overnight while you slept. That baseline is the quiet hum of, 'I can handle today'.

The moment you grab your phone and start scrolling—checking notifications, news and social media—your brain gets flooded with rapid-fire dopamine spikes. Every notification, every like, every headline triggers a hit. For about ten minutes, you feel stimulated and engaged. Your brain loves it.

After every spike, however, your dopamine doesn't just return to baseline—it drops below it. Your brain has to pay for every high with a corresponding low. So, by the time you've spent 15 minutes scrolling in bed, your motivation tank is already running on empty. You haven't even put pants on yet. (And you know how I feel about pants.)

This is why you can wake up feeling fine and then, after ten minutes on your phone, feel flat, anxious or unmotivated for no obvious reason. It's not in your head it's neurochemistry. As neuroscientist Dr Andrew Huberman explains, when you spike dopamine artificially first thing, everything that follows feels less rewarding by comparison. The workout feels harder. The conversation feels duller. The work feels more draining. Those things haven't changed, but your brain's capacity to enjoy them got burned before breakfast.

The fix is stupidly simple: don't touch your phone for the first 30 minutes after waking. I started charging mine in a different room. If it's not within arm's reach, the automatic grab doesn't happen. Within a month, the difference was undeniable.

Protect your dopamine baseline the way you'd protect your sleep. It's the fuel that powers every clear decision, every present conversation and every productive hour of your day. Don't let an algorithm burn through it before you've even opened your eyes.

Here are my morning habits (roughly 30 minutes in total, roughly grouped together):

- Wake at a consistent time (5.30 am)—a little later on weekends, within a 30-minute window. (This also depends on whether my kids decide to wake up early or not.)
- Do five to ten minutes of reflection while still lying in bed, one hand on my heart and hand on my stomach—gratitude, intention and priorities, and my best essence.
- Read a paragraph out of a book related to inspiration or motivation.
- Step outside and just breathe for five minutes; look around, take in the birds, planes, sounds, smells and ground for a moment and just smile to think how amazing this is all around us.
- Don't look at my phone for the first 30 minutes after waking. This is non-negotiable
- Drink a full glass of water before eating or drinking anything else.
- Do ten minutes of movement—stretching, walking, anything.

And here are my evening habits (15 minutes total):

- Complete a daily review—what worked and what didn't? What did I learn?
- Prepare for tomorrow—lay out my gym clothes, check my calendar, work out my top priorities.
- Put away all screens 30 minutes before bed. This is non-negotiable.

- Outline three gratitudes—tell them to Jules or write them down.
- Go to bed at a consistent time (10 pm)—within a 30-minute window.

That's it; 45 minutes of practice distributed across the day's transitions.

Now, I get it, you will have different scenarios in your life. You may be dealing with aspects such as kids' bedtimes, work and relationships, which can all affect your routine. You may be thinking, *There's no way I can do all of that before work.* I had the same reaction the first time someone showed me a morning routine. My brain instantly said no before I'd even considered it. That pushback is worth noticing because it's not logic talking. It's comfort protecting itself. Go back and re-read the time. It's 40 minutes. You probably spend longer than that scrolling before you get out of bed or when you go to bed. The real question isn't whether you have time. It's whether you're willing to give that time to yourself instead of giving it to an algorithm. So why wouldn't you prioritise this if you *know* it will make you feel better? You dictate your morning and the rest of your day, no-one else.

I'm not saying it has to be perfect all the time; I'm just saying keeping these intentions somewhat in your control gives you a much better chance at building small habits that can serve you wherever you may be in whatever scenario that presents to you. Those 40 minutes, done consistently, have changed my life more than any retreat, therapy session or single insight ever did.

So, what do you need to create your personal force field in the morning?

> *If you change your daily routine, and stay consistent, you can change your entire life.*

The habit foundation builder

Back in chapter 5 I asked you to complete a habit audit. Time now to look again at that audit and work out where you could make some changes. Again, grab a pen and your journal (or Clarity Workbook) because this works better on paper.

Current state audit

What do you currently do every single day without fail, both helpful and unhelpful? Write down every habit you have in the morning and the evening. (Go back to your audit from chapter 5 if needed.)

Against each habit, put + if it serves who you're becoming or – if it doesn't serve.

The identity question

Ask yourself:

- Based on your work on the Identity Pillar in the previous chapter, who are you becoming?
- What habits would that person absolutely have?
- What habits would that person absolutely *not* have?

Add one habit

Think about one habit that would make the biggest difference in your life if you did it consistently. This is the habit you are going to add to your daily routine.

Choose the two-minute version

Whatever habit you chose, make your implementation of it embarrassingly small. So small you can't say no. Write down the full habit and your two-minute version of it.

The implementation

Time to get specific. Write down responses to the following:

- When will you do it? (Specific time)
- Where will you do it? (Specific location)
- What will you do immediately before it? (Habit stack)

The environment

Now think about your environment. What one change to your environment would make this habit easier? Make that change today. Right now, if possible.

The commitment

Now commit! Write the following in your journal or Clarity Workbook:

'I commit to *[two-minute habit]* every day for the next 30 days, regardless of how I feel, regardless of circumstances, regardless of whether I want to.'

Sign it and date it to really make your commitment official.

Your clarity rituals

The morning Jules told me she was pregnant, I almost missed it. I don't mean the announcement, she made sure I heard that. She burst through the bathroom door at 6.47 am, pregnancy test in hand, tears streaming down her face, laughing and crying at the same time. I definitely heard and saw that. What I almost missed was being the person who could receive that moment fully.

I'd been awake since 5.30 that morning, following my ritual—the same ritual I'd followed every single day for nearly three years at that point:

- breathwork on the bedroom floor
- light movement to wake my body
- a review of my intentions for the day.

By the time Jules burst through that door, I was regulated, grounded and present. My nervous system was calm and my mind was clear. I wasn't groggy or disoriented or half-asleep. I wasn't reaching for my phone or lost in yesterday's worries or tomorrow's anxieties. I was there.

So, when she showed me that test—when she said the words that changed our lives—I caught her. I held her. I cried with her. I was completely, fully present for one of the most important moments we would ever share.

Three years earlier, that moment would have gone differently. The old Cam—pre-rituals, pre-consistency—would have been half-conscious at 6.47 am; probably hungover and definitely dysregulated. He would have been reaching for his phone before his eyes were fully open, flooding his brain with other people's emergencies before he'd even oriented to his own life.

That version of me would have been physically present but emotionally unavailable. I might have said the right words, hugged her at the right moments, performed the appropriate response, but I wouldn't have felt it, not fully and not in the way that moment deserved.

The rituals not only help me function better but also make me available for my own life, for the people I love and for the moments that matter most.

These aren't productivity hacks or morning routines designed to help you get more done. These are practices that shape who you are and who you're capable of being in your peak moments, and in the ordinary moments that turn out to be extraordinary. The rituals create the person who can show up.

> *Rituals don't just change what you do; they change who you're available to be.*

The three anchors

I mention my morning and evening habits earlier in this chapter. I'd now like to dive into all of my daily clarity rituals a bit more deeply.

I organise my clarity rituals around three daily anchors:

1. Morning ritual: Sets the foundation for the day.
2. Midday reset: Helps me recalibrate and prevent drift.
3. Evening ritual: Gives me time to process, release and prepare for renewal.

These three anchors create a rhythm, giving me predictable touchpoints when I reconnect with myself, assess my state and course-correct before drifting too far from clarity.

Think of a ship crossing an ocean. The navigator doesn't just point toward the destination and hope. They check their position regularly, adjust for currents and compensate for winds. They continually realign the ship with its intended course. Without those navigation checkpoints, small deviations compound into massive misdirection.

Your day works the same way. Without anchors, the currents of distraction, reaction and external demand pull you off course. With anchors, you catch the drift early.

The morning ritual (30 minutes)

The morning is sacred territory. Neurologically, you're at your peak. Your prefrontal cortex is fresh and your willpower reserves are full. This is your most valuable cognitive real estate.

The tragic mistake most people make is handing this precious time to other people. They wake up, grab their phone and immediately immerse themselves in emails, news and social media—other people's priorities and other people's emergencies. They start the day reactive.

When you take the clarity approach, you protect your morning fiercely. Before the world gets access to you, you get access to yourself.

Here's the expanded version of my recommended morning stack:

- *The mindful transition (two minutes):* Before getting out of bed, lie still with your eyes closed and take ten conscious breaths. Don't look at your phone or start to plan your day. Just breathe and arrive. With each exhale, silently say, 'Thank you. I am here. This is today'. This tiny practice prevents the reactive cascade that can ruin your morning.
- *Hydration before stimulation (one minute):* Drink a full glass of room-temperature water before having a coffee, or eating or drinking anything else. Rinse your mouth out and get rid of that morning breath. (I don't have any science for you there—just no-one likes morning breath, do they?) The order matters: hydration before stimulation. Water before coffee; care before productivity.
- *Movement (ten minutes):* Don't see this as a workout but an activation. Start with gentle stretching, include some dynamic movement and then add light activation. I do this on my bedroom floor, but you could even do it in bed if you have the room. The specific movements matter less than the consistency of moving.

- *Breathwork (five minutes):* I do box breathing most mornings, but if I'm feeling sluggish, I'll use the energising breath; if anxious, I'll use the extended exhale. Five minutes of conscious breathing establishes a regulated nervous system baseline for the entire day. (For more on these different types of breath techniques, refer to chapter 7.)
- *Clarity mindfulness or journaling (ten minutes):* Focus on the following three components:
  1. *Gratitude:* Write down or say to yourself three specific things you're grateful for; not vague categories but specific instances (for example, 'The conversation with Mum when she really listened'). Specificity creates felt gratitude, not just the concept.
  2. *Intention:* Choose one to three priorities for your day. Focus on the vital few things that, if accomplished, will make the day successful regardless of what else happens.
  3. *Best essence:* Decide on one quality you'll embody today; for example, 'Today I will embody patience'. This sets a filter for the day.

- *The Clarity Pause (two minute):* Close your eyes and take three deep breaths. Notice what your body is feeling, your emotional state and what your mind is doing. Ask yourself, 'Am I ready to meet this day with clarity?' I finish by saying, 'Today is going to be a great day' and then, when I step consciously into the day, I usually look for evidence to prove it will be.

Of course, in a perfect world I get to the gym in the morning and then head to the local ocean pool for a swim, followed by a five-minute meditation and just sitting and appreciating the world around me before heading home. However, I'm also aware that for all of us, life obstacles can get in the way, so this can't happen every day.

If I do manage it, though, my force field is at full power—so look out day, I'm coming for you. More importantly, I just feel so at ease and at peace with myself and the world around me, and that's a pretty beautiful feeling to get used to.

> *How you start the day is how you live the day. How you live the day is how you live your life.*

The midday reset (seven to nine minutes)

By midday, entropy has begun its work. In other words, a feeling of lack of energy to do useful work that has crept in. The intentions you set in the morning have been tested by reality. Without a midday anchor, you can drift through the afternoon on whatever momentum the morning created, which can often be the wrong kind. (I'm actually feeling this right now, at home at 12.52 on a Friday afternoon, one eye on the baby monitor as I pray my son stays asleep for just a little longer, the other eye on the keyboard as I write this and deal with some, *Hit the couch, mate. You'll be fine* thoughts. Luckily, I can put into action what I'm about to share with you ... Okay, I'm back—it works!)

Here's my recommended midday reset:

- *Pattern interrupt (one minute):* Physically change your state. Stand up, shake your body, do ten jumping jacks, splash cold water on your face—anything that breaks the pattern. Your body and mind get locked into the mode of the morning. A physical interrupt releases that mode.
- *The check-in (three minutes):* Do a quick assessment across the following three dimensions:
    1. *Body:* Ask yourself, 'What is my body telling me right now? Am I tense, hungry or tired?'

2. *Emotions:* Ask, 'What am I feeling?' Name it specifically. Is this feeling from now or leftover from earlier?
3. *Mind:* Is your mind calm or chaotic, focused or scattered? Is it present or lost in the past or future?

- *Recalibration (two to three minutes):* Reconnect with your morning intention. Are you embodying that quality or have you drifted? Are you working on what matters, or have you been hijacked by what's urgent? If you've drifted, don't judge, just correct.
- *Reset breath (one to two minutes):* Complete five to ten cycles of extended exhale breathing or three physiological sighs (refer to chapter 7). Discharge the morning's accumulated stress so you don't carry it into the afternoon.

I do this reset at around 1 pm after lunch. The specific time matters less than doing it consistently. The midday reset is where you catch the drift before it becomes disaster.

The evening ritual (15 minutes plus wind-down)

If the morning is about preparation, the evening is about completion, processing what happened, releasing what you're carrying and preparing for renewal.

If you're like most people (and how I used to be), you may have no evening transition. You might go from work to screens to bed. If you have kids, I certainly understand that whole scenario of also trying to get them settled. Whatever you are dealing with, without an evening ritual, you are carrying the stress of the day into your sleep.

Here's the expanded version of my recommended evening ritual:

- *The shutdown ritual (two minutes):* This sets a clear marker that work is over. Review your task list, write down any open loops, and then say, 'Shutdown complete. The day is done'. Close your laptop. The work will be there tomorrow. This seems almost too simple, but it's not. The ritual creates a psychological boundary that your mind respects.

- *Daily review (five minutes):* Write down your responses in the following three areas:
  1. *'What worked today?'* What went well and what progress did you make?
  2. *'What didn't work?'* Where did you fall short and what would you do differently?
  3. *'What did I learn?'* What insight will you take forward and what will you let go?

- *Gratitude and acknowledgment (two minutes):* Write down three specific gratitudes from the past 24 hours plus one acknowledgment—something you did well today, even if small. This isn't arrogance; it's accuracy.
- *Release and forgiveness (two minutes):* Ask yourself, 'What am I still carrying from today that I'm ready to release?' Acknowledge it, accept it and then release it with the following: 'I'm choosing to put this down now. I can pick it up tomorrow if I need to, but I don't have to carry it through the night'. If you're carrying self-criticism, say to yourself, 'I forgive myself. I did the best I could with what I had'.
- *Tomorrow preparation (two minutes):* Glance at tomorrow's calendar and identify one to three priorities. Set out anything you need. Give yourself just enough orientation that you wake up with a sense of what's important.
- *The wind-down (30+ minutes):* Don't look at any screens for at least 30 minutes before bed (I do 60 minutes). Charge your phone outside the bedroom. Instead, use the time to read, stretch, listen to music or a calming podcast (no true crime podcasts, please) or talk to your partner or housemate.

Remember: a problem shared is a problem halved. You can even just share your wins or ask your partner or housemate about theirs. This is the practice people most resist and most benefit from.

> *How you end the day determines how you wake up tomorrow.*

Building your ritual stack

I'm not saying you need or can do all the rituals I've just outlined. However, you now have options and some ideas for one or two different rituals that you could implement into your life that may just work for you. Do some trial and error and see what works, what's beneficial and what you can fit into the busy schedule I know you already have. Importantly, give yourself a chance to find something that could help.

Work through the following to get a better idea of what might work for you.

Assess your current state

Identify your current rituals with the following:

- *Morning:* What time do you wake? What do you do in the first hour? Rate your typical morning for intentionality out of ten.
- *Midday:* Do you have any midday transition rituals? What happens to your focus and energy by afternoon? Rate yourself out of ten.
- *Evening:* What time do you go to bed? What do you do in the last hour before bed? Rate your evening for restoration out of ten.

(continued)

Identify your constraints

Work out the constraints on what you might be able to implement by considering the following:

- What time must you be 'on' for work?
- What's the earliest you could realistically wake up?
- How much morning time could you protect?
- Is a midday break possible?
- What time must you stop to get enough sleep?

Design your morning ritual

Choose one ritual from my recommended morning stack. Write down how much time this ritual will add to your morning routine.

Design your midday reset

Choose one ritual from my recommended midday reset. Write down what time you will adopt this ritual.

Design your evening ritual

Choose one ritual from my recommended evening transition. Write down when you will turn off all screens as well as your target bedtime.

The commitment

Now, make a commitment to yourself by writing down the following: 'For the next 30 days, I commit to *[morning ritual]* starting at *[time]*, *[midday ritual]* starting at *[time]* and *[evening ritual]* starting at *[time]*. I understand that consistency matters more than perfection. If I miss a practice, I won't abandon the system. I'll simply return to it the next day'.

Sign it and date it to really make your commitment official.

The ritual protection policy

Your rituals will be attacked. Life will constantly offer reasons to skip them. If you don't protect your rituals, they will erode and with them, everything they create.

To protect your rituals, keep the following in mind:

- *Rituals are non-negotiable, not optional:* I don't ask, 'Should I do my morning ritual?' any more than I ask, 'Should I brush my teeth?'
- *Imperfect execution beats perfect skipping:* If I only have five minutes instead of 30 for my morning routine, I do a five-minute version. Something is infinitely more than nothing.
- *Travel and disruption have adapted versions:* You can create a hotel room version or an airport version of your rituals. You can even create an 'everything went wrong' minimum viable version. Doing so means the ritual survives even when the environment changes.
- *The first day back is sacred:* If life does force a disruption, make sure the first day life is back to normal, the ritual resumes—no 'I'll start again Monday'.
- *The ritual protects the ritual:* The clarity I gain from doing the rituals is what protects my commitment to them.

> *Protect your rituals, and your rituals will protect you.*

The restart protocol

At some point, you won't just slip. You'll fully collapse. The morning ritual will disappear. The journaling will stop. You'll look up and realise you haven't done any of your rituals for weeks. And the loudest voice will say, 'See? You can't sustain anything'.

That voice is lying. A collapse is not evidence of who you are. It's evidence of being human. It happened to me multiple times during my recovery. The first few times, I let the shame spiral win. Then I learned something that changed my relationship with failure permanently: the restart is part of the system. It's not a bug; it's a feature.

The restart protocol has three steps, and you can do all three in a single day:

1. *Name it without making it mean something about you:* 'I stopped. Here's what happened'. Name the circumstances, and then add, 'This doesn't mean I'm someone who can't stick with things. It means life happened'.
2. *Pick one practice, not the whole stack:* Pick the one habit that felt most impactful. For me, it's always morning breathwork—when that's back, everything follows.
3. *Do it for three days before adding anything else:* Three days of one practice rebuilds the identity of someone who shows up, without triggering the perfectionism that caused the collapse.

The measure of your practice is not whether you maintain it perfectly. It's how quickly you come back when you don't. The restart is part of the practice.

Habits and Discipline Pillar summary

Pillar 6: Habits and discipline is where clarity becomes a way of life, not just a concept. Here's what to keep in mind:

- *Prioritise what works:* Why wouldn't you prioritise what you know will make you feel better? You dictate your morning and the rest of your day, no-one else.
- *Clarity without consistency is entertainment:* Insights fade but habits remain. You are not transformed by what you understand; you are transformed by what you do every day. Every action is a vote for the person you're becoming. The compound effect means a 1 per cent improvement daily produces a 37 times improvement in a year. Discipline is not punishment — it's care for your future self.
- *The three anchors — morning, midday, evening — create predictable touchpoints where you reconnect with clarity:* The morning ritual sets the foundation through breathwork, movement, journaling and intention. The midday reset catches drift before it compounds. The evening ritual processes the day and prepares for renewal. Start with a smaller change than feels meaningful and remember that consistency beats intensity. Design systems for yourself in which willpower isn't required.
- *Rituals change more than what you do:* They also change who you're available to be.
- *Remember that life happens:* Tap into your non-negotiables, those things you have control over doing at any time or stage. The real flex is saying, 'I'm still showing up for my future self, no matter what'. That's when you get rewarded.

Chapter Ten

Pillar 7: Connection and contribution

> The wound you're hiding is the bridge someone else is looking for.

His name was Glen, and he helped save my life without knowing it. We met in the facility common room on my third day. I was sitting in the corner, trying to make myself invisible—which is hard to do when you're a reasonably well-known face in a psychiatric ward. I'd been avoiding everyone, eating alone, skipping group sessions and retreating to my room whenever possible.

I didn't want to be seen like this: broken, medicated and shuffling around in hospital slippers. I had spent my entire adult life being the guy who had it together, the entertainer, the one who lifted others up. The idea of anyone seeing me at rock bottom was unbearable. So, I hid; even in a place specifically designed for people who were struggling, I hid.

The healing power of connection

Glen didn't let me hide. He was maybe 60, with kind eyes and a weathered face that suggested he'd seen some things. He walked straight over to my corner, pulled up a chair uninvited, and sat down across from me.

'You're Cameron', he said. It wasn't a question. I nodded, already planning my escape. 'I'm Glen. I've been here three weeks. Depression. Third time in a place like this.' He said it matter-of-factly, like he was telling me he'd been to the grocery store. I didn't know what to say. I mumbled something about being sorry to hear that.

He waved it off. 'Don't be. It's just what it is. But I noticed you've been hiding out, and I wanted to tell you something.' I braced myself for advice. Everyone had advice—tips for recovery, perspectives on mental health or inspirational quotes they'd read somewhere. Instead, Glen said, 'I tried to do it alone too. The last two times. I thought I had to figure it out myself, that needing people was weakness, that showing anyone the truth would destroy me'.

He paused, looking at me with those kind eyes. 'It almost did destroy me. The isolation. Not the depression, the isolation. The depression wanted me dead, but it was the loneliness that nearly delivered me.' I felt something crack in my chest; a wall I didn't know I'd been holding.

'For this third time', he continued, 'I decided to try something different. I decided to stop hiding, actually talk to people, let them see me. I decided to let them help'. He smiled slightly. 'It's the only thing that's ever actually worked.'

I wanted to argue. I wanted to explain that my situation was different, that I had reasons for hiding, that he didn't understand. But I couldn't. Because something in me knew he was right.

'You don't have to perform in here', Glen said, standing up. 'Nobody's watching except people who understand. And we're all too busy fighting our own battles to judge you for yours.' He put his hand on my shoulder for just a moment. 'Let people in, mate. It's the only way out.'

Then he walked away, leaving me alone with a truth I'd been running from my entire life: I was never meant to do this alone.

The isolation epidemic

Isolation is where suffering goes to multiply. When you're struggling, the instinct is to withdraw and hide. You want to protect others from your mess and protect yourself from being seen in it. This instinct feels like self-preservation; it's actually self-destruction.

Human beings are not designed for isolation. We are social creatures down to our neurobiology. Our nervous systems are wired to co-regulate with other nervous systems. Our brains develop through relationships. Our sense of self forms in the mirror of others' eyes.

Connection isn't about proximity or communication volume. Connection is about being truly seen, truly known and truly held by another human being.

> *Isolation is where suffering goes to multiply; connection is where healing begins.*

Your nervous system doesn't regulate in isolation but in relationship. When you're dysregulated, the presence of a calm, regulated person helps your nervous system settle. They don't do this through advice or problem-solving. They do it just through their presence. Their regulated state literally influences your state.

I learned this viscerally in the facility. The days I isolated were the days I spiralled. The days I sat in group, let people see me and stayed present with others, even when I didn't feel like it, even when I felt I had nothing to offer, were the days I stabilised.

The age of everything — and no-one

Here's the strangest paradox of our time. We are the most connected generation in human history but we're also the loneliest.

You can video-call someone on the other side of the planet in three seconds. You can message 100 people without leaving your couch. You can even talk to an AI chatbot that remembers your name, asks how your day was and never gets tired of listening. And yet, somehow, we've never felt more alone.

In 2023, Dr Vivek Murthy, at the time US Surgeon General, called loneliness an epidemic, warning that chronic loneliness is as damaging to health as smoking 15 cigarettes a day. And this epidemic is affecting us all. Even though we live in the most connected time in human history, with endless social media and constant communication, we're lonelier than ever.

Two years later, the World Health Organization reported that one in six people worldwide is affected by loneliness, contributing to an estimated 871 000 deaths every year between 2014 and 2019. That's roughly a hundred deaths every hour, not from disease or conflict, but from the quiet absence of genuine human connection.

And the numbers keep climbing. According to 2025 AARP research, four in ten US adults now report being lonely. Men in their 40s and 50s, blokes conditioned their whole lives to 'handle it themselves'—are reporting higher rates than women (at 42 per cent versus 37 per cent). Here in Australia, the 2023 *State of the Nation Report* found almost one in three of us (32 per cent) feels lonely some or all of the time. Among young Australians aged 18 to 24, that rose to 38 per cent. And, according to a report from Bankwest Curtin Economics Centre, the economic cost of loneliness in Australia alone is up to $2.7 billion a year. Yes, that's billions—for loneliness.

So how did the most technologically advanced era in history produce the most disconnected humans? Because we confused communication with connection, and they're not the same thing. Communication is the exchange of information while connection is the exchange of humanity. Getting 100 messages doesn't equal one genuine conversation, and 1000 followers don't equal one real friend. Social media promised us the world's biggest community, but what it often delivered was the world's biggest audience. And the difference between having an audience and having a village is massive. An audience watches you but a village knows you.

Now layer on artificial intelligence, and the paradox deepens. AI companion apps have surged by 700 per cent since 2022. Millions are turning to chatbots for friendship, emotional support and even romance. A recent Harvard Business School study led by Julian De Freitas found that talking to an AI companion reduced loneliness as effectively as talking to another human, in the short term. That should stop you in your tracks, not because AI is evil, but because it reveals how starved for connection we've become. When a machine feels as comforting as a mate, something fundamental has broken.

And look, I'm not on a high horse here. I've done it myself. I've typed something personal into an AI chat late at night, and got back this beautifully worded, warm and empathetic response, and for about 45 seconds I genuinely felt like I'd just had a deep and meaningful with my best mate. *Wow, this thing really gets me.* Then I put my phone down, looked around the room and remembered my 'best mate' was a server in California running on electricity and code. The warm feeling evaporated almost instantly. Deep down, my nervous system knew: nobody was actually there. No-one had chosen to show up. It was convenience dressed up as companionship, and my body wasn't fooled for long, even if my brain was for a moment.

The research confirms this. While AI can temporarily ease the *feeling* of loneliness, it cannot address the *cause*. Heavy reliance on AI companions actually increases loneliness over time, creates dependency and reduces real-world socialising. Again, your nervous system is wired to co-regulate with other humans—lowering cortisol, calming the threat response—in ways no algorithm can replicate.

Every human being on this planet needs one thing and it's not money, success, a bigger house or a viral moment. It's other human beings. That's it. We need each other. We heal and grow through each other. Strip everything else away and what remains is relationship. That truth has sustained our species for hundreds of thousands of years, and no amount of technological advancement will change it.

Meeting on the park bench

I want to tell you about a moment that will stay with me for the rest of my life.

I was grabbing lunch one afternoon. The restaurant was packed, so I grabbed my food as takeaway, headed outside and found a park bench. A young man was already sitting there with his phone in his hand. He was shaking.

I asked him if he minded if I sat with him. He looked up with tears in his eyes and just nodded. I put down my phone and my food, and did the simplest thing a human being can do for another human being. I checked in. 'My name's Cameron. What's yours? Are you okay, mate?'

He looked at me with this puzzled expression, like he was confused. And he said, quietly, 'I've never really been asked that question before'. A young man, sitting on a park bench in the middle of the day, and nobody had ever genuinely asked him if he was okay.

'Well, I'm asking', I said. 'Are you okay?' He told me his name was Ben, and what then poured out of him in the next few minutes was the kind of pain I knew intimately. He'd lost his job that week. A relationship had ended. He'd lost his sense of purpose and felt useless. He didn't know where to go.

I thanked him for sharing and then said, 'Can I tell you a story? Once upon a time, I lost a career. Cricket was my everything, and then it was gone. My relationship ended. I was dealing with trauma. I was homeless. Mate, I couldn't even put pants on'.

He looked at me. 'Pants?'

'Yeah, pants. Got pants on, Ben?'

He looked down. 'Yeah.'

'Well, you're ahead of me, buddy.' He smiled, almost.

I told him that if he could just hold on and give himself a chance to open up to someone, share what he was going through, he'd give himself an opportunity to be supported, to be heard and to find some solutions. I said, 'I'm a walking, living, breathing example. I've been where you are. I asked for help and I got it. And I'm here right now, sitting on this bench with a smile on my face, telling you that everything can be okay. What do you need?'

He put down his phone. He looked at me and for the first time in our conversation he smiled. 'Thank you, Cameron.'

'What for?'

And then he said something that knocked the air out of me. 'I want you to know that on my phone right now, in my notes, I had a plan to take my own life tonight. I had a list of people I wanted to say goodbye to. But from this conversation, from you just sitting down and caring enough to check in, I've just deleted that note. You've given me hope. You've reminded me that things can get better if we give them the right opportunity.'

I sat there, unable to speak. Here was every statistic, every piece of research and every pillar in this book—made real in one moment on a park bench over a missed lunch.

No app, chatbot, algorithm or perfectly worded AI response could have created that moment. What saved Ben in that moment wasn't technology. It was a human being putting down his phone, sitting down beside another human being, and saying four words: *Are you okay, mate?*

That's the power of connection. This isn't the curated, filtered, optimised version, but the real, messy, unscripted, showing-up-when-it-matters version. It's the kind you can't download; the kind that saves lives.

This is why Pillar 7 exists. In a world getting louder and more digitally sophisticated by the day, the most radical thing you can do is put your phone down, look another human being in the eye, and ask: 'How are you? No, really. How are you?'

That's not old-fashioned. That's the most urgent, evidence-backed, life-saving act available to any of us. Ben is living proof.

> *We built machines that can think, but we forgot to protect the thing that makes us feel: each other.*

The performance trap

I spent most of my life in what I now call the 'performance trap'. This trap is when you only let people see the curated version of yourself—the highlights, the successes, the put-together persona—while hiding everything that's messy, struggling or real. It feels like protection but it's actually prison.

When you only show people the performance, you can never be truly known. You might be admired, liked and applauded, but you won't be known—because the person people are responding to isn't really you. It's a character you're playing.

And, deep down, you know this. So every bit of positive feedback feels hollow. Every relationship feels conditional. Every success feels fraudulent. Through it all, you hold on to what you think is the truth: if they saw the real me, they wouldn't love me like this.

The performance trap kept me isolated even when I was in crowds. I could be at a party with 100 people, being the entertainer, making everyone laugh, and feel completely alone. None of them knew me. They knew Cameron the character, while Cameron the human was hiding backstage.

You can be surrounded by people and utterly alone. Connection isn't about proximity; it's about being truly seen. The only way out of the performance trap is terrifying. You have to let people see the real you, not the highlight reel or the curated version, but the actual, messy, imperfect and struggling human being. While this feels like the most dangerous thing in the world, it's the only path to genuine connection.

The vulnerability paradox

You believe that showing your struggles will push people away. The opposite is true. We don't bond over each other's highlight reels. We bond over our shared humanity—the fears, the failures and the wounds we all carry.

I experienced this firsthand after I left the facility. For months, I told almost no-one where I'd been, because I was ashamed. Slowly, I started telling the truth, first to close friends and then more broadly. Eventually, I started talking about my experience publicly. And something remarkable happened: instead of pushing people away, the truth drew them closer. People told me about their own struggles. Relationships deepened. Strangers reached out to say they understood because they'd been there too. My greatest source of shame became my greatest source of connection.

This connection even happened as I wrote this chapter. I was sitting in a little cafe overlooking the beach, tucked away with my head down as I tried to get my thoughts out, when a woman sat next to me. 'Hi Cam', she said. 'We did a breathwork class together.' I immediately recognised her and said hi. She then saw my laptop was on and went to leave, telling me she didn't want to disturb me, but I told her she wasn't and asked her how she was.

What started with a surface-level conversation about the weather and what a beautiful day it was quickly rolled into a conversation about what I was writing about, why I was writing it and the impact it can have if people become vulnerable and allow themselves to connect on an honest and deeper level.

She then told me she was a recovering alcoholic for over seven years and had come from a recovery meeting only an hour before. In that moment, we were both vulnerable and open. I said to her, 'Vulnerability is the fastest way to connection and trust in a relationship'. She agreed. That morning, we had a choice: we could continue our conversation about the weather and she could then go on her merry way, or we could choose to share something a little deeper. Yes, this second option came with the risk of judgement but it also came with so many possibilities. I shared my story and she shared hers, and together this gave us an opportunity to connect on another level.

I said to her, 'If you look around, every single person you see here has some shit going on. We are all facing challenges, so why aren't we connecting more and sharing our stories to help each other heal and to inspire? By sharing your story, you simply help someone else feel like they are not alone'. She agreed. We both thanked each other for sharing and gave each other a hug. She told me she looked forward to reading the book and then left. It was a beautiful moment of connection and just one of many conversations that I have had with so many people that I am truly grateful for.

> *“What you're hiding because you think it will push people away is often what will bring them closer.”*

The four types of connection

Perhaps you've noticed that connection is becoming more sparse and relationships are becoming more fleeting. In part, this is because we often don't know exactly what kind of relationships we are in need of during certain seasons of our lives. Understanding this a little more can make connections easier to engage in.

Not all connection is created equal. The four different levels of connection are as follows:

1. *Surface connection:* This is small talk and pleasant exchanges. It's the 'How are you?'/'Good, you?' interactions. This level of connection has its place, but it doesn't nourish. You can have hundreds of surface connections and still be profoundly lonely.
2. *Functional connection:* This covers task-oriented relationships, and includes colleagues and perhaps neighbours. (Although some neighbours can be closer than this.) These relationships are useful and necessary, but they don't meet the deeper human need for being truly known.
3. *Emotional connection:* These are the relationships where you share how you actually feel and emotions are welcomed rather than managed. These connections begin to meet your need for genuine relationship.
4. *Soul connection:* This is the deepest level of connection. In these relationships, you are fully known—your light and your shadow, your strengths and your wounds. Nothing is hidden, and you are loved not despite your humanness but because of it. I truly love, appreciate and am so grateful for these connections. When things go pear-shaped, these relationships are there for you. When things are good for you both, the conversations had are truly life-changing and forever stimulating.

Soul connection is rare, and most people have only a handful in their entire lives. But these connections are the ones that heal and that hold you when nothing else can. They're the ones that simply don't have to understand completely but support entirely.

> *Surface connections fill time; soul connections sustain life.*

My circle transformation

Before the hospital, I had many acquaintances and few genuine connections. My calendar was full but my soul was empty. I had people I partied with, people I worked with and people I performed for, but almost no-one who actually knew me.

When I fell apart, most of those acquaintances disappeared. They didn't do this maliciously; they just didn't know what to do with a version of me that wasn't entertaining and successful. The relationships had been built on a persona and when the persona cracked, nothing was underneath to sustain them. Even some real close friends who I thought were by my side closed their doors. Some people come into your life to build you, others to reveal you but not all are meant to stay, and that's okay.

While this was painful at the time, looking back, it was a gift. The few people who remained loved me beyond my performance. This included my family and a handful of real friends from school who saw my pain and hurt. These friends weren't sure how I could return to the person I was, but they stuck by me and supported me regardless. They were people who had somehow seen past the character to the human, and cared about the human. But even so, repeating the same conversation with those friends eventually created a point of friction. They had their own lives to get on with. I realised the only person who could make some change and get myself healthy again was me. The moment I picked myself up off the floor after finally accepting I needed to go to mental rehab, I walked into the lounge room to tell Tom, my best mate. He simply hugged me with the kind of embracing hug I hadn't experienced in a while and told me he was proud of me. He didn't have any judgement or questions; just pure support and love that told me, regardless of what happened, he would be there for me. Tom was best man at both of my weddings with Jules. When he was going through a similar time, I was there for him without question to get him back to himself too. Since being at school together as 13 year olds, he remains my best friend in the world today and I am so grateful for him.

Coming out of the hospital, I made a decision: I would only invest in relationships where I could be fully myself. No more performing from me, and no more people in my life who only wanted the highlight reel. Either we could be real with each other, or we wouldn't be close. Some people left and that's okay. Some stayed and that was okay too. This narrowed my circle dramatically, and was the best thing I ever did for my relational life.

And then something interesting happened: as I became more authentically myself, I started attracting people who resonated with that authenticity and energy. These were growth-oriented people, people doing their own inner work and people who wanted real connection, not social performance. These are the people you want in your life, who align with who you are and the same is reciprocated. That's simply a good train to be on. The question is who is on your train? Some people come into your life for a reason, some for a season and a few for a lifetime, and every one of them serves a purpose in who you become.

In my speech at my 40th birthday, I thanked the people who were there to celebrate with me, not just for the evening but for my life up to that point. They had gone through it all with me and had stayed to support me, and I will be forever grateful for that. In my speech, I simply said (paraphrasing Marilyn Munroe), 'If you can't support me at my worst then you don't deserve me at my best'.

> *When you become fully yourself, you attract people who love your full self.*

The connection audit

Life is simply so much better when you know you have the right people around you, because those people are simply affecting your existence.

They say that you are the sum of the five people you most hang around. Take some time now to consider the levels of connection in your life. List the five people you spend the most time with. For each person, ask yourself the following:

- 'Can I be fully myself with them?'
- 'Do they support my growth?'
- 'Do I feel energised or depleted after time with them?'
- 'What type of connection is this — surface, functional, emotional or soul?'

Now check in with what traits the people in your circle have. I like to have the people who have the most influence on me to possess certain traits. Ask yourself if your circle has the following traits:

- positive
- dedicated

(continued)

- activational
- inspiring
- encouraging
- value-adding.

How many of these relationships are at the soul connection level? In how many can you be fully yourself? What does this tell you?

Your circle should want to see you win. They should clap loudly when you have good news. Your circle should be there when you need them most. If not, get a new circle.

The upgrade

Now think about one relationship that could deepen if you showed up more vulnerably. Also consider the one relationship that's draining you that needs a boundary. What's one action you could take this week to deepen your closest relationships?

Having the courage to reach out

Reaching out for help when I knew I needed it was certainly one of the hardest things I ever had to do. However, looking back, it was also one of the strongest things I ever did. Reaching out when you're struggling is incredibly hard. Every instinct tells you to withdraw. You don't want to be a burden and you convince yourself that needing support is weakness. But the people who love you want to help.

Think about it this way: when someone you care about opens up to you, how do you feel? Burdened? Or do you feel honoured and grateful they trusted you? The people who love you want to be there. Letting them in isn't a burden—it's a gift.

You don't have to have it figured out before asking to help. Simply saying, 'I'm struggling and I don't know what I need, but I didn't want to be alone' is enough. Sometimes it's everything.

Start with one person. One genuine conversation is worth more than 100 surface interactions. And remember that reaching out is a skill. If you've spent years hiding, it will feel awkward at first but each time after, it will be a little less hard.

The bravest, wisest people I know are the ones who can ask for help. They understand that independence isn't strength—interdependence is.

> *Reaching out isn't weakness but wisdom. It says, 'I value my life enough to let others help me live it'.*

Reaching out to repair

Reaching out to someone new takes courage. Reaching out to someone you've hurt takes a different kind entirely. It takes the courage to be wrong, to be rejected, and to sit in discomfort without knowing how the other person will respond.

If a relationship in your life needs repair—perhaps a friendship that faded, a family member you've been avoiding or someone you left things badly with—here's a framework that helped me:

- *Lead with ownership, not explanation:* Don't open with why you did what you did. Open with what you did. 'I wasn't there when you needed me.' Explanation can come later, if they ask. Ownership comes first.
- *Name what you did, not what they did:* Resist the temptation to balance the scales. A repair conversation is not a negotiation. It's an offering.

- *Don't ask for forgiveness—offer accountability:* 'I see what I did, and I'm committed to showing up differently.' Then let them respond however they respond. They might be grateful, angry or silent. None of those responses changes the value of what you've done.

Not every relationship can be repaired. Some bridges burned for good reason. But the ones that can be rebuilt often become the strongest connections in your life—because they've been tested by honesty and survived.

How contribution heals the giver

About 18 months after leaving the facility, I met this legend named Jimmy. I was doing better, not perfect, but better. The rituals were established and clarity was returning. I'd started tentatively sharing my story with small groups, testing whether my experience might help others.

After one of these talks, to maybe 20 people in a community centre, a young man approached me. He was tall and athletic-looking, but his eyes were hollow in a way I recognised immediately. The lights were on but something essential had dimmed. 'Can I talk to you?' he asked. His voice was barely audible.

We found a quiet corner and, for the next hour, Jimmy told me his story. He was now 23 and had been a promising rugby player, state representative at 17, dreams of professional contracts. His entire identity was built around the sport and the future he could see so clearly. But then came the injury, a tackle that went wrong and spinal damage that ended not just his career but also his ability to play at any level. At 18 years old, everything he'd built his life around was gone in a single moment.

What followed was a descent I knew intimately:

- the depression that crept in when the initial shock wore off
- the drinking that started as coping and became its own problem
- the isolation as friends drifted away, uncomfortable with his pain
- the dark thoughts that visited more and more frequently.

'I don't know why I'm telling you this', he said at one point, staring at the floor. 'I haven't told anyone.'

'Because you recognised something', I said. 'You heard my story and you saw yourself in it.'

He looked up. 'How did you get through it? How did you come back?'

I didn't have a neat answer, because recovery isn't neat. But I shared what I could about the facility, the pillars I was still discovering and the slow rebuilding that was possible even when it seemed impossible.

And then something happened that I hadn't expected. As I talked, as I watched Jimmy's face shift from hopeless to something like hope, I felt something moving in my own chest. I felt warmth and a sense of purpose. This was a feeling I hadn't experienced in years, maybe ever. I realised I was useful, not performing useful but actually useful. My pain—the very thing I'd been ashamed of, the experience I'd hidden, the wound I'd wished I could erase—was helping someone.

That hour with Jimmy did more for my recovery than months of therapy. I don't mean I didn't need therapy, I did. But something unlocked when I stopped focusing exclusively on my own healing and instead turned outward and started using what I'd learned to help someone else.

Walking to my car afterward, I called my therapist. 'I think I understand something', I told her. 'I think helping him helped me more than it helped him.'

She laughed softly. 'Now you're getting it. That's one of the oldest secrets of healing. The helper heals.'

> *Your wound is not your weakness. It's your qualification to help others who are bleeding in the same place.*

The wounded healer

Something is uniquely powerful about someone who has walked through darkness helping another who is currently lost in it. When Jimmy looked at me, he wasn't seeing a credentialed expert. He was seeing someone who had been where he was and who understood his experience viscerally. He saw someone whose presence said, 'I know this territory. I've survived it. You can too'.

That's the gift of the wounded healer. They're not offering expertise from above, but companionship from alongside. They're not saying, 'Here's what you should do' but 'Here's what helped me, fellow traveller'.

And the gift goes both ways. When you help someone, your brain releases dopamine, serotonin, oxytocin and endorphins. Giving is good medicine and the benefits are often strongest for people who have experienced significant adversity themselves. Those who've been through darkness and then helped others in similar darkness report the most profound healing from the act of giving.

The wound that nearly destroyed you can become the wisdom that helps others survive.

From mess to message

Your mess can become your message. The past is your platform to build what it is that you were placed on this earth to build. Every struggle you've been through, every failure you've survived and every wound you've carried is not just pain to be healed and forgotten but also material to be transformed and shared.

The addiction you overcame qualifies you to help others fighting the same battle. The grief you've processed becomes a map for those newly lost in sorrow. The mental health crisis you navigated lights the path for those still in the dark. None of this minimises the pain. Instead, it transforms it and gives it purpose. It makes meaning from what otherwise would be meaningless suffering.

In the acknowledgments of this book, I include my younger self, thanking them for turning pain into purpose. When I think about this, I get very emotional because I would never wish the pain and suffering that I experienced on anyone. However, as I sit here right now, I know I had to go through it to be able to step into my purpose and turn my mess into my message. If I only help one person, it was all worth it.

Sometimes the fastest way out of your own darkness is to bring light to someone else's. What you survived is not just your history; it's your curriculum for helping others.

The ripple effect

After that first conversation, Jimmy and I stayed in touch. I checked in on him as he started therapy and began doing some of the practices I shared with him—imperfectly, inconsistently, but he began. Slowly, he stabilised. The drinking stopped, the dark thoughts retreated and he found a new direction, not playing rugby but coaching young players who were dealing with injuries and helping them find their identity beyond the sport.

About a year later, Jimmy sent me a message. He'd just finished talking with a young woman who'd suffered a career-ending injury. He'd shared his story with her. She cried. He'd cried. And something had shifted in her, he could see it. 'I finally understand what you meant', he wrote. 'Helping her helped me more than it helped her. It's like my whole struggle suddenly made sense.' Jimmy's pain had become purpose. And now he was passing it on to someone else.

I helped Jimmy. Jimmy helped this young woman. This young woman will, eventually, help someone else. Each act of contribution creates ripples that spread far beyond the initial moment.

You will never know the full impact of your giving. The person you help might help ten others. Those ten might help 100. The ripple you start today might still be moving through the world long after you're gone.

> *Every act of contribution creates ripples you'll never fully see.*

The village in India

A moment in India deepened this lesson on connection for me even further, and it had nothing to do with stages, microphones or healing from heartbreak.

I was in India through my cricket marketing work, moving between stadiums, meetings and factories, with noise and colour and movement everywhere. India is alive in a way that gets your head spinning: chaotic and beautiful all at once.

One afternoon, I found myself in a small local community. Kids were playing cricket in the dust with makeshift bats and worn tennis balls. There was no grass and no boundary rope, just pure joy. I decided to walk past with a smile and ask if I could join them.

We played for hours with no agenda and hardly any rules, but plenty of laughter, louder-than-necessary appeals and wild celebrations for even the smallest runs. Their smiles were enormous and the moments were perfect.

Later, they invited me to visit their own family village. I arrived to brick homes, cement beds with thin mattresses and astonishing heat. Chickens wove between our feet. It was the kind of setting many people in the Western world can't even imagine, but nothing about it felt lacking.

I had brought dinner for the family, a small gesture from my perspective. We sat together, cross-legged, sharing food and exchanging stories in the best broken English and Hindi we could piece together. Our words were clumsy, but the connection was effortless.

They kept thanking me as they smiled and nodded, hands on heart. The gratitude in their eyes was overwhelming. And yet, quietly, I knew something they didn't. I was the one receiving the greater gift.

Their happiness without excess stripped away the illusion that fulfilment is found in accumulation. They had so little by material standards, yet so much richness in spirit. Laughter flowed freely, potentially at my expense. (I wasn't too sure because I couldn't understand but I went with it and laughed too.) Appreciation was immediate and community was unquestioned.

In that small village, contribution stopped being about 'helping' and became about shared humanity. It became about remembering that what we all crave isn't status, applause or possessions but connection. We want to be seen and valued. We want to sit across from another human and feel we matter to each other in this moment.

That night, as I left the village, I realised something profound: contribution is not a transaction. It is an exchange of dignity.

Those children playing cricket in the dust didn't need a better pitch to be joyful. They didn't judge my past, my mistakes, my life and my story. They just needed each other and appreciated the time and energy I gave them. And, for a few hours, I was lucky enough to be part of that. Contribution healed me in ways I didn't even know I needed healing.

Finding your contribution

The following four questions helped me find my unique way of contributing:

1. *What have I survived?* Your struggles have given you specific wisdom that others need. Someone out there is going through what you've been through, and they need someone who understands.
2. *What do I know?* You have knowledge—professional, personal and practical—that others lack. You don't have to know everything in order to help. You don't have to wait to get to 'level 100' in knowledge. Even if you have knowledge of level 1, someone out there who's willing to learn and be helped is at level 0. Don't let your perceived lack of knowledge hold you back from contributing to someone who needs you most.
3. *What do I have?* Beyond knowledge, you have resources. You have time, energy, connections, perhaps a platform and a skill set. How could these benefit others?
4. *What breaks my heart?* Compassion is your compass. The suffering that moves you most isn't random—it's pointing you toward where your contribution might live.

The intersection of these four questions is where your unique contribution lives.

The balance of giving and receiving

A word of caution: contribution should not become another form of self-abandonment. Keep the following in mind when contributing to others:

- *Give from overflow, not from deficit:* Make sure your own cup is being filled. You can't sustainably give what you don't have.
- *Receive as well as give:* Let others help you too. When you refuse to receive, you deny others the gift of giving.
- *Set boundaries:* You can't help everyone and you can't fix everything. Knowing your limits isn't selfishness; it's sustainability.
- *Serve, don't save:* Your job is to contribute, not to rescue. I know we all want to have the answers and save so many souls, but you can't save everyone. You can walk beside people, but you can't carry them. Sometimes we/they just need to figure it out on their own in order to grow.

Whatever you've been through, it's not just your history; it's your curriculum and your credentials. It's the raw material and your purest intentions for a contribution that only you can make.

> *The very thing you most want to hide might be the very thing the world most needs you to share.*

Don't be afraid to start lighting flames. In a dark room, light two people's candles and then allow them to light two more people's candles. Eventually, you can turn a dark room into a light one. That's how we make genuine change in this world.

Connection and Contribution Pillar summary

Pillar 7: Connection and Contribution is where clarity turns outward. Here's what to take with you:

- *Isolation is where suffering goes to multiply:* Connection is where healing begins. Your nervous system doesn't regulate in isolation but in relationship. The performance trap keeps you surrounded by people who don't really know you. The only way out is terrifying and liberating: let people see the real you. What you're hiding because you think it will push people away is often what would bring them closer.
- *Contribution heals the giver:* Your wound is not your weakness; it's your qualification to help others who are bleeding in the same place. Your mess becomes your message. The person you help might help ten others, creating ripples you'll never fully see. Find your contribution at the intersection of what you've survived, what you know, what you have and what breaks your heart. Give from overflow, not deficit. Serve, don't save.
- *Surface connections fill time:* Soul connections sustain life.

Chapter Eleven

∞ Pillar 8: Integration

Clarity is not something you find once. It's something you come home to, again and again.

I was woken up by Jules at 1.47 in the morning. Jules and I had been married for two years and we were expecting our first child, 28 weeks and counting. Life was good, better than I'd ever imagined it could be. The work was meaningful, the relationship was deep and the daily practices were holding. I'd started to believe that maybe, just maybe, everything we had dreamed of was coming true.

Then she rolled over and grabbed my arm with a hysterical cry, lying in bed sheets covered in blood. *This can't be good. Surely this is a nightmare.*

'It's the baby. I don't know what's happening', she said, her voice cracking in a way I'd never heard.

Sustaining clarity when life gets loud

The next 12 hours were a blur, starting with the frantic drive to the hospital. Rain was pouring down and the windscreen wipers were frantic, faster than the thoughts in both our minds, yet the car was silent. We were both thinking the same thing, not just of the situation but also of the horrendous hate message Jules had received just days before from an anonymous follower on social media. *'I hope you have a miscarriage and your baby dies a painful death.'* (Oh, the joys of social media and humans who live behind the keyboard. As I write this, it still brings up so many emotions.) We looked at each other and I knew we were thinking the same thing, that poor excuse for a human had gotten their wish.

We pulled into emergency and raced into the sterile waiting room with its fluorescent lights and plastic chairs, Jules in a wheelchair. Jules was understandably distressed, but I had to hold it together and remain calm.

Through test after test, doctor after doctor, and moments that felt like hours on end, we tried to prepare ourselves for the worst potential outcome. Then, finally, good news: our baby was healthy and okay but needed to be monitored.

For the next 24 hours, we stayed in that hospital. I slept in chairs and mostly ate from vending machines. I watched monitors and held my breath every time an alarm sounded. I tried to be strong for my wife and our baby.

And here's what I discovered during those 24 hours:

- Everything that I continued to show up for in life and that had kept me going all those years ago had now been threatened.
- Everything I'd built was being tested—every pillar, every practice and every piece of clarity I'd worked so hard to establish.

The morning rituals I'd maintained religiously for years? Gone. Finding a quiet space for reflection and setting priorities is impossible when you're sleeping in a hospital corridor. The regulation tools? Pushed to their absolute limit. My nervous system was in sustained activation. The breathwork helped when I remembered to do it but, most of the time, I forgot. The identity work? Shaken to its core. Who was I when I couldn't do any of the things that had come to define me? When I was just a scared husband watching over his wife and our child fight for their life.

Every single thing I'd learned was stress-tested under the most brutal conditions. But here's another thing I discovered: the pillars held. I didn't implement them perfectly or elegantly, and not in the way I did in normal life when I had time and space and energy, but they held.

The pillars didn't prevent the pain—nothing could have done that. But they gave me something to hold onto when everything else felt like it was chaos. They provided a foundation that bent but didn't break, and a core of clarity that flickered but never went completely dark.

On what could have been the worst night of our lives, as I drove through the rain and darkness or sat on the floor of the waiting room, I breathed. I took four counts in, held for four counts, four counts out. The box breathing I'd done a thousand times in easy moments was now the only thing keeping me from completely unravelling.

And, between breaths, a question from the awareness work surfaced: what is true right now, in this moment?

What was true was that something may happen to our first child. Everything that had allowed me to keep going in life was threatened. I was terrified and sad and angry at the unfairness of it all.

And what was also true was that I was still here. I was still breathing and still capable of being present with Jules in whatever came next. I was still the person all this work had shaped me into, even when I couldn't do any of the practices in full.

That's when I understood what integration really means. It's not about maintaining perfect practices when life explodes. It's about the work becoming so much a part of you that it holds even when you can't consciously hold it. It's about the pillars becoming bones—structural, internal and present even when invisible.

Our baby survived and we were so, so grateful. Months later, we walked out of that same hospital with a healthy newborn baby, Ollie. Today, five years later, we are still so thankful, present and grateful for every day.

But that crisis taught me something I couldn't have learned any other way: the point of all this work isn't to prevent life from being hard. It's to become someone who can meet the hard parts without losing themselves and their ability to remain calm in the face of the unknown.

> *Clarity isn't about having a perfect life; it's about having a steady centre when life is anything but perfect.*

The inevitability of storms

Life will test you, nothing is surer. No matter how much work you do, no matter how clear you become and no matter how solid your foundation, storms will come. The question is never, 'Will I face adversity?' The question is always, 'Who will I be when I do?'

Integration means the work has become part of who you are, not just what you do. It means the pillars have moved from practice to identity, and from conscious effort to unconscious competence. You've built something that can withstand storms, not just something that works in sunshine.

Anyone can be calm when life is easy. The work is building a calm that survives when life isn't.

The three phases of crisis

Crises move through three distinct phases, and each demands something different:

1. *Impact:* This is the initial shock—the early morning phone call or the diagnosis. In the impact phase, all bets are off. Your nervous system activates fully. Don't expect yourself to be clear. Focus only on immediate necessities. Let yourself feel. Reach out for help. If you can access one regulation tool, even just breathing, use it. But don't beat yourself up if you can't.
2. *Navigation:* This is the sustained period of dealing with the crisis, and it could last days, weeks or months. During this period, you have slightly more capacity, but you're running a marathon you didn't train for. Maintain minimum viable practices and lower your standards temporarily. Accept help. Take breaks when possible. Remember: this is a season, not forever.

3. *Recovery:* The acute crisis has passed and you can begin building a new normal. Rebuild your practices gradually as you process what happened. Give yourself grace and be patient with yourself. Learn from the experience. Watch for delayed reactions, sometimes the emotional impact hits after the crisis is 'over'.

> *Crisis moves in phases, and each phase needs a different response.*

Maintaining your minimum viable practice

During Jules's hospitalisation, I couldn't maintain my full practice. I did, however, discover something crucial: you don't need your full practice to survive. You need your minimum viable practice (MVP).

Your MVP is the smallest set of actions that keeps you connected to your clarity when everything else falls apart. It's what keeps the thread intact when you can't weave the full tapestry.

My MVP during that crisis was:

1. Three conscious breaths whenever I noticed I was spiralling, which was often.
2. One text per day to someone outside the crisis, just to stay connected.
3. Five minutes outside to breathe whenever I could manage it, even if this was just standing in the hospital parking lot. I used the time to practise my gratitude for what was around me, what we did currently have and what was going well. This included gratitude for the incredible and caring nurses and doctors who gave so much to help.
4. Asking 'What's true right now?' when my mind started catastrophising about the future. And answering with, 'I am safe, I am calm, I am loved'.

5. Letting myself feel rather than suppressing—crying when I needed to, being scared when I was scared—and knowing this was okay. Being brave for your family is one thing but suppressing emotions that need to be released when they can be is so important.

That's it. These five tiny practices were a fraction of my normal routine, but they kept the thread intact. They prevented complete collapse into old patterns of numbing, isolating and spiralling.

When you can't do everything, do something. When you can't do something well, do it badly. The thread matters more than the tapestry in these moments.

Building your crisis protocol

Build your own crisis protocol now, before you need it. When you're in crisis, you can't think clearly enough to figure out what you need. If you've built a protocol in advance, you don't have to think. You just follow it.

Grab a pen and your journal (or Clarity Workbook), and write down your responses to the following:

- *Your warning signs:* What are the early signs you're entering crisis mode? List your physical, emotional and behavioural signs.
- *Your minimum viable practice:* What are the absolute essentials you'll maintain no matter what? Pick three to five essential rituals.
- *Your support team:* Who can you reach out to when crisis hits? Write down two or three people.

(continued)

- *Your shutdown permission:* What are you giving yourself permission to let go of during crisis? What standards will you lower?
- *Your recovery trigger:* How will you know the acute crisis has passed and it's time to begin rebuilding?
- *Your first recovery step:* When the recovery trigger happens, what's the first practice you'll restore? Pick just one.

The relapse reality

Relapse is part of recovery. This isn't failure or evidence that the work didn't take; it's part of the process. Despite everything you've built, you will at certain times fall back into old patterns. I certainly did. You'll skip the practices. You'll numb out instead of feeling. You'll isolate instead of connecting.

I used to worry that a relapse would mean I would fall back to where I once was. I now firmly believe this won't happen, because I have created a new baseline of resilience and understanding of myself. I know that if things slightly fall off track, I'm smart enough and aware enough to recognise it and put in place the solutions that will help me continue to build mental strength inside whatever I'm facing.

The same is true for you. Remember that awareness is seeing a pothole up ahead when you're driving a car. Once you spot it, you're able to swerve out of the way. If you haven't done the work, you stay unaware—and you drive straight over that pothole. You've now done enough work to be able to swerve.

The difference between someone who's done the work and someone who hasn't isn't that the first person never relapses. It's that they notice faster, judge less, return quicker and learn something.

I've slipped multiple times since my original breakdown and still do (and still will), but I recognise in that moment that it's okay. Life is a cycle and I now understand when it's time for me to rest and recover, and recognise when things are flowing and it's time to go. I just give myself a little extra love during the down cycle.

Your goal isn't to never fall. Your goal is to always get back up—and to get back up quicker each time. Relapse isn't failure; it's feedback. The question isn't, 'Did I fall?' but, 'How quickly did I return?

Post-traumatic growth

Some of the worst experiences of my life have produced the best growth.

I'm not advocating toxic positivity here—pain is pain and loss is loss. Some things that happen are simply terrible. However, as well as completely acknowledging post-traumatic stress, I also think post-traumatic growth is possible. I love this reframe and it's a topic I believe we should be talking more about.

Research has found that trauma survivors often report greater appreciation for life, deeper relationships, increased discovery of new possibilities, improved personal strength and increased spiritual development. Not everyone who lives through trauma experiences these benefits, and they don't happen automatically. They require the kind of processing and integration we've been building throughout this book.

Jules's hospitalisation while pregnant with Ollie was terrifying, and I wouldn't wish those feelings and fear on anyone. But something happened in that hospital, something I couldn't have accessed any other way. I underwent a deepening of my faith, not in any particular religion but in the process of life itself. I developed a visceral understanding that I could survive more than I thought.

And I found a gratitude for my wife, little bub, health and life that I'd always felt intellectually but now felt in my bones.

Sometimes what feels like breaking is actually breaking open. Every difficult season I've survived has left me with something I didn't have before. Capacities I couldn't have built in easy times, depths I couldn't have reached on the surface and clarity that only comes from being tested.

> *Difficult seasons aren't interruptions of the work but accelerations of it.*

Your clarity compass

The opportunity arrived at the worst possible time: six months after Jules had given birth to our first son, Ollie. He was healthy and happy and, as first-time parents, Jules and I were still finding our footing and figuring this whole new chapter out day by day. Then came the offer: a major media opportunity and a chance to accelerate our lives in all facets. It would be a new adventure, a way to 'renovate' our lives and share our story and current lives on a platform that would reach millions. It was the kind of challenge and 'once in a lifetime' experience that could be so hard yet so fulfilling, giving us the chance to transform so many lives. We could build on our impact and our reach, and increase our ability to help people with our mission along the way.

On paper, it was exactly what we had been working toward and thinking about. However, as exciting as the opportunity was, something felt wrong. The opportunity was legitimate and the platform aligned with our values. The potential end result was something we'd been dreaming about. The experience, tough as it would be, was potentially life changing and memorable. Every rational analysis said yes. Yet the timing, and my gut, screamed no.

I was confused and couldn't seem to access my usual clarity. The months of new parent duties had depleted me. No-one can prepare you for late nights and early wake ups. Yes, when you're in your 20s and going out every Saturday night with friends you seem to be able to handle the lack of sleep, but that's a whole different life. My practices had become inconsistent and my mind was foggy. Jules told me 'baby brain' was a thing for mothers due to the hormones, but I'm pretty sure dads experience it too. Some days felt like I couldn't even spell my own name.

Was the feeling in my gut my intuition protecting me from something I couldn't see? Or was this self-sabotage and the old patterns trying to keep me small? I didn't know. And we had 72 hours to decide. That's when I developed what I now call my Clarity Compass.

I was sitting at home underneath our tree in the backyard, the deadline looming, feeling completely lost. My anxiety was building. Will we make the right decision? Will we regret it? I'd made pro-con lists. I'd talked to Jules, to friends. Everyone had opinions, but none of them resolved the knot in my stomach.

So, I tried something different. I stopped trying to figure out the decision and started trying to figure out myself. I just sat, breathed and allowed silence to surround me. I then asked myself the questions I outline in the following section. I didn't ask them about the opportunity; I asked them about me.

> *“When you can't see the path, you can still find your direction. Give yourself a moment of silence and the answers will appear.”*

The seven directions on your Clarity Compass

The Clarity Compass has seven directions, formed through your answers to seven questions. Together, the compass allows you to find your true north. The seven directions of the compass, along with the questions for each one and what it assesses, are shown in the following table.

Direction	Question	What it accesses
Values	What do I actually value here?	Your authentic priorities
Fears	What am I afraid of?	Your hidden obstacles
Love	What would love do?	Your highest wisdom
Regret	What will I regret?	Your future perspective
Worst case	What could happen if it goes wrong?	Perspective that reduces catastrophic thinking
Best case	What could happen if it goes right?	Expanded possibility and potential
'Am I okay?'	Am I capable of both scenarios?	Your self-trust and capacity

Here's a little more detail on each of the directions and their questions:

- *Values:* 'What do I actually value here?' Don't think about what you should value or what would impress others. What do you actually care about most deeply? When I asked this about that opportunity, I discovered I valued depth more than reach. I valued showing up fully more than showing up fast. The opportunity prioritised reach over depth. It wasn't wrong; it just wasn't aligned.

- *Fears:* 'What am I afraid of?' Your first answer here is usually the surface fear, while your real fear often hides beneath. I was afraid of missing the opportunity *and* afraid of building on a shaky foundation. Both fears were real, but they pointed in opposite directions. Recognising both allowed me to choose consciously rather than being driven by whichever fear was louder. The fear you can name has less power than the fear operating in shadows.
- *Love:* 'What would love do?' I don't mean romantic love, I mean something closer to genuine care for yourself, your family, others and the future. Love would counsel healing first and building second. Love wasn't being soft. Love was being wise, and seeing that saying yes from where I was would ultimately serve no-one well.
- *Regret:* 'What will I regret?' Focus on your potential regrets in ten years or on your deathbed. For me, I knew I wouldn't regret saying no to an opportunity that came at the wrong time. But I might deeply regret saying yes and showing up as a shadow of who I could be. Imagine yourself at 80, looking back over your life. What choice would that future self wish you'd made?
- *Worst case:* 'What could happen if it goes wrong?' Be specific rather than dramatic or vague. If that worst-case scenario happened, what would you do next? Would this still matter in five years? What's within your control when it comes to reducing unnecessary risk? The worst case for me wasn't ruin but discomfort. This would be survivable but costly.
- *Best case.* 'What could happen if it goes right?' Let yourself think bigger than your fear. What growth, opportunity or impact might open up? Who would you need to become to hold that success well? For me, the best case was exciting but premature. I wasn't fully resourced to maximise it.

- *'Am I okay?':* 'Am I capable of both scenarios?' Do you trust yourself to handle disappointment if it goes wrong? Do you trust yourself to handle responsibility if it goes right? What support or preparation would strengthen your capacity? When I asked honestly, I knew I wasn't yet equipped for either extreme. I needed to strengthen first.

The compass in action

The Clarity Compass isn't about answering one question. It's about using multiple perspectives to find where they converge. Here's a summary of what my compass told me when I was considering this opportunity:

- *Values:* Depth overreach. Direction: wait.
- *Fears:* Afraid of staying small (go) *and* afraid of building on shaky foundation (wait). Tension acknowledged.
- *Love:* Heal first, build second. Direction: wait.
- *Regret:* Would regret showing up depleted. Direction: wait.
- *Worst case:* Survivable, but unnecessary.
- *Best case:* Exciting, but premature.
- *'Am I okay?':* Not yet. Build capacity first.

While my compass may not have converged perfectly and some uncertainty still existed, it had provided enough clear direction for me and Jules to act. We turned down the opportunity. Once we had accessed the required clarity, it became a relatively easy decision.

Of course, parts of us still felt like we were making a mistake and wondered whether we would ever get another chance like this. And, for the people who did take the opportunity in our place, the end result was life changing. However, we were also comfortable in our choice and happy for them because we knew we had made the right decision for our life in that moment.

Our life values aligned and it all made sense.

Six months later, different opportunities emerged, and we were ready for them and could show up fully.

> *When the compass points converge, trust them. When they diverge, the tension itself is teaching you something.*

The Clarity Compass exercise

Think of a decision you're facing that you feel uncertain or conflicted about.

In your journal or Clarity Workbook, write down your responses to the following:

- *Values:* What do you actually value here? What choice would be most aligned?
- *Fears:* What are you afraid of? Remember: your first response is likely your surface fear. What are you really afraid of? Keep asking 'and then what?' to get to your deeper fears.
- *Love:* What would genuine care for yourself, others and the long term look like here?
- *Regret:* In ten years, what choice would you wish you'd made?
- *Worst case:* What could realistically go wrong? How would you respond? Would it still matter in five years?
- *Best case:* What could go right? What growth might open up? Who would you need to become?
- *'Am I okay?':* Are you equipped for either outcome? What would strengthen your capacity?

(continued)

> Now consider:
> - Where do the directions converge?
> - Where do they diverge?
> - What does your compass suggest?
> - What is one concrete action you could take in the next 24 hours?

When the compass isn't enough

Sometimes you do the Clarity Compass exercise and you're still uncertain. When this happens, check in with the following:

- *The body compass:* Imagine you've made choice A. Really inhabit this choice—you've decided, it's done. Scan your body and check how you feel. Tension? Relief? Expansion? Contraction? Now imagine choice B and repeat the process. Sometimes the body is clearer than the mind. Go with that intuition and those feelings.
- *The coin flip:* Assign each choice to one side of a coin and then flip it. When the coin is in the air, notice which side you're hoping it lands on? How do you feel when it lands? That hope and that reaction tell you something your conscious mind couldn't access.
- *The minimum viable decision:* If you truly can't decide, ask what is the smallest step you could take that would give you more information. You don't have to make the whole decision. You just have to learn something. Then decide again with new data.

Sometimes the path reveals itself only as you walk it.

Living by the compass

For a few weeks after turning down that opportunity, I second-guessed myself. The fear of staying small was loud, and I wondered if I'd made a terrible mistake. But, as the months passed, something became clear: I had made the right choice. I could feel it in my body. I felt the relief of not having overcommitted when depleted, the joy of having space to actually rebuild my practices, and the integrity of waiting until we were ready.

When the next opportunity came, I was a different person and we were in a different position. We had rebuilt and I felt clear and settled. I was ready to show up fully. This became a turning point—not just for our family and my work, but also for how I, and we, made decisions going forward.

Now, years later, I use some version of those seven questions in my Clarity Compass for almost every significant decision. What do I actually value here? What am I afraid of? What would love do? What will I regret? What is the worst and best scenario and am I okay regardless of what happens?

This compass has never led me astray. It might not always give easy answers, but it always brings me back to myself and makes things clearer.

Another benefit is that the more you use the compass, the less you need it. The questions become internalised and the compass becomes intuitive. Eventually, it just becomes how you make decisions. And that's when you know the integration is complete.

> *The destination changes but the compass remains. Learn to trust it.*

Integration Pillar summary

Pillar 8: Integration is where the work becomes who you are. Here's what to keep in mind:

- *Life will test you:* The question is never 'Will I face adversity?' but 'Who will I be when I do?' Integration means the pillars have moved from practice to identity, and from conscious effort to unconscious competence. They become bones — structural, internal and present even when invisible.
- *Crisis moves in three phases:* These phases are impact, navigation and recovery. Your minimum viable practice keeps the thread intact when you can't weave the full tapestry. Build your crisis protocol before you need it. Relapse isn't failure; it's feedback. The question isn't, 'Did I fall?' but, 'How quickly did I return?'
- *The Clarity Compass finds your direction when you're lost:* The compass asks you to consider your values, fears, love, regret, worst-case and best-case scenarios, and whether you will be okay. When the directions converge, trust them. The compass doesn't give you wisdom; it helps you access the wisdom you already have.
- *Clarity isn't about having a perfect life:* It's about having a steady centre when life is anything but perfect.

Conclusion

The life of clarity

My son was born on a Monday morning. I was there—fully there—holding Jules's hand through every surge, breathing with her and dancing with her. I was present in a way I couldn't have been five years earlier. When Ollie finally arrived, he hit the deck and didn't move. You can imagine then what was going through our minds after so much already. The nurse hit the emergency alarm, which was terrifying, and doctors came rushing in, but I was able to remain calm as our baby started to move and come to with a cry. We were, once more, so grateful. The nurse placed our son on Jules's chest and I watched my wife become a mother. It was the most surreal and incredible feeling, and I had so many emotions running through me.

Then they handed my son to me for some skin-on-skin time. I held him for the first time, this tiny life we'd created, and something happened that I need you to understand. I felt it all. I felt the overwhelming love and the primal terror of being responsible for something so fragile. All my life learnings, wounds and beliefs were there to carry with me into this new role. I felt a joy so intense it was almost painful. And I felt the weight of every generation before me, every parent who'd held their child and wondered if they'd be enough.

I felt it all. And I didn't run.

Five years earlier—before the breakdown, before the hospital, before any of this work—I would have numbed. I would have smiled for the photos while dissociating from the intensity. I would have performed fatherhood while hiding from its reality. The feelings would have been too much, so I would have felt nothing at all.

But standing in that delivery room, holding my son, I was present for the full catastrophe of the moment, the terror *and* the love; the grief *and* the joy; the overwhelm *and* the gratitude. I cried real tears, from somewhere deep, tears I couldn't have accessed before I learned how to feel but tears of so much joy.

And in that moment, I understood why I'd done all this work. I hadn't done it for productivity or success, or even for mental health as some abstract concept. I'd done it for the ability to be fully alive when life hands you its most precious moments. I'd done it for the capacity to feel the things that matter most and the presence to actually experience your own existence instead of watching it from a distance.

That's what clarity gives you. It doesn't give you a perfect life, absent of pain, or some enlightened state beyond human struggle. But it does give you access to yourself, to others and to the moments that matter. It gives you the capacity to be there, really there, for your own life that you built, your life that at one stage may have never felt possible.

Everything we've built in these pages—the eight pillars, the frameworks, the practices and the tools—all exist for moments like that one. They exist so that when your child is born, you can hold them and you can be present with them. Or when your marriage hits its hardest season, you can stay. Or when your dreams finally come true, you can actually experience them. And when life breaks your heart, you can feel it break, and heal.

This is the life of clarity. This life is not a destination you arrive at, but a way of being you grow into. It's about presence, not perfection. It's about knowing yourself and creating an inner peace you are incredibly proud of.

> *The point of this work isn't to build a perfect life. It's to be present for the imperfect, beautiful, heartbreaking, miraculous life you actually have — and be proud of it all.*

The long view

When I look back at my journey, I see a 20-something performer who didn't know he was dying inside; who smiled for cameras while suffocating in silence and tried to please everyone while neglecting himself. I see someone who achieved everything he thought he wanted and felt nothing but emptiness.

I see the breakdown, the moment when the performance finally collapsed and I ended up in a hospital, unable to pretend anymore. It was the worst thing that ever happened to me, and the best thing that ever happened to me.

I see the slow, unglamorous work of rebuilding, the therapy sessions where I said things I'd never said aloud, the mornings I sat trying to be present yet wanting to be anywhere else, and the journals filled with confusion and pain and gradual, almost imperceptible, progress.

I see the setbacks—the relapse six months out when I thought I'd made it, the crisis with life's challenges that tested everything, and the seasons when clarity felt distant and I wondered if any of this work was real.

I see the breakthroughs from courage. The first time I felt genuine peace instead of just numbness, the moment I told Jules who I really was and she didn't leave, and the day I shared my story publicly and discovered my wound could help others heal.

And I see now—this life I'm living, my marriage and two sons. I see the work that allows me walk alongside others in their own journeys toward clarity. What do you now see?

None of this would exist without the breakdown and without the willingness to begin. None of it would exist without every single step of the path, including the steps backward, including the falls, including the times I wanted to quit.

But there is an arc, I promise you there is. The work compounds, the practices accumulate and the tiny choices add up. One day, you're holding your child and you realise, *This was the moment that kept me going all these years. It was all worth it. I'm here. I made it through and I'm so proud of myself.*

You can't see the arc while you're in it—just trust that it exists.

What I want you to know

We've walked through all eight pillars together, each built on the last. Together, they form something I believe can change your life the way they changed mine. Before we finish, I want you to know a few things. They're not frameworks or practices, just truths I've learned that I wish someone had told me.

Remember:

- *You are not broken:* You may be wounded and you may be struggling. You may be lost, uncertain, unclear or lacking a certain direction in ways that may feel permanent and unfixable. But you are not broken. You are certainly worthy and enough. You are a human being having a human experience, which includes pain and confusion and the feeling of being shattered. Broken things can't heal. You can.

- *The work is worth it:* At certain moments you will wonder if any of this matters. Progress will seem invisible and the practices will feel pointless and you will be tempted to give up. Remember that what you're doing matters. It's working. The changes that matter most are often the ones you can't see yet. Take some rest. Take a moment. Just keep going.
- *You will fall down:* We all do and that's okay. This isn't failure. It's part of the journey. Every fall contains a lesson. Every return makes you stronger.
- *You are not alone:* Right now, as you read these words, millions of others are on the same journey. We all have shit going on, every single one of us. You are part of a vast human community of people trying to become more conscious, more present and more alive. The key to that is 'trying'. We are all trying our best and that's all we can do.

> *"You are not broken and you are not alone — and the work is worth it."*

The life that becomes possible

You wake up in the morning and you're there, not immediately reaching for your phone or dreading the day, but actually present in those first moments of consciousness. You're grateful for another day focusing on the things you do have in your life as opposed to what you don't. You smile. You do your practices not because you have to, but because you've experienced what happens when you don't and what happens when you do.

You move through your day with intention and a centre. As things happen—stress, frustration or unexpected challenges—you feel them without being destroyed by them. You respond instead of react.

Your relationships are different. You're not performing anymore; you're connecting. People experience the real you, and the right people love what they find. Your conversations have depth. Your conflicts have repair. Your love has room to breathe, and the energy and light you give off is contagious to those around you.

You know who you are and you like it. You like you, not your titles or your achievements or your roles, but the you beneath all that. This knowing gives you an unshakeable core that external circumstances can't touch.

You're contributing. Your struggles have become wisdom and your wounds have become gifts. Somewhere, someone's life is better because you did this work, because you showed up, healed yourself and turned around to help others.

And, perhaps most importantly, you're actually experiencing your life. The joy registers and the beauty lands. The moments that matter find you present to receive them. You're not watching your life from a distance; you're living it and you inspire not just those around you but also yourself.

This is the clarity life. It's not always easy or pleasant. Presence means being there for the hard stuff too. But it's real. And real is better than numb. Alive is better than performing. Present is better than absent and being you, authentically you, is better than being anyone else.

Find your seed

As we near the end, I want to tell you about a moment from those early days that I haven't shared yet. I was living and working in London with my cricket gear company, trying to build the business. I was starting to feel more stable in who I was and what I was doing, and to move on from the past. I was certainly not out of the woods, I was still shaky and uncertain, but no longer in complete free fall.

It was a Tuesday evening and I had just finished a presentation at a cricket store in Yorkshire in the UK when I secured a meeting with another highly valued retailer in Torquay. The problem was I could only get in to see them at 9.30 the following morning. A quick search told me Torquay was over 400 kilometres away—and about a six-hour drive. It was late but I knew what I had to do: get in my little two-door hire car and go for it. I didn't have a hotel booking and had virtually no petrol but it didn't matter. I was confident I could figure it out along the way.

That's how I ended up on the M1 with torrential rain buffeting my tiny car. I remember being about halfway there, propped on the steering wheel doing my best to see with the windscreen wipers on full. The winds were picking up, the traffic was hectic and, for the first time in as long as I could remember, I felt something I didn't have a word for at the time. I remember looking at myself in the rear-view mirror, staring myself in the eye for a moment, and then saying something I had never said to myself in my entire life: 'I'm proud of you mate'. What I felt in that moment wasn't happiness or joy exactly; it was something more subtle as my eyes began to well up and tears began to stream down my face. I realised what I was feeling was a state of peace. It was me being finally proud of me.

Now, tearing up while driving at a decent clip on the M1 in torrential rain is certainly not safe but I had to welcome this moment. So, I pulled off and parked safely on the side of the motorway, and just sat there, existing. Just a human being, sitting in a car, looking at myself in the rear-view mirror, emotional, raw, vulnerable, proud.

I wasn't crying from sadness, but from something like recognition. I felt like I was meeting someone I'd forgotten existed; like I was coming home after being lost for so long I'd forgotten I had a home.

That moment lasted maybe five minutes and, within it, came memories of all of the challenges I had faced, and all the hardship and pain I had once experienced. I remembered my lowest points that I'd had to fight my way back from, even when nothing seemed to be working out. And I acknowledged where I was in this exact moment as my achievements flooded my mind, flickering like a movie highlight reel. I was simply proud of myself, not my performances or my achievements; just simply me and all that I had overcome to be here at this moment. It wasn't elegant, it wasn't pretty, it certainly wasn't expected but it was the moment that overcame me when it was right.

To anyone else it may have seemed like a straightforward decision but for me, making the decision to drive six hours south just typified how far I'd actually come. Around four years prior, I'd had moments when I couldn't even put pants on; 12 months prior I was still a shell of a human. So, realising I was now able to do what I was doing in that moment, something came over me. Call it grace, call it peace, call it acceptance, call it what you will, but it was a moment that I am incredibly grateful for and will always remember.

I knew I hadn't reached the finish line, but I also knew that all the work I had so far put in had led to that moment on the M1. And every practice I've built since, every pillar we've explored, every word in this book—it all traces back to that moment in the car. That five-minute window when I experienced what it felt like to simply sit and be proud of myself.

Being able to sit with yourself and be present, here, alive, proud and at ease with a sense of peace is the clarity life. That's what becomes possible. You'll find it, maybe not all at once, and not perfectly or permanently, but you'll find it. Glimpses will become moments. Moments will become stretches. Stretches will become your life, consistently.

And one day, you'll be sitting somewhere—maybe a garden, maybe a car on the side of the M1, maybe a delivery room, maybe in front of your bathroom mirror, maybe in your office or bedroom, or maybe just in your living room on an ordinary Tuesday, and you'll realise that you're there. You're really there, present and proud of your own existence.

You just needed to give yourself permission and a chance to find your way home.

A letter to you

We've spent this entire book together. I've told you things I've never really told anyone. I've shown you my worst moments and my most vulnerable truths. I've given you everything I have. And now you have a choice. You can close this book and let it become another thing you read once and forgot, or you can let this be a beginning.

I don't know what you're carrying. I don't know what brought you to this book, what you're struggling with or what you're hoping to find. But I know this: you picked up this book for a reason. Something in you is ready, and it's reaching for something different. That something is not random, and it's not weakness or desperation. It's life itself, trying to live through you more fully. How incredible is that?!

The path won't be straight and the journey won't be easy. You will have moments when you wonder why you started, when giving up seems reasonable and when clarity feels impossibly far away. In those moments, I want you to remember something: I was where you are. I started where you're starting or where you might currently be. I had the same doubts, the same fears, and the same voice saying, 'This won't work for me' and 'What am I doing with my life?'

And now I'm holding both my sons, present for my own life, writing these words to you. The distance between where you are and where you want to be is not as far as it seems. It's walked one day at a time, one practice at a time, one moment at a time, one choice at a time.

I know it's not easy, I'm getting emotional right now writing this, but I know it's possible. Every step counts and every attempt matters. Every time you try and fail and try again, and every time you continue to get up, you're building something that will eventually hold.

You can do this because you are you and you are magnificent. You have your own special ingredients and gifts that are yours and yours only. You are confident because you now believe in your abilities, and because you're human. Humans have been finding their way from darkness to light since the beginning of time. It's what we do. It's what you'll do too. It's what I did and I'm proud of it and you will be too.

> *"I was where you are. I started where you're starting. And I'm living proof that the path leads somewhere worth going."*

Your first step

I'm not going to end this book with a summary or a comprehensive action plan. You have everything you need in the chapters behind you. Instead, I want to leave you with a single question and a single invitation: what is the one practice from this book that, if you did it consistently, would change everything?

Don't think of five practices or a complete system. Think of the *one* thing from this book that resonated most deeply, that you know in your gut would make the biggest difference.

Maybe it's the morning ritual. Maybe it's being the observer of your emotions. Maybe it's the Clarity Compass. Maybe it's just creating your strong enough why. Maybe it's something else entirely.

What is it? Name it now. And then do that one thing tomorrow, and the next day, and the next. You don't have to do it perfectly or with grand ambition. You just need to do that one thing, imperfectly but consistently. One practice, done daily, will change your life more than 100 practices done once.

Start small. Start there. Start tomorrow. Start before you're ready.

We began this journey with a question: what do you actually want? I hope that you might be a little clearer on this now. What would your life look like with real clarity? Now you know the answer isn't a destination but a way of walking. Clarity isn't something you achieve and then have. It's something you practice and then embody. It's something you lose and then find again. It's something you build and rebuild, day by day, choice by choice, breath by breath.

You will forget and you will fall. You will wonder if any of this matters. And then you'll remember. You'll return. You'll begin again and, once more, that's okay. That's the practice. That's the path. That's the Clarity Life.

I believe in you—not because I know you, but because I know this work. I know it reaches the people who need it. I know that something brought you to these pages, and that something knows what it's doing. The methods are there; you just need to now go and use them.

Trust it. Trust yourself. Trust the process. And when you're ready, when you've walked far enough down this path to have something to offer, turn around, reach back and help someone else find their way.

The Clarity Method isn't mine, it's ours. It belongs to everyone who uses it, everyone who adapts it and everyone who passes it forward. Your clarity isn't just for you. It's for everyone your life touches.

Go live it and share it. Go be the proof that transformation is possible.

I was once running from something that followed me everywhere I went. No matter how fast I moved, no matter how far I travelled, no matter how many versions of myself I tried on, it was always right there: behind me, beside me and inside me. What I didn't understand then, what I couldn't have understood, was that the thing I was running from and the thing I was searching for were the same thing: me.

Through the work I've shared with you in these pages, I stopped running. I turned around and found a version of myself that I like and love, and that I am genuinely proud of. This isn't a perfect or finished version of myself. I still have many flaws and I'm okay with that. I'm still a 'work in progress' because the work is always ongoing. But I've found a real me that I don't need to hide from anymore.

For so long, I felt empty. I felt like something was missing; some final piece that would make everything click. I looked for this missing piece in achievement, approval and distraction. I searched for it in other people's opinions of who I should be. It was never there. Once you give yourself the opportunity and the permission to do the work, truly do it, you realise that nothing was ever missing. It was all within you from the start, buried under the noise, fear, performance and stories you'd been told about who you were supposed to be. But it was there. It was always there. That's what I was looking for all along. And I hope, with everything in me, that you find the same.

Thank you for walking this journey with me. Thank you for trusting me with your time, your attention and your willingness to look inward. That takes courage, more courage than most people will ever know.

The biggest compliment you can give—not to me or anyone else, but to yourself—is to now go and live it. Close this book and open your life. Take what you've learned, felt and uncovered and give yourself the chance to become who you were always meant to be. I wish you nothing but love as you do so.

And I hope that one day, whether it's via a message, a conversation or a moment on a park bench somewhere, you can tell me where you came from, what you did and where you ended up. Tell me about the life you built and the people you helped along the way. Tell me how many others are now finding their own clarity because you had the courage to find yours. That would make me so, so happy.

Please know that the end of this book is just the beginning of your practice. The pillars don't stop here. They live in your mornings, your conversations, your decisions, your relationships and your quiet moments when no-one is watching. They live in you now.

So, take what you need. Close these pages and give yourself permission to open your life up to something truly spectacular: a life of clarity, connection and purpose; a life you are incredibly proud of. This is most certainly not the end, for this is just the beginning for you.

Thank you for being here. Sending you so much love,

— Cam

Acknowledgements

To my younger self, thank you for turning your pain into purpose. I love you.

To my beautiful wife, Jules, thank you for being my rock, my support, my sounding board, my cheerleader and my best friend. Thank you for encouraging me always and supporting me when, at times, you knew my value, worth and impact more than I did. Thank you for encouraging me to keep going and allowing me to step into my purpose fully. Thank you for having the courage to show up and marry a stranger on a day that will shape and change our lives forever. We both did the work individually and fate allowed us to connect and now lead the life we live. For that, I am forever grateful. I love building and doing life with you and am so proud of you in all that you are doing. I love you.

To my children, Ollie and Carter, thank you for saving my life well before you were even born. The vision of holding you kept me alive and kept me striving when I was in my darkest hours. You are precious (most of the time, anyway!) and I love you dearly. One day, when you need me most, please know I will always be there for you and we can work through life together.

To my mum, Marg, and dad, Russ, thank you. I now know what it's like to be a parent and feel what your child is feeling as you feel it with them but have no control. You would do anything in your power to take away the pain and suffering but can't. Thank you for standing by me at the most difficult part of my life. Thank you for being there for my entire life but also when I needed you the most. You didn't need to understand because you couldn't; all you had to do was show up and that's exactly what you did. I am truly grateful for you and the beautiful life you have helped me create and the person I have become. I truly hope you are proud of me. I love you.

To my friends and family who have been there from the start and have seen the ups and downs of my life but remained by my side, thank you for accepting me for me, being loving and supporting, continuing to inspire and encourage me, and making me smile and laugh along the way. Your friendships and our experiences remain one of the greatest gifts and joys of my life. Thank you for sticking around and for you I will be forever grateful.

To Wiley Publishing, thank you for believing in me and this project. Thank you for taking a punt on me and seeing that my intentions have the potential to change lives for the better. Never in my wildest dreams, especially when I was at my lowest, would I have ever thought to myself, *Hey I know you're not feeling the best right now but someday you'll write a book on it and hopefully help and inspire many people.* And yet here we are—and I hope we inspire many others to find their own personal clarity and find life just a little lighter and brighter, the way they deserve it to be. Thank you for helping with that.

Lastly to you, the reader, thank you for taking a chance and picking up this book with the thought that something in it might help you in your season of life right now. I certainly hope and trust that it will. I'm so lucky to be able to meet people on the street, in public or online and share conversations with them. I am forever grateful for these moments of connection when we talk about life. The work and conversations I strive to do and have every day is to simply help someone feel just a little better than they did before they started talking to me. I have continued this approach with this book, and I am truly grateful to you for reading it. You are the reason I have put everything into these pages, and I hope I can continue to help, inspire and meet so many more beautiful people along the way. Thank you.

Cam's Treasure Chest

Books I've read that helped me on my journey to clarity.

The Seven Spiritual Laws of Success by Deepak Chopra

The Four Agreements by Don Miguel Ruiz

The 5am Club by Robin Sharma

The Wealth Money Can't Buy by Robin Sharma

The Everyday Hero Manifesto by Robin Sharma

The Universe Has Your Back by Gabrielle Bernstein

Self Matters by Dr Phil McGraw

The Power Of Now by Eckhart Tolle

How to Win Friends and Influence People by Dale Carnegie

Atomic Habits by James Clear

The Let Them Theory by Mel Robbins and Sawyer Robbins

I Can Make You Confident by Paul McKenna

Greenlights by Matthew McConaughey

References and further reading

Chapter 1

Australian Bureau of Statistics (ABS) (2023), 'National Study of Mental Health and Wellbeing, 2020–2022', Australian Bureau of Statistics, Canberra.

Hari, J (2022), *Stolen Focus: Why You Can't Pay Attention*, Bloomsbury Publishing, London.

Iyengar, SS & Lepper, MR (2000), 'When choice is demotivating: Can one desire too much of a good thing?', *Journal of Personality and Social Psychology*, 79(6), 995–1006.

Killingsworth, MA & Gilbert, DT (2010), 'A wandering mind is an unhappy mind', *Science*, 330(6006), 932.

Mark, G, Gudith, D & Klocke, U (2008), 'The cost of interrupted work: More speed and stress', Proceedings of the SIGCHI Conference on Human Factors in Computing Systems, 107–110.

Newport, C (2016), *Deep Work: Rules for Focused Success in a Distracted World*, Grand Central Publishing, New York.

Schwartz, B (2004), *The Paradox of Choice: Why More Is Less*, Ecco/HarperCollins, New York.

World Health Organization (WHO) (2022), 'Mental health and COVID-19: Early evidence of the pandemic's impact', World Health Organization, Geneva.

Chapter 2

Clear, J (2018), *Atomic Habits: An Easy & Proven Way to Build Good Habits & Break Bad Ones*, Avery/Penguin Random House, New York.

Huberman, AD (2021–2025), Huberman Lab Podcast, Scicomm Media.

Kahneman, D (2011), *Thinking, Fast and Slow,* Farrar, Straus and Giroux, New York.

Seligman, MEP (1975), *Helplessness: On Depression, Development, and Death,* WH Freeman/Times Books, San Francisco.

Chapter 4

Buettner, D (2008), *The Blue Zones: Lessons for Living Longer from the People Who've Lived the Longest,* National Geographic Society, Washington, DC.

Buettner, D & Skemp, S (2016), 'Blue zones: Lessons from the world's longest lived', *American Journal of Lifestyle Medicine,* 10(5), 318–321.

Frankl, VE (1946; English translation 1959), *Man's Search for Meaning,* Beacon Press, Boston.

Goggins, D (2018), *Can't Hurt Me: Master Your Mind and Defy the Odds,* Lioncrest Publishing.

Jacobson, NS, Martell, CR & Dimidjian, S (2001), 'Behavioral activation treatment for depression: Returning to contextual roots', *Clinical Psychology: Science and Practice,* 8(3), 255–270.

Martell, CR, Dimidjian, S & Herman-Dunn, R (2010), *Behavioral Activation for Depression: A Clinician's Guide,* The Guilford Press, New York.

Nietzsche, F (1889; translation 1968), *Twilight of the Idols (Götzen-Dämmerung),* trans. RJ Hollingdale, Penguin Classics, London.

Chapter 5

Lieberman, MD, et al. (2007), 'Putting feelings into words: Affect labeling disrupts amygdala activity', *Psychological Science,* 18(5), 421–428.

Siegel, DJ (2010), *Mindsight: The New Science of Personal Transformation,* Bantam Books, New York.

Tolle, E (1997), *The Power of Now: A Guide to Spiritual Enlightenment,* New World Library, Novato, CA.

Chapter 6

Pennebaker, JW & Smyth, JM (2016), *Opening Up by Writing It Down: How Expressive Writing Improves Health and Eases Emotional Pain* (3rd ed), The Guilford Press, New York.

Rotter, JB (1966), 'Generalized expectancies for internal versus external control of reinforcement', *Psychological Monographs: General and Applied,* 80(1), 1–28.

Seligman, MEP (1990), *Learned Optimism: How to Change Your Mind and Your Life,* Vintage Books, New York.

Chapter 7

Balban, MY, et al. (2023), 'Brief structured respiration practices enhance mood and reduce physiological arousal', *Cell Reports Medicine*, 4(1), 100895.

Hof, W (2020), *The Wim Hof Method*, Rider Trade.

Porges, SW (2011), *The Polyvagal Theory: Neurophysiological Foundations of Emotions, Attachment, Communication, and Self-Regulation*, WW Norton, New York.

Siegel, DJ (2012), *The Developing Mind: How Relationships and the Brain Interact to Shape Who We Are* (2nd ed), The Guilford Press, New York.

Van der Kolk, BA (2014), *The Body Keeps the Score: Brain, Mind, and Body in the Healing of Trauma*, Viking/Penguin, New York.

Chapter 8

Clance, PR & Imes, SA (1978), 'The imposter phenomenon in high achieving women: Dynamics and therapeutic intervention', *Psychotherapy: Theory, Research & Practice*, 15(3), 241–247.

Kruger, J & Dunning, D (1999), 'Unskilled and unaware of it: How difficulties in recognizing one's own incompetence lead to inflated self-assessments', *Journal of Personality and Social Psychology*, 77(6), 1121–1134.

Chapter 9

Duhigg, C (2012), *The Power of Habit: Why We Do What We Do in Life and Business*, Random House, New York.

Hofmann, W, et al. (2012), 'Everyday temptations: An experience sampling study of desire, conflict, and self-control', *Journal of Personality and Social Psychology*, 102(6), 1318–1335.

Chapter 10

Choi-Allum, L & Rainville, G (2025), 'Disconnected: The escalating challenge of loneliness among adults 45-plus', AARP Research.

De Freitas, J, et al. (2026), 'AI companions reduce loneliness', *Journal of Consumer Research*, 52(6), 1126–1148.

Duncan A, et al. (2021), *Stronger Together: Loneliness and Social Connectedness in Australia*, Bankwest Curtin Economics Centre Focus on the States Series, #8.

Ending Loneliness Together (2023), *State of the Nation Report—Social Connection in Australia 2023*, Ending Loneliness Together.

Holt-Lunstad, J, Smith, TB & Layton, JB (2010), 'Social relationships and mortality risk: A meta-analytic review', *PLoS Medicine*, 7(7), e1000316.
Murthy, VH (2020), *Together: The Healing Power of Human Connection in a Sometimes Lonely World*, HarperCollins, New York.
World Health Organization (WHO) (2025), 'Social connection linked to improved health and reduced risk of early death', World Health Organization Commission on Social Connection, Geneva.

Chapter 11

Tedeschi, RG & Calhoun, LG (2004), 'Posttraumatic growth: Conceptual foundations and empirical evidence', *Psychological Inquiry*, 15(1), 1–18.